Women in Charge
Policing, gender and leadership

Marisa Silvestri

WILLAN
PUBLISHING

Published by

Willan Publishing
Culmcott House
Mill Street, Uffculme
Cullompton, Devon
EX15 3AT, UK
Tel: +44(0)1884 840337
Fax: +44(0)1884 840251
e-mail: info@willanpublishing.co.uk
Website: www.willanpublishing.co.uk

Published simultaneously in the USA and Canada by

Willan Publishing
c/o ISBS, 920 NE 58th Ave, Suite 300,
Portland, Oregon 97213-3786, USA
Tel: +001(0)503 287 3093
Fax: +001(0)503 280 8832
e-mail: info@isbs.com
Website: www.isbs.com

First published 2003

ISBN 1-84392-046-8

British Library Cataloguing-in-Publication Data

A catalogue record for this book is available from the British Library

Typeset by TW Typesetting, Plymouth, Devon
Project management by Deer Park Productions, Tavistock, Devon
Printed and bound by TJ International Ltd, Trecerus Industrial Estate, Padstow, Cornwall, PL28 8RW

Contents

Acknowledgements

I am grateful to a number of people who have been involved in different ways and at various stages in the writing of this book. I owe a huge debt of thanks to Frances Heidensohn who has been and continues to be a mentor, critical commentator and a dear friend. She has consistently provided unwavering support throughout the development of this book. Given that, as my supervisor, she knew this work well in its previous life as doctoral work, her patience in reading various drafts is unsurpassable, as is her ability to continuously offer valuable observations and new insights. I am also grateful to friends and colleagues, Jennifer Brown, Chris Crowther, Sharon Pickering, Dorothy Schulz and Richard Wild who have generously given of their time by reading drafts and providing important advice and comments. I owe an especial debt of gratitude to Chris Crowther who has demonstrated an unfailing patience over the years, expending a considerable amount of effort to ensuring the realisation of this book.

I am also thankful to the various forums that have stimulated discussion and debate. In particular, I would like to thank the third Australasian Women and Policing Conference on *Women Policing Globally*, held in Canberra in October 2002, for kindly inviting me to share my thoughts and findings with them. Such an occasion provided a remarkable opportunity to explore the international experiences of policewomen – it was also tremendously enjoyable. My appreciation also goes to the *British Association of Women Police* for being a wonderful resource, in particular, thanks to Irene Divine who has always responded to my queries so efficiently.

My thanks also go to my friends and colleagues, in particular, Brian Clark, Gary Fooks, Chris Gifford, Constantinos Phellas, Shaminder Takhar, Robert Cook and Carol Williams who have offered much moral support and provided meaningful and welcome distractions.

The enduring support and encouragement of my parents and Annette has been fundamental, as was the help of Karola Quade in the early stages. More importantly, family assurances to purchase copies of the book will hopefully have a significant impact on increasing circulation figures. Especial thanks to Stef, for the many lost weekends, for tolerating the unpredictable emotions that accompany the process of writing and above all, for reminding me of the importance of life beyond work. Also, for his meticulous care in proof reading the bibliography. Thanks must also go to Brian Willan and the production team for ensuring the smooth passage of the book.

Lastly, the study itself would not have been possible without the pioneering policewomen who agreed to participate in this study. My thanks go to them for engendering a fascination within me to want to know more about the gendered nature of policing and power.

Although I have drawn on the help and work of others, it simply remains to say that the usual caveat applies: all responsibility for misguided interpretations or omissions that follow remain my own.

Chapter 1

Introduction

The gendered world of police leadership is the focus of this book. It comes at a time when calls are being made for a different kind of police leader to guide the police organisation through the twenty-first century. Pagon (2003: 167) notes that 'Different times call for different people. Not only has police work changed, so have the public and the communities into which it is separated ... Police leaders have to change themselves, their organisations and their people.' It also comes at a time when we can see the face and faces of police leadership literally changing. In 2002, England and Wales could lay claim to four female chief constables, and twelve female assistant chiefs.[1]

The concept of change then is central to this book. Its enquiry has been shaped by two fundamental ideas about organisational change. First is the idea which suggests that by increasing the number of women in organisations greater and more sustainable forms of change will result (Itzen and Newman 1995). With reference to policing, there is a growing body of work which suggests that policewomen are engaged in the project of policing in a distinctly different way to their male counterparts (Homant and Kennedy 1985, Saunders and Size 1986, Bloch and Anderson 1974, Sherman 1975, Grennan 1987, Lunnenborg 1989, Prenzler 1997, Neiderhoffer 1974, Linden 1983, Spillar 1999). Second is the idea that leaders and managers have a significant role to play in bringing about change to organisations. This idea is central to current debates about change within policing. Police leaders have been awarded a pivotal role in driving forward organisational change (Adlam and Villiers 2003). More specifically, police leaders have been tasked with the job of developing 'ethical policing' (Neyroud and Beckley 2001, Adlam and Villiers 2003, Alderson 2003, Bunyard 2003, Richards 2003, Quinton and Miller 2003). A combination of these ideas has led directly to the focus of this book – that is, that women in police leadership positions may offer significant contributions to the project of organisational change within policing.

Women in leadership have come to be seen as both a symbol of and indeed a *measure* of organisational change. Affirming this, Wall's (1998) historical study of chief constables ends in 1996, with the arrival of Pauline Clare, Britain's first woman chief constable at Lancashire Constabulary. He notes the significance of 1996 as symbolising the end of the 'traditional symbolic male dominance of the office of chief constable', together with the 'end of patriarchy' (*ibid.*: 6). Though Wall's proposal that the appointment of a woman chief constable hails the end of the male dominance of the office is unquestionable, the idea that this signals the end of patriarchy may be somewhat premature and overstated. Nonetheless, this book is premised on the belief that things *can* and *might* be changing in the police organisation, and it is grounded in the idea that individuals are both creative and transformative agents (Giddens 1984), that despite structural constraints, individuals have the ability to bring about change, to *make a difference*.

Over the past few decades, there has been a proliferation of police research that has attempted to investigate and map out the nature and extent of organisational change in the police service. There is also a small but growing body of research that demonstrates the gendered nature of the police organisation. Instrumental in exposing the varied forms of discrimination that both men and women encounter in their work, such work remains firmly grounded in the argument that the 'cult of masculinity' (Reiner 1992), characteristic of rank-and-file culture, is a prime culprit for women's continued exclusion from policing. Those at the top of the police organisation continue to remain relatively absent from academic discourse, with the majority of studies focusing almost exclusively on the lowest levels of the organisation, favouring the lives of the rank and file than those of their managerial counterparts.

More recently, however, there does appear to be an increased interest in police leaders and leadership with some notable works emerging (Reiner 1991, Charman *et al.* 1999, Densten 1999, Loader and Mulcachy 2001, Wall 1998). An edited collection by Adlam and Villiers (2003) perhaps offers the most systematic investigation to date of those occupying senior positions. While such texts contribute much to our lack of knowledge of police leadership, none, with the exception of a chapter by Jennifer Brown in the aforementioned collection, considers gender as a variable – an analysis of masculinity and, by implication, femininity does not form part of their investigations. While leadership studies continues to be an important and prominent area of study for organisational theorists (Avolio 1999, Conger and Kanungo 1998, Northouse 1999), it still remains the case that relatively little is known about those involved in management and leadership in policing, even less about the ways in which management and leadership in the police organisation are gendered.

There are important reasons for exploring and deconstructing the experiences of senior policewomen. The most obvious one remains the need to 'plug' gaps in our academic knowledge (Reiner 1998, Stanko 1998). Senior policewomen remain relatively unchartered territory in terms of research and analysis. Exploring the diversity among women, among police officers, will also allow for more sophisticated analyses of the experience of policing to develop. More significant, perhaps, is the fact that much of the work that considers organisational change in policing fails to examine its gendered context. This book attempts to provide a conceptual bridge between these emerging discourses through an exploration of senior policewomen's careers and their engagement with the project of change.

As women move forwards and upwards in organisations, the tensions between organisations and leadership as mediated by gender have become an increasingly topical area of study. The issue of women's careers, more generally, and women's opportunities for promotion, more specifically, has recently been high on political and social agendas in Britain. A report by the Hansard Society in 1990 demonstrated a concern about the lack of women in top positions in public service. In particular, it noted women's absence from corporate management and in key areas of influence such as the media, universities and trade unions, claiming that women are 'bunched together just under the glass ceiling, with only the few breaking through this intractable barrier' (Hansard Society Commission 1990: 11). Over a decade later, we can hear such sentiments echoed in an almost parallel discourse in which the New Labour government has voiced its concern over the position of women in public life, calling for a redress of the balance of power between women and men.

Coupled with this call, the 1980s and 1990s witnessed considerable change throughout public and private sector organisations, with attempts to reorganise their directions, functions, and structures. The ability to bring about sustainable change in the police organisation continues to cause problems for those involved in implementing the processes of change. The strength and persistence of police culture continues to be routinely blamed for the failure of police reform. But while there is much to suggest that the police organisation is highly resilient to the forces of change, there is no doubt that since the 1990s we have observed a substantially altered agenda for the police organisation, both in terms of policing philosophy and in policing practice. A new managerialist order based on economy, efficiency, and effectiveness prevalent in the public sector has been ushered into policing (McLaughlin and Murji 1995, 1997, Morgan and Newburn 1997, Leisham, Loveday and Savage 1996, Waters 1996, Charman *et al.* 1999) forcing a service-wide commitment to achieving greater 'quality' of service. Such changes have also been accompanied by a number of welcome changes in equal opportunities policy in the police organisation. Collectively, Brown (2003) argues that the ideas from equal opportunities, new public sector management, and police reform offer the possibility of a 'paradigm shift', with the potential to revolutionise the police organisation and its leadership.

Given the challenges facing individuals as a result of the reorganisation of functions, directions, and structures in organisations, it has been proposed by some commentators that women may be in a particularly good position to take advantage of these opportunities to work towards transformation and change. It has been argued that such changes can transform existing structures and hierarchies, offer new ways of doing things and open up spaces in which women can seek to influence the organisations of the future (Itzen and Newman 1995), offering women the opportunity to become more active partners in the reshaping of organisations. Inherent within such discourse, women have been awarded a transformative status, with the potential to both effect and benefit from such organisational change. If we are to believe the new management forecasters, 'feminine is in – masculine is out' (Brumlop 1994: 88). Indeed, the increased number of women returned to parliament following New Labour's success at the General Election in 1997, not only provided the tabloid press with a great photo opportunity and headlines hailing the arrival of 'Blair's Babes', it also provided government with a perfect opportunity to demonstrate its new feminist credentials.

A key starting point for this book is that it is rational to recognise senior policewomen as *knowledgeable agents* who can contribute to the current state of knowledge about the police organisation. In her analysis of British and American policewomen, Heidensohn (1992: 115) argues that 'We now, certainly as far as the advanced western countries are concerned, inhabit a knowing world. Women know they are interesting and they are interested in themselves.' The term *knowledgeable agent*, within Giddens's (1984) structuration theory, involves recognition of the realities and symbiotic connections of both structure and action. Action cannot be viewed from the perspective of universal laws, because 'the causal conditions involved in generalisations about human social conduct are inherently unstable in respect of the very knowledge (or beliefs) that actors have about the circumstances of their own actions' (ibid.: xxxii). Nor can structure be assumed, in social systems, to exist outside of actions or to be determinative of outcomes; rather, it is 'the medium and outcome of the conduct it recursively organises' (ibid.: 374). For Giddens, individuals create meaning and social reality from within social settings. There is a purposive notion of human agency in which there is the ability to make a difference, and thus individuals are both creative and transformative agents. In defining senior policewomen as agents, I do not claim that they move wholly purposively through organisational life, exercising subjective choice and decision making, only that, despite structural constraints, they possess the ability to bring about change, to *make a difference*. In discussing what counts as agency, Giddens rejects the idea that human action can only be defined in terms of intentions. Rather, he argues that:

> Agency refers not to the intentions people have in doing things but to their capability of doing things in the first place (which is why agency implies power). Agency concerns events of which an individual is the perpetrator, in the sense that the individual could, at any phase in a given sequence of conduct, have acted differently. (*Ibid*.: 8)

In drawing out the power of structural elements more fully, this book is informed by Acker's (1990) fundamental principle that organisations are not gender neutral. Organisations are a key site where gender divisions are routinely created, exploited, perpetuated, and preserved. Drawing on a gendered organisation approach, together with an appreciation of human agency, this book argues that senior policewomen have the potential to be active gendering agents, with the ability to develop, reinforce, resist or transform cultural knowledge and structures in policing. At the same time, it acknowledges that structure has the potential to work towards enabling as well as constraining gendered change.

Existing theorisations of policing continue to disregard the centrality of police officers as active participants in the construction and reproduction of cultural knowledge and institutional practices. Greater appreciation of the importance of individuals as active participants is emphasised by Chan's (1997) study on organisational reform in

Australian policing. In her analysis she critiques existing conceptualisations of police culture for 'their neglect of the active role played by officers in the reproduction or transformation of culture' (*Ibid.*: 12). It is through exploring the careers of senior policewomen and raising questions about the extent to which such women in leadership positions *are* agents of change and *can become so*, that we can begin to engage with some of the more complex debates concerning leadership, gender, policing, and change.

The conduct of police officers and the performance of police organisations have increasingly come under public scrutiny in recent years following revelations of systematic corruption and malpractice in some police forces (Newburn 1999). Calls for reforming the police have become urgent items on police agendas world-wide, as evidenced in a number of damning reports, including: the *Scarman Report* (1981) following the Brixton riots; the *Mollen Report* (1994) into the New York City Police Department; the *Christopher Commission Report* (1991) following the beating of Rodney King in Los Angeles; the *Fitzgerald Report* (1989) on the Queensland Police Force; the *Wood Royal Commission Report* (1997) into New South Wales Police; the *Macpherson Inquiry* (1999) into the Metropolitan Police following the murder of black teenager Stephen Lawrence; and more recently, Lord Laming's (2003) report into the murder of eight-year-old *Victoria Climbié* and the *Stevens Enquiry* into the murder of Patrick Finucane in Northern Ireland.

These reports have explicitly condemned the nature of police culture in contributing to unacceptable police behaviour. In addition, such reports have drawn attention to the link between police malpractice and those who are involved in the work of policing, highlighting the potential implications of having policing reside in the minds and hands of a predominantely white and male organisation. In doing so, they have emphasised the need for further attention to be given to the recruitment, retention, and career progression of women and ethnic minority officers. They have also highlighted a growing concern over the quality and calibre of police leadership by drawing attention to the gap that exists between management and the rank and file.

Charman *et al.* (1999) note that it is against a background of concern over police corruption and police racism following the *Macpherson Inquiry* of 1999 that a 'crisis of police leadership' began to emerge. Rumours began to spread that the then Home Secretary, Jack Straw, was less than happy with 'the quality of police leaders' and the Home Office launched a review of recruitment, training, and selection which considered, among other things, the selection of senior officers. Indeed, the creation of the National Police Leadership Faculty and the Police

Leadership Development Board in 2001 is further evidence of the growing disquiet over the quality of police leadership.

Interestingly, such calls for change, both in terms of developing more effective leaders and in terms of increasing the number of women in policing, have, for the most part, emerged from external pressures. Women's increased presence in police agencies throughout the world has often been preceded by some contemporary crisis or controversy – the result of which has seen women being called upon as 'desperate remedies' (Heidensohn 1996b). This is consistent with the work of Fleming and Lafferty (2002) who argue that visible movements towards achieving greater gender equity owe much if not more to organisational crises than to measures explicitly designed to achieve greater equality such as equal opportunities legislation and policy. They cite the powerful effects of the *Fitzgerald Report* (1989) and the *Wood Royal Commission Report* (1997) in influencing and driving forward the debate about women in policing in Australia. Concerned with bringing about change to the heavily male-dominated 'cop culture', both reports point to the direct association between increasing the number of women police officers and reducing the levels of complaints against the police organisation. Following the number of 'formative controversies' (Savage and Charman 1996) and 'integrity lapses' (Mitchell 2003) of police organisations in Britain and throughout the world in recent decades, we should perhaps expect a continued call for more women in policing.

Despite the increased numbers of women in policing, research continues to confirm a picture of continued sexual harassment, discrimination, and differential deployment for policewomen globally (Heidensohn 1992, 2000, Mckenzie 1993, Prenzler 1997, Brown 1996, Brown and Heidensohn 2000). The issue of sex discrimination involving female senior officers was placed firmly on the agenda in 1992 when Alison Halford, then the highest serving woman as assistant chief constable, pursued a sex discrimination case against Merseyside Police relating to her failure to be appointed to a position of higher rank. The significance of this case is emphasised by McKenzie (1993) who notes that Alison Halford's sex discrimination case was to police sexism what the Brixton riots and the subsequent Scarman inquiry had been to police racism (cited in Brown, 1996).

Brown's (1998: 278) work demonstrates the continued limited access of women officers to high rank and certain specialist roles, noting that 'progress towards integration and gender equity has been glacially slow, the numbers, role and status are still marginal . . . women are still underrepresented both laterally and horizontally within the service'.

7

Given the lack of any real structural change in the numbers and positions of women, Brown (1997a) has argued that it may still be somewhat premature to measure the change that gender equity and women may bring. In this view, few gender differences will be evident so long as women remain a distinct minority, but the situation may be transformed once women reach a critical mass.[2] In an interesting model of the developmental stages of women's progression in the police service, Brown (1997b) asserts that as the number of women in the police increases, the ratio moves towards a 'tip-over' stage from minority to gender balance. It is at this 'tip-over' stage that women may have a greater impact on the nature of policing. Fielding (1999) terms these kinds of analyses as 'threshold' arguments and suggests that once women have reached the magic threshold, change will follow.

Recent figures from Social Trends (2000) demonstrate that women's presence in the labour force has been increasing. One of the most striking overall features of the labour market is that women are taking an increasingly central role. In 1971, 56 per cent of women in the UK were economically active (that is, either in work or seeking work); this had risen to 72 per cent by 1999. Despite an increase in the number of women in managerial and professional occupations, women still represented only 33 per cent of managers and administrators in 1999 (*ibid.*: 72).

The number of women police in England and Wales continues to show an upward trend, with women forming 18 per cent of total officer strength in 2002. Despite this increase, women nationally continue to find themselves under-represented at senior rank, occupying only 8 per cent of leadership positions (of the rank inspector and above) in 2002. The small numbers of senior policewomen continue to pose a problem for those wishing to engage in the debates on gender, leadership and organisational change. Despite this, my position is one that concurs with Colgan and Ledwith (1996), who argue that the increasing movement of women in the labour market is in itself a significant source of change and that simply by 'being there' women will inevitably bring new and different perspectives on employment issues and so become catalysts for change within their organisation. Though their numbers are small, there are now some women to talk to, some women who, through their presence as managers and/or leaders, may be engaged in the dynamic processes of change in the police organisation. Before outlining the scope of the book, the next section details briefly some of the methodological considerations that have shaped this study.

A methodological note

The characteristics of senior policewomen raise interesting and challenging questions for the study of methodology. All of the participants in the study are women, they are all police officers and to a certain degree they can be considered as part of an 'elite'. In many ways, senior policewomen fulfil the criteria of being a 'minority within a minority'. By virtue of their sex, they are distinct and set apart from the rest of a predominantly male organisation; they are also a minority among their 'elite' counterparts. By virtue of their rank, they are distinct and set apart from the rest of the non-elite officers in the police; they are also a minority among their female counterparts in the police organisation.

The lack of literature on chief police officers reflects the enduring problems involved in studying and trying to gain access to elite-type groups. The lack of gendered knowledge of women in police management is further compounded and perhaps better understood by the small number of women in top positions. In addition, the absence of knowledge about women in leadership may also be a result of the conflicts within feminism itself. There remain notable sources of tension within feminist theorising regarding a range of issues including: what qualifies as suitable areas of research; who should be researching them; and how they are to be researched. There are still awkward groups who pose problems for the researcher who hopes to adopt 'feminist' values. Wajcman (1996) notes a reluctance on the part of feminist sociologists studying women and work to delve into women in management. She argues that:

> Women managers have not been feminism's favourite daughters
> . . . the more pressing problem for feminists has been research into
> the continued prevalence of low pay, the failure to break down
> gender segregation of the labour market, and the concentration of
> women in under-valued part-time work. (*Ibid*.: 260)

Feminist researchers have been much more concerned with 'researching down, rather than researching up' (Puwar 1997). In the same vein, but with respect to policewomen, Heidensohn (1992: 109) notes that:

> The study of women as social control agents does not fit as easily
> into the various feminist paradigms which have informed much
> modern research on women and from women's perspectives . . .
> [W]omen who are, in some way 'part of the problem', who share,
> however meagrely, in the system of oppression are not, therefore,

easily assimilated into feminist politics or happily explained in the framework.

One of the challenges of this study has been to overcome some of the contradictions and problems encountered when exploring the lives and positions of high-status and potentially non-feminist women from a feminist perspective. Equipped with the recipe for conducting feminist research (Roberts 1981, Maynard and Purvis 1994, Oakley 1981, Stanley and Wise 1990), I was keen to establish a research process that minimised the power relations between the researcher and the researched. The experiences that were to follow, however, did not always correspond to other feminist accounts of doing research. My own experiences of the difficulties involved in developing a 'woman to woman' rapport or sharing experiences based around the notion of 'womanhood' were to provide vital clues for my analysis of the nature and extent of women's activism in policing. In policing, the sharing of womanhood is compounded and heavily demarcated by rank, hierarchy, and the power that this brings. My own experience as a female researcher of women has shown that acquiring the label of 'feminist' is an easy accomplishment in the police organisation; this was secured simply by my interest in women. More importantly, 'feminism' and 'feminists' have no place in the police organisation.

The problematic nature of 'researching up' has been echoed by other women conducting work on women in power (Puwar 1997, Millen 1997). In her analysis of interviewing female MPs, Puwar (1997: 11) argues that

> feminists who are 'researching up' come across a whole set of distinctive problems during the course of their fieldwork. Issues related to space, talk, access, control and empowerment have a bearing upon the research relationship in quite a different way to when feminists are 'researching down'.

The power asymmetry is in many ways reversed when researching women elites. Exploring the dynamics of the interview situation itself offers many clues to the distinctiveness and meanings of power in the creation of (gendered) identities in the police organisation. An appreciation of the meanings of police work and the implications that these may hold for police officers in the construction of their identities goes some way in accounting for the dynamics I encountered.

Police officers are by their very nature symbols of authority; through their position they are the possessors of legitimate power. As legitimate agents of social control, they are skilled interrogators; they are the ones who ask the questions. They have the power and are able to control and set the agenda in interactions with those they police; this is true even for those officers occupying the lowest rank of constable. Waddington (1999a) notes that when police intervene in some situations,

> they do so *authoritatively*; *they* structure conversation around *their* concerns; *they* are expected to display certainty and not to equivocate; *they* find it difficult to apologise, since this is tantamount to demeaning themselves; and most of all *they demand deference*. (*Ibid.*: 20, original emphasis)

Police officers have come to expect a degree of respect and deference from those who are not members of the police organisation. Expecting and accepting deference and respect play a key part in their daily existence and in the construction and maintenance of their identities. Combining their status as police officers with the possession of rank serves to produce a powerful identity rooted in notions of power, authority, and superiority. Such an identity poses serious challenges to the conceptualisations of power relations addressed by feminist theory. Traditionally, it is the researcher who is defined by the interviewee as *an expert*. As a result, the 'deference effect' may come into play, causing problems preventing the interviewer from gathering good data (Bernard 1994). The case is somewhat reversed in this research; being an academic does not necessarily equate to being cast into the role of 'expert'. On the contrary, it can be argued that academics are often portrayed as those with no knowledge of the 'real' world, and certainly no knowledge of what is involved in 'real' policing. In my case, the display of deference and the conferring of 'expert' status to participants appeared a more successful strategy in working towards the creation of a good research relationship.

The research is based on in-depth, semi-structured interviews carried out with thirty senior policewomen in Britain, including officers from inspector to chief officer ranks – that is, those belonging to the Association of Chief Police Officers (ACPO). The fieldwork was carried out within four police service areas in England and Wales and was conducted over a ten-month period in 1998. The choice of police areas was informed by a number of considerations; above all, the forces chosen were noted for their progressive thinking on equality issues together with their good intake of women. Searching for, and gaining access to, elite women in the police organisation proved to be problematic from the outset. There are considerable difficulties in gaining access to minority groups in policing – in this case, 'women' and 'elites'. Both groups are few in number, more easily identifiable and yet harder to locate than their male non-managerial counterparts. Their small number affords them a higher degree of visibility which, in turn, causes potential conflicts for the maintenance of anonymity.

Given their small number, it became obvious at the outset that a focus solely on women of ACPO rank would have proved methodologically problematic. A wider representation of 'seniority' has therefore been adopted. One of the realities of a hierarchical organisation is that there are many forms of leadership that deserve recognition. The power to bring about change does not lie exclusively in the hands of chief constables. Rather, leaders and managers, 'mini-chief constables', exist at many levels of the organisation (Reiner 1991). The idea that other members of the managerial hierarchy can bring about cultural change can be clearly evidenced in Foster's (1989) work in which she points to the solid commitment and support of the entire management hierarchy in accounting for successful changes in police style and practice. Skolnick and Bayley (1986) also reach a similar conclusion, demonstrating the vigour of innovative US police chiefs, and other managers lower down the police hierarchy, who have successfully reoriented their departments towards a community policing culture.

There was a good mix of uniformed and CID officers within the sample, a ratio of 20:10 respectively. Women's service length ranged from under ten to over thirty years. In terms of their personal characteristics, twenty-one women were married and, of those, eleven had children. Of the nine women who were not married, none had children. Educationally, there were seventeen graduates including four post-graduates. All of the policewomen in this study are white.

In emphasising the need for a gendered reading of organisational life, I am conscious of the partial picture that may result, given the diversity of women in policing. Research has demonstrated the potential richness that may result from accounts that combine the interactive effects of race, ethnicity, class, and gender. At the time the fieldwork for this study was carried out, the highest rank attained by ethnic minority women was chief inspector, of which there was one; there were also three inspectors. In 2002, this stood at one superintendent, one chief inspector, and ten inspectors. The lives of black and ethnic minority women remain relatively unexplored both in the women in management literature, more broadly, and in the women in policing literature, more specifically. Although some research has been attentive to the policing of ethnic minority groups, the racialisation of relations within the police service remains an under-researched topic of study. Studies by Holdaway (1996), Holdaway and Barron (1997) and Bland *et al.* (1999) on the experiences of ethnic minority officers remain male centred. The value of a more integrated gendered and racialised approach can be found in some of the American works of Belknap and Shelley (1992), Martin (1992, 1994), Felknes and Schroedel (1993) and Pogrebin *et al.* (1999), who have all explored the intersection of race and gender more specifically. Research conducted by Pogrebin *et al.* (*Ibid.*: 55) illustrates well the complexity of diversity among women. They argue that women from ethnic minorities in policing face a threefold occupational dilemma, in that 'they are members of a minority group in a white dominated organisation; they are female in a male dominated work place; and often they are resented by black community members they come into contact with while on the job'. A detailed analysis of the racialised and gendered experience of policing in Britain remains absent, but the case of former constable Sarah Locker (who achieved a compensation package worth £1 million in June 2000 from the Metropolitan Police, following a barrage of sexual and racial discrimination) serves to remind us of the issues raised by the combined effects of a sexist and racist cop culture. Understanding the experience of ethnic minority women may also hold the key to illuminating debates about the potentially unintended divisive effects of activism among women in organisations. I will return to some of the debates about women organising across difference in Chapter 6.

Asking senior policewomen to reflect about their careers gave them an opportunity to talk at length about themselves, to offer in effect their 'life stories' (Chase 1995). When respondents talked about their past careers and their futures within the organisation it frequently became difficult to disentangle their accounts from issues of personal identity, but such reflections have served to give context to the gendered nature of their lives. It was through these 'stories of the self' (Halford *et al.* 1997) that women began to map out the processes of marking time. Nicholson and West (1989) emphasise that career narratives are stories of transitions, punctuations, pauses, and turning points that mark work histories. One of the key themes from women's narratives of their career was the significance of 'time' both as a defining feature of their identity and as a key resource for managing a successful career in policing. The way in which time is constructed, manipulated, and experienced is central to our understanding of the police organisation. It is women's reflections and conceptualisation of time that have helped to shape the broad themes of this study. In the main, senior policewomen's narratives were characterised by three significant moments in time: the *past*, which I conceive of in terms of the processes involved in 'getting there'; the *present*, making reference to 'being there'; and the *future*, inextricably bound with the processes involved in 'staying there'.

Mindful of the potential problems and critiques that accompany the recounting and reflection of 'life stories' (some of the women inter- viewed had a career that spanned more than thirty years), an array of official documentation was also consulted. This centred around policy documents and data that provided information on: the changing gender composition and deployment of the workforce; formal express- ions of equality; organisational competence and skill; and documenta- tion from various minority networks in policing including the: British Association of Women Police (BAWP); National Black Police Associ- ation (NBPA); Lesbian and Gay Police Association (LAGPA); Action E; European Network of Policewomen (ENP); International Association of Women Police (IAWP); Feminist Majority Foundation (FMF). Such consultation has helped to provide some form of 'reality check' on women's potential reflexive reading of the past.

In presenting women's narratives throughout the book, I make no reference to their names, ranks, or force areas. My decision to present data in such a way relates directly to the relatively small number and high visibility of these women. An important condition of conducting the research was the assurance of confidentiality. Although much social research remains governed by such conditions, the depth of senior policewomen's concern about being identified tells us much about the precarious position in which they may perceive themselves to be. It is also worth reiterating here that an acknowledgement of the timing of this study will give greater context to its findings. Despite the current push towards change for women being advocated by the Gender Agenda,[3] at the time of conducting this fieldwork there was little evidence of a coordinated approach towards pushing forward gender issues among British policewomen. Methodologically, the study of elite women, or women who hold some measure of social power, has above all highlighted the need for a more subtle and detailed characterisation of power within feminist research than has so far been available.

Scope of the book

Chapter 2 situates the book within ongoing theoretical debates that govern the study of gender and organisations, drawing on the valuable work of Acker (1990, 1992). Out of a growing dialogue between feminist theory and organisation theory, a concern with the way in which organisations are themselves gendered has emerged (Ferguson 1984, Acker 1990, Mills and Tancred 1992). One of the key features of this approach is that it provides an understanding of the ways in which gender divisions are actively created and sustained in the processes of organisational life. In particular, this chapter focuses on the way in which gender is socially constructed and institutionalised within the police organisation. It emphasises the importance of culture as a site of gendered meaning and challenges existing conceptualisations of that culture. In doing so, it points to the inadequacies of existing theorisations for the study of police leaders. Calls to shift our monolithic perception of police culture (Chan 1997, Reiner 1992, Waddington 1999a) continue to be made but largely remain unheard and unanswered. This chapter goes some way towards responding to that call, in this case investigating how culture may be shaped by both rank and gender.

It proposes an appreciation of a multiplicity of police culture(s) for understanding the construction(s) and meaning(s) of police work and police identity(ies). In the same way that lower-ranking officers inhabit a shared world of meanings, it follows that police leaders also inhabit a world of shared rituals, symbols, languages, practices, rationales, and values that translate into scripts. In doing policing, officers demonstrate 'customary ways of doing things', passing on customs from one generation to the next (Panzarella 2003). Such scripts are, in turn, drawn upon in the construction of their identities and work. The cult of masculinity to which we have become so routinely accustomed, characterises and refers predominantly to the culture of those at the bottom, the male rank and file. Such an analysis of masculinity remains inadequate when trying to explain the gendered identity of those at the top in policing. As women progress through the ranks, they join new circles, new groups, each with its own distinct set of behavioural prescriptions, and each with its own set of gendered identities. Senior policewomen face a different kind of gendered environment than their non-managerial counterparts, one in which 'managerial masculinity' dominates. Changes brought about as a result of the movement towards greater quality of service have served to create a new 'smart macho' culture (Maddock and Parkin 1993) of police management. In occupying this new territory, its inhabitants are fierce, tough, forceful, and quick thinking, displaying ruthlessness, competitiveness, and risk taking. Above all the police leader remains male. The lack of acknowledgement of the existence of multiple masculinities in policing serves to seriously underestimate the effects for senior women in policing. An appreciation of multiple masculinities will enable us to make better sense of why women continue to be absent from the higher echelons of policing, with the 'smart macho' culture of policing providing ample opportunities for social closure.

In much the same way that organisations have been viewed in gender-neutral terms, so too have the processes of change. The extent to which organisational changes in policing may affect women has not been a topic of investigation. The processes of change and organisational restructuring in policing are themselves better understood as gendered processes. Chapter 3 contributes to debates about organisational change in policing by considering the concept of 'change' through an insight into the gendered effects of change through the doctrines of 'quality' and 'equality'.

Although slow in responding to policy initiatives and lagging behind other public and private sector organisations, the police service has gone some way towards introducing equality initiatives for its officers. There is much to suggest that through such change the police service of the twenty-first century is able to lay claim to a changed identity for both its organisation and its officers. In support of their proposition of 'epochal' change within police organisations across developed economies, Bayley and Shearing (1996) cite the police service's search for a new identity as evidence of this change. The movement towards developing diversity through equal opportunities appears an obvious site for exploring a changing police identity. The significance of equal opportunities as a possible site for forging police officer identity becomes even more convincing if we look at the way in which the police organisation has vociferously resisted attempts to introduce equality for its officers.[4]

The inclusion and movement towards more flexible working practices are being hailed as indicative of organisations that are serious about developing and managing diversity successfully within their organisations. The potential effects of flexible working practices are wide and far-reaching and raise important questions for the career progression of police officers. More specifically, the gendered effects of such change may hold significant implications for the progression of women in policing. Much of the work that concerns itself with issues of equality takes the 1970s and the wave of equality legislation that ensued as a starting point for its analyses. Organisational change concerned with issues in equality, however, has a much longer history in policing.

A recurrent theme throughout the research on women in policing is the conception of policewomen as 'pioneers' (Heidensohn 1992, Schulz 1995). Such a conception remains useful in examining the careers of senior policewomen at the beginning of the twenty-first century. There are still pioneer women in policing, women who are now occupying new spaces and new territories. An awareness of policewomen's early experiences in policing adds a valuable dimension to contemporary debates about policing and change. It could also offer important lessons for those women who might be currently involved in the change process. Drawing on what we already know from their historical counterparts, the prognosis is mixed. Historical analyses demonstrate that policewomen encountered resistance in gaining admittance and progression in policing, that above all it was policemen on the whole who most vehemently opposed their presence and progression (Lock 1979, Carrier 1988, Heidensohn 1992, Schulz 1995, Appier 1998). On a more positive note, the power of individual agency exercised by policewomen themselves is clearly visible through their campaign to achieve a permanent place for women in policing. The continued belief in their skills, their perseverance, and fighting spirit all provide grounds for future optimism for police-women today.

In bringing into focus senior policewomen's experiences of organisa-tional life, Chapter 4 provides an insight into the 'making' of police leaders, focusing more closely on the processes involved in getting to the top. If we are to fully engage with debates about why women are not reaching senior ranks, it is crucial to explore more deeply the route they face in their progression through the ranks. It is not my intention here to provide an in-depth account of the selection and training procedures for police officers,[5] but rather to critically consider the organisational arrangements for progression in policing by going beyond the assumption that a neutral administrative logic prevails. It offers an account of the gendered nature of the climbing frame available to police officers for their progression through the ranks, and more specifically it details how policewomen themselves make sense of the climbing frame by highlighting some of the strategies they have employed to rise through the ranks.

The managing of both 'time' and 'place' is central to women's narratives, both as a defining feature of their identity and as a key resource for achieving a successful career in policing. Through managing 'time' and 'place', police leaders are able to accomplish organisational commitment and credibility, two fundamental yet essentially informal competencies. These elements tell us much about the practical and symbolic meanings that characterise the journey of 'becoming' a police leader. It also tells us much about some of the more complex ways in which gendered processes operate within the police organisation, taking account of both explicit and institutional as well as more subtle and cultural forms that are submerged in organisational decisions.

An important aim of this book is to offer an assessment of the potential changes that gender equity, more generally, and the increased presence of women in police management, more specifically, might bring to the police organisation. Chapter 5 explores the ongoing processes involved in the *doing* of leadership, through an investigation into how women in police leadership positions see themselves both as women and as organisational members. There appears to be a consensus among organisational theorists that the autocratic style of leadership, which once characterised most organisations, is now outdated and counterproductive. There are also those who have pushed forward the idea that the police service of the twenty-first century requires a much more 'democratic and less dictatorial style' (Villiers 2003a: 29). The new policing agenda requires officers to rely on interpersonal rather than crime-fighting skills, 'more brain, less brawn' (BAWP 2002, Quirk 2002), a change that has been regarded by some commentators as the 'feminising' of the management of social control (Martin 1996). Heidensohn (1992: 244) notes that social control has become 'feminized' in nature, that 'organizations and issues have operated in less confrontational, less informal and more negotiated ways'.

Yet, despite the call for a different kind of police leader, recent work by Villiers (2003a: 29) continues to advocate a position where

> the old style ... has so far survived all attempts to achieve its extirpation ... [and that] ... in reality, the bulk of senior police commanders remain autocrats – even those who advanced changing the culture when they occupied a position of middle management within it.

While studies have demonstrated the various ways in which women offer substantial and significant benefits for the police organisation of the twenty-first century, Villiers reminds us, 'we do not know what a police service *led* by a proportionate representation of women police officers would be like or what it could achieve' (*ibid.*: 31, emphasis added). This chapter addresses such a concern by focusing more closely on investigating the extent to which senior policewomen are involved in developing new styles and conceptualisations of leadership. An investigation into how senior policewomen characterise effective leadership, together with an analysis of how their own style fits with the broader organisational style, reveals important gendered notions of competence. It also reveals something of the negotiations taking place and the experiences women have in making their work effective in the organisation.

Debates concerning organisational change have routinely centred on the idea that by increasing the number of minority groups in organisations, change will inevitably follow. Such a proposition can be found most notably in Kanter's (1977) model of organisational change. Kanter's thesis is based on the idea that as the number of minority groups in organisations rises, discriminatory treatment should decline and gender balance will 'bureaucratize' out the inequalities that minority groups face. That organisations would be more representative and democratic should a more equitable ratio between groups be achieved is undeniable; it does not, however, necessarily serve to better the position in which minority groups may find themselves. With regard to women in policing, Brown and Heidensohn's (2000: 156) study challenges Kanter's thesis, finding that 'there is no bureaucratizing out of discrimination and harassment by dint of numbers alone'.

While there continues to be a call for more women in management, it is worth remembering that women in management are highly diverse and difficult to classify as a group in their career patterns, leadership styles, and policy agendas. The perception that women managers enter organisations with the intention of representing other women and their interests is a naïve one. Such a position has much to do with the nature of their consciousness and their willingness to take action to address organisational inequalities (Ledwith and Colgan 1996). Mindful of this, Chapter 6 examines some of the resources that exist in the police organisation to promote women's status. It also considers the extent to which senior policewomen themselves are actively working to make gender and equality issues visible and central to police organisational agendas. In short, it assesses the extent to which senior policewomen may be acting as 'femocrats' (Sawer 1995) and challenges the idea of sisterhood as a valid basis for working with women in the twenty-first century. The Conclusion reflects more broadly on the issue of change, assessing the extent to which the police organisation can legitimately claim organisational change through an agenda of equal opportunities. It also reviews the role that women as police leaders are playing in the change process and offers some observations on the potential of current change initiatives.

Notes

1 Statistics from Smith *et al.* (2002) claim there are six female chief constables, and ten female assistant chiefs in England and Wales. Such a claim is misleading and a distortion of the numbers of actual female chief constables. The record number of female chief constables has been calculated by including deputy and assistant commissioner posts in the Metropolitan Police within the category of chief constable.
2 Critical mass theory suggests that once the proportion of minority groups rises to around 30 per cent, the policy agenda will shift, reflecting more accurately the interests of all groups.
3 Launched in 2001, the Gender Agenda has been developed by an executive group representing the British Association of Women Police (BAWP), Action E, the Senior Women Officers' Conference, the Police Federation, the Association of Chief Police Officers (ACPO) Women's Group, the Metropolitan Association of Senior Women Officers, and the European Network of Policewomen (ENP).
4 Calls to be exempt from the provisions of the 1975 Equality Act came from the three police staff associations. Powerful objections against the integration of women into policing were made on a number of grounds including: the unsuitability of police duties for women; their physical and emotional deficits; the risks they posed to male colleagues (both in terms of the possible distractions caused by potential sexual liaisons and their inability to provide back-up to male colleagues); and the economic feasibility of women, related to their likelihood of leaving the police after marriage and/or childbearing (Brown 2003).
5 For an interesting insider's view, see Adlam's (2003a) account.

Chapter 2

The police organisation: a gendered site

Research on organisations has historically paid little attention to the significance of gender with the field almost exclusively dominated by malestream approaches and ways of viewing and understanding organisational reality. In recent years, however, a concern with the way in which organisations are themselves gendered has emerged. A considerably large body of research has documented the pervasiveness of gender beliefs, constructions, and practices in organisations (Baron and Davis-Blake 1986, Bielby and Baron 1987, Boyd *et al.* 1991, Cockburn 1988, Cohn 1985, Hearn and Parkin 1987, Hearn *et al.* 1989, Reskin and Hartmann 1986, Reskin and Roos 1990, Ferguson 1984, Acker 1990, Mills and Tancred 1992). Some have adopted a historical perspective, demonstrating how certain jobs and occupations came to be seen as appropriate for women or men (Cockburn 1983, 1985, Davies 1982, Mills 1989, Pringle 1989, Witz 1990, 1992). Other studies have taken an ethnographic approach, looking at the ways in which interactions between workers or individual strategies for identity maintenance serve to engender work and workers themselves (Collinson and Collinson 1989, Hall 1993, Leidner 1991, Pierce 1996, Williams 1989, 1992, 1995).

The absence of enquiry into the significance of gender for policing is evident within police literature, with only a handful of researchers taking gender as their main focus. Indeed, even the chapter on 'Policing and the Police' in the most recent edition of the *Oxford Handbook of Criminology* (Maguire *et al.* 2002) pays scant, if any, attention to gender issues. There is now a small but strong caucus of research on gender issues and policing. Much of this work points to the importance of studying police culture as a site of gendered meanings. The study of culture as a site of gendered meanings has become a major theme in the study of organisations more broadly. With enormous variation in the use of the term 'culture' in organisation theory, I have found the definition offered by Strati (1992: 578) a useful one, encompassing a broad base and incorporating both conscious and unconscious dimensions:

> An organizational culture consists of the symbols, beliefs and patterns of behaviour learned, produced and created by the people who devote their energies and labour to the life of an organization. It is expressed in the design of the organization and of work, in the artifacts and services that the organization produces, in the architecture of its premises, in the technologies that it employs, in its ceremonials of encounter and meeting, in the temporal structuring of organizational courses of action, in the quality and conditions of its working life, in the ideologies of work, in the corporate philosophy, in the jargon, lifestyle and physical appearance of the organization's members.

Gender not only provides a key for the interpretation of organisational cultures, it is one of their distinguishing features. Police organisational cultures are powerful sites where symbols, images, and forms of consciousness that explicate and justify gender divisions are created and sustained. It is here that gender symbols are attached to actions and behaviours, which have little to do with biological sex (Hunt 1984).

Various aspects of police culture have been cited for their damaging effects on the internal relations between police officers and on relations with citizens, but, for the purpose of this book, a key element of that culture – the cult of masculinity – has been noted for its ruinous effects on women and on some men (Burke 1993). The police culture is one that is hostile to women and continues to have a strong influence in defining and structuring policing and police work (Holdaway 1983, Fielding 1988, Feinman 1986, Reiner 1978, 1992, Smith and Gray 1983, Young 1991, Anderson et al. 1993, Heidensohn 1992, Fielding 1994a, Chan 1997, Cain 1973, Manning 1977, 1989, Waddington 1999b). Efforts at police reform have therefore been directed at breaking up, or at least attempting to dilute, elements of police culture.

Despite the fact that policing scholars have come to acknowledge that police culture is 'neither monolithic, universal nor unchanging' (Reiner 1992), the majority of work continues to neglect the diversity and multiplicity of organisational culture in the police. Reflecting on the lack of change following enormous organisational reform in Australian policing, Chan (1997: 12) critiques existing conceptualisations of police culture for 'their inability to account for differences in culture'. In response, she proposes that a full and comprehensive theory of police culture should account for internal differentiation and jurisdictional differences with multiple cultures. It is the potential differences brought about by rank, together with an appreciation of the impact that gender may have on such divisions, that is at the centre of my enquiry. This chapter addresses the calls made by Chan (*ibid.*) and Reiner (1992) to develop our understanding of police culture through a greater appreciation of the multiplicity involved in understanding culture(s) as site(s) of gendered meaning(s). Before doing so, it is worth outlining in more detail the theoretical framework that governs this study.

A gendered reading of organisations

It was Acker (1990, 1992) who made one of the first systematic attempts to theorise the processes through which organisations and occupations are gendered at both institutional and individual levels. The usefulness of Acker's approach lies in its ability to unlock the role of both structure and individual agency. In 1990, Acker outlined the inadequacies of organisational theory and asserted that a systematic theory of gender and organisation was necessary. In particular, she pointed to the way in which the gender segregation of work and the inequality between women and men in terms of income and status are created through organisational processes and practices. Organisations provide forums within which cultural images of gender are invented and then reproduced.

For Acker (1990), organisations are arenas in which both gender and sexuality have been obscured through gender-neutral, asexual discourses, concealing the embodied elements of work. As a result, she argues, job positions and management hierarchies assume a universal, disembodied worker. In thinking about the ways in which organisations reproduce gendered identities, she suggests that the bureaucratic organisation has a 'gendered substructure' – that is, the social practices that are generally understood to constitute an 'organisation' rest on certain gendered processes and assumptions. In defining this substructure, Acker (1992: 255) argues that:

23

> The gendered substructure lies in the spatial and temporal arrangements of work, in the rules prescribing workplace behaviour and in the relations linking work places to living places. These practices and relations, encoded in arrangements and rules, are supported by assumptions that work is separate from the rest of life and that it has the first claim on the worker.

Here Acker is arguing that organisational designs and established norms are far closer to men's lives and assumptions about men than to women's lives and the assumptions made about women. It is men's bodies, men's sexuality, and men's relationships to procreation and production that are subsumed in the image of the disembodied worker. As a result, gender is difficult to see when only the masculine is present. Inherent within her theory of gendered organisations is the proposition that the feminist project should work to make large-scale organisations more democratic and supportive of humane goals.

Acker's approach emphasises that men and women encounter gender meanings, relationships, and identities which are embedded in the social setting itself, as part and parcel of the roles and scripts deemed appropriate for that setting. Hence gender is defined here as a contextually situated process and is conceived of as an emergent property of social situations rather than as an individual characteristic. Instead of a characteristic that people have, gender is something that individuals *do* with their behaviour and organisations *do* through the gendering processes and structures. Here individuals create social constructions of behaviour, among them the gender differences between men and women. Such gendering processes mean that 'advantage and disadvantage, exploitation and control, action and emotion, meaning and identity, are patterned through and in terms of a distinction between male and female, feminine and masculine' (Acker 1990: 146). Concepts of masculinity and femininity are socially learned and reinforced, not biologically determined or reflective of natural differences (West and Zimmerman 1987). *Doing* gender, then, involves a 'complex of perceptual, interactional and micropolitical activities that cast particular pursuits as expressions of manly and womanly "natures" ' (West and Fenstermaker 1995: 9).

The extent to which the work of policing has been cast and constructed as an expression of 'manliness' is explored later in this chapter. There is a considerable body of research that confirms the notion that organisations are not made up of empty, gender-neutral positions, filled in accordance with the dictates of rationality or efficiency based on applicants, objectives, and qualifications irrespective of gender. On the contrary, research demonstrates that practically all jobs and job ladders are gender specific and practically all job searches are gender searches. Research on flight attendants (Hochschild 1983); fast food counter clerks and insurance agents (Leidner 1991); radiologists (Cockburn 1988); nurses (Williams 1989); computer specialists (Kiesler *et al.* 1985, Wright 1996, Turkle 1984, 1988); table servers (Hall 1993); and prison officers (Jurik 1985, 1988, Owen 1988, Pollock 1986, Martin and Jurik 1996, Zimmer 1986, 1987, Britton 1997) all document the way in which job tasks, and not just the workers performing them, are loaded with gender meanings. Women are sought for women's jobs; men are sought for men's jobs (Acker 1990, Williams 1989). More significantly, women are rarely employed to manage men whereas many men manage women (Reskin and Ross 1992).

For Acker (1992), understanding the gendered nature of organisations more fully requires an appreciation of various elements and processes. The first set of processes involve the production of gender divisions, which can, for example, be evidenced in the gender patterning of jobs, tasks, and hierarchies. These gendered processes operate on many levels from the explicit and institutional to the more subtle cultural forms that are submerged in organisational decisions. They include the way men's influence is embedded in rules and procedures, formal job definition, functional roles, and the accumulation of competence, skill, and merit. Ideas about femininity and masculinity are embedded in organisational arrangements, and the opportunities to accumulate 'merit' are structured along gender lines (Burton 1992). The organisational arrangements for achieving merit in the police organisation are examined more closely in Chapter 4 with an insight into the processes involved in the making of police leaders. The second set of processes involve the creation of symbols and images that explain and justify gender divisions. In reproducing gendered organisations, interactions between individuals are crucial as they enact dominance and subordination and create alliances and exclusions; images here are constructed and confirmed. Lastly are the processes in which individuals consciously construct their own understandings of the organisation's gendered structures of work and hence provide the appropriate gender response, in terms of behaviours and attitudes (Acker 1992: 252–3). This might, for example, include the creation of the correct gendered persona with roles and scripts deemed appropriate for that setting (Hall 1993).

Consisting of both a cognitive element (inferences that permit understanding and comprehension) and a behavioural element (activated performances) in a particular social setting, the concept of scripts describes a 'predetermined, stereotyped sequence of actions that defines a well known situation' (Schank and Abelson 1977, cited in Hall 1993: 457). Hall's (1993) research on restaurants and servers, for example, demonstrates that restaurants *do* gender by defining the smiling, deferring, and flirting scripts in gender terms and by demanding appropriate behaviour. Male and female servers *do* gender by differentially enacting gendered scripts of 'good service'. Attention to scripts serves to demonstrate how organisations and their participants encompass, construct, and maintain gender differences. Chapters 5 and 6 scrutinise in more depth the processes through which policewomen consciously and sometimes unconsciously construct their own understanding of the organisation's gendered structures of work, by detailing the responses that women offer in terms of their behaviours, scripts, and attitudes in *doing* leadership.

The construction of police work as 'manly'

To propose that the nature and substance of police work and identity are characterised by a cult of masculinity remains uncontested within the police literature. It has been argued that the cult of masculinity is strongly grounded in heterosexuality where particular notions of masculinity govern. In deciphering the cult of masculinity, Fielding (1994a) argues that its stereotypical values may be read as an almost pure form of 'hegemonic masculinity'. Hegemonic masculinity refers to the currently dominant form of masculinity as constructed in relation to (and therefore dependent on) femininities and subordinated, marginalised masculinities (Connell 1987). In support of his argument, Fielding (1994a: 47) asserts that stereotypical values serve to highlight:

> (i) aggressive, physical action; (ii) a strong sense of competitiveness and preoccupation with the imagery of conflict; (iii) exaggerated heterosexual orientations, often articulated in terms of misogynistic and patriarchal attitudes towards women; and (iv) the operation of rigid in-group/out-group distinctions whose consequences are strongly exclusionary in the case of out-groups and strongly assertive of loyalty and affinity in the case of in-groups.

What remains ambiguous within the policing literature is the explanatory power of the cult of masculinity, as described above, for making sense of the experiences of policing for those who do not occupy rank-and-file positions – that is, for senior officers. While policing scholars may be guilty of failing to acknowledge and realise the potential effects that a gendered reading might hold for women, it remains the case that masculinity is often a taken-for-granted feature of the police organisation.

Indeed, much of the work on gender and organisations can be critiqued for its essentialist nature regarding men, with many writers tending to treat masculinity as if it were homogenous. There is, however, a small but growing body of work that develops a more sophisticated appreciation of masculinities in organisations. Themes that persistently emerge from this work include the plurality of masculinities and management styles (Collinson and Hearn 1994, Hearn and Collison 1996, Hollway 1996, Kerfoot and Knights 1993, Roper 1994, 1996) and the centrality of notions of control, rationality, and expertise to discourses of masculinity (Burris 1996, Hearn and Collinson 1996). In combating the problems of reification and essentialism in criminology, Newburn and Stanko (1994) also urge an appreciation of the multiplicity of masculinities.

In documenting multiple masculinities, Maddock and Parkin (1993) outline six varieties of masculinities that have shaped the working practices of organisational cultures. These include: the 'gentlemen's club', an extremely exclusive culture based on old-fashioned principles where women are patronised in a paternalistic way; the 'barrack yard', a culture in which bullying is a key feature of working relations; the 'locker room', where men build relationships based on a series of shared assumptions; the 'gender blind' culture, in which a level playing field is assumed where women can excel if they simply try; the 'feminist pretender' culture, where the practices of women have not really changed yet men salute equal opportunities policies; and finally the 'smart macho' culture, where the pressure is clearly on corporate performance. In offering different interpretations of 'maleness' and 'masculinity', these cultures continue to reflect the commonality of patriarchal values prevalent within the organisation.

Alongside the need to recognise the existence of multiple masculinities is an understanding of the concept of masculinity as something that is accomplished. As Messerschmidt (1993: 80–1) writes:

> masculinity is accomplished, it is not something done to men or something settled beforehand. And masculinity is never static, never a finished product ... Masculinity must be viewed as structured action – what men do under specific constraints and varying degrees of power.

The nature of enacted masculinity may take on different forms, with the ability to *do* masculinity being influenced by a range of elements including, race, class, age, and sexuality.

In a review of the literature on occupations, Connell (1987) observes, for example, that the masculinity in working-class jobs focuses on physical prowess and sexual contempt for men in managerial or office positions. In his study of the management team of the Space Shuttle *Challenger* disaster, Messerschmidt (1996) demonstrates a middle-class display of masculine prowess. He argues that for the corporate managers of Morton Thiokol Inc., risk taking became the situation-defining feature of managerial masculinity. For these men, 'doing risk was simultaneously doing masculinity'. Facing economic pressures that focused on the present and the near future, male managers concentrated on 'the next milestone, the next contract, the next stockholder' (*ibid*.: 40). In acknowledging the importance of multiple masculinities, Cheng (1996) stresses that gender writers who intentionally disregard diverse types of masculinities, especially marginalised, subordinated, and colonised ones, are playing a 'zero-sum, hegemonically masculine game of "oppression Olympics"', which mistakenly assumes that acknowledging the oppression of other groups will detract from one's own oppressed group. Such inter-group conflict colludes with and strengthens the existing hegemonically masculine system. Drawing on the notion of multiple gendered identities, together with the idea of gender as an accomplishment, serves to remind us that there are different ways of *doing* gender and that both men and women have the potential to *do* masculinity and femininity. Masculinities need not be about the male sex, as masculinity can be, and is, performed by women. Baril *et al.* (1989) and Cheng (1996), for example, argue that women who are successful managers can be seen to be performing hegemonic masculinity.

To what extent and in what way do senior policewomen experience the cult of masculinity? Do their experiences of being in leadership positions share anything in common with their past experiences of being rank-and-file officers? Do women confront different gendered scripts for masculinity and femininity as they progress through the ranks? If so, how do they read and decipher such scripts? More fundamentally, are they involved in the rewriting of scripts? Such questions challenge the long-standing association between the cult of masculinity and women's negative experiences of policing, and propose more reflexive readings of masculinity and femininity within policing. Before addressing these questions, it might be useful to detail what we already know about the experiences of women in policing.

The research on women and policing continues to provide substantial evidence of the continued discriminatory gendered nature of policing. Despite the formal integration of women into policing in the mid-1970s, and a barrage of new directives and systems to develop more creative and all-encompassing equal opportunities for police officers, research continues to confirm the idea that while theoretically, integration has occurred, women are not fully accepted by their male colleagues and continue to be subject to sexual harassment, discrimination, and differential deployment.

An extensive review of practices conducted by the Equal Opportunities Commission in 1990 into the Metropolitan Police Service reported that women were excluded from a number of specialisms. The Commission found that women were unlikely to be employed in public order duties and were more likely to be assigned to inside station duties, communication departments, or to have responsibility for young people, women victims or offenders. In 1992, a thematic inspection by Her Majesty's Inspectorate of Constabulary (HMIC) on the progress made by forces in implementing equal opportunities policies demonstrated continued blatant breaches of equal opportunities policy and a serious problem of sexual harassment (HMIC 1992). It also stressed that while all forces had written equal opportunities policies, the majority of forces inspected had no grievances recorded. In 1993, research by Anderson *et al.* (1993) went on to suggest that fewer than a third of police officers had sufficient confidence to use grievance procedures. They also found that women officers reported sexual harassment and high levels of discriminatory practices in career advancement, deployment practices, and access to benefits. Above all, they firmly assert that whatever their rank, women officers are more likely to be differentially deployed compared to their male equivalents. The Kinsey Lord (1994) report also recounts the less than satisfactory impact of equal opportunities in the Metropolitan Police.

Of greater concern, perhaps, is Heidensohn's (1994b) finding that women officers found dealing with harassment by male colleagues a greater problem for them than violent encounters on patrol. Feinman (1986) also argues that the limited progress made by women in law enforcement is, in part, a result of the continued overt and covert resistance by their male colleagues. Young (1991) agrees and notes that it is policemen who are overtly and consistently hostile to women. Following an internal survey on the Cleveland Police in 1994, HMIC found 'widespread incidents of sexual harassment ... involving uninvited derogatory and degrading jokes' (HMIC 1994: 7). This pattern continues in 1996, with HMIC reporting that 'alongside praise worthy examples of good practice, there is also scepticism, tokenism and indifference ... a worrying lack of faith in the grievance system and evidence of continuing high levels of sexist and racist banter' (HMIC 1995: 9). Gregory and Lees (1999) provide a review of sexual harassment cases that have made the headlines in recent years. They point to a bleak picture of the impact of equal opportunities policies in the police and provide a catalogue of both recent and past cases in which female police officers have been verbally, sexually, physically, and racially abused by their male colleagues. It seems that although the quota system operating in the recruitment of female officers exposed by the Policy Studies Institute (PSI) study some twenty years ago has disappeared, the report's observation that 'it is the group values of men that have the greatest effect on the women in the force' (Smith and Gray 1983: 374) remains valid.

Such findings are not exclusive to Britain, with research pointing to a global picture of discrimination. Heidensohn's (1992) and Mckenzie's (1993) comparative analyses of the US and UK, Prenzler's (1997) work on Australia, Brown's (1996) review of Eastern Europe, Continental Europe, the US and UK, together with Brown and Heidensohn's (2000) wide-ranging international study, all confirm a picture of continued harassment, discrimination, and differential deployment for police-women across the world. Drawing upon a European comparative data set, Brown (1996) suggests that women from all jurisdictions believe that they have been discriminated against in terms of deployment, promotion prospects, training, and opportunities for overtime payments. Works also report varying levels of sexual harassment across Europe, including at least one Scottish force (Brown 1994), the Royal Ulster Constabulary (Brewer 1991), the Belgian Police (Corryn 1994, cited in Brown et al. 1999) and the Dutch Police (Eikenaar 1993, cited in Brown et al. 1999). Data from Brown's (1996) study indicates that those in Eastern European countries appear to suffer less discrimination and harassment than their counterparts in Continental Europe, the British Isles, and the US. At the same time, she reports bearing witness to a 'Miss Hungarian Policewoman' competition in 1995 (Brown 1997b). In noting jurisdictional differences, she argues not only that equality legislation and policy implementation hold greater enforcement power across Continental Europe and America, but that the women's movement and feminist consciousness-raising have given women a heightened awareness of behaviour that is considered discriminatory and the analytical tools and vocabulary to help make sense of their experiences (Brown 1996). The resounding message of such research is that, despite organisational change throughout police organisations, women in policing across the world continue to experience discrimination in various forms; nothing much has altered, attitudes remain unchanged, and sexism and inequality persist.

Gendered images – gendered meanings

Earlier in this chapter I pointed to the importance of understanding the creation of symbols and images that explain and justify gender divisions in organisations (Acker 1992). It is through the creation of such divisions that the working styles, practices, and images of both male and female police officers are constructed and confirmed. *Doing gender* in policing involves the creation of distinct differences between men and women by maintaining and emphasising their respective 'maleness' and 'femaleness', thus emphasising and preserving a peculiar form of masculinity – that of street cops. Police work becomes a means whereby men differentiate masculinity from femininity, a reason for constructing oneself as a real man (Messerschmidt 1993: 182). With the perception that police work involves 'strength, action, danger and male fellowship' (Flynn 1982), the work of policing becomes securely defined as 'men's work'. As Heidensohn (1992: 73) notes 'an elision which is frequently made [is that] *coercion* requires *force* which *implies physique and* hence policing by *men*' (original emphasis). In this way, Messerschmidt (1993: 175) contends that policemen are able to secure their status as the owners of legitimate authority whose power is 'deemed an authentic and acceptable part of social relations'. It is also within such discourses that police work is defined culturally as an activity only 'masculine men' can accomplish (*ibid.*). Those who do not fit this definition are perceived to be 'outsiders' in the project of policing – in this case, women. As a result, the policewoman remains the 'ultimate oxymoron' (Brown and Heidensohn 2000).

Burke's (1992, 1993) work on the significance of sexuality in policing corroborates the significance of a police culture that is grounded in heterosexism, with police officers holding stereotypical notions about homosexuals. Here two forms of masculinity strongly emerge – 'the effeminate, limp wristed, ambisexual, handbag carrying, weak and rather pathetic "queen", or the butch, leather/denim clad, heavily moustached and closely cropped "clone" ' (Burke 1992: 35) – neither of which have a place in policing. As Burke (*ibid.*: 38–9) reminds us, homosexuals '... rank among the most formidable of natural police adversaries. Tolerating homosexual colleagues, let alone condoning their recruitment, would represent the most serious kind of contamination and the worst possible threat to the integrity of the service.' Not only do such findings serve to confirm a picture of police masculinity grounded in heterosexuality, they also confirm the need to explore the variations of masculinity within the police service. What follows is an analysis of some of the gendered meanings and images of police work that have helped to define policing as a function to be carried out principally by, and residing in, the domain of men.

When exploring the construction of the police image, much can be gleaned from fictional representations of the police. Reiner (1994: 18) notes that while television watching is primarily a means of entertainment, it is 'not innocent of profound ideological effects in the images it constructs and conveys'. In his distinctly British account, he traces the changing image of police in Britain through television fiction. Constructed around the dialectical progression through three distinct phases, his analysis begins with *Dixon of Dock Green*. Here he notes the police are primarily constructed as carers, with PC George Dixon becoming the 'quintessential image of the traditional British Bobby'. His analysis progresses through to *The Sweeney* where, in line with the tough law and order politics of the late 1970s, police are portrayed primarily as controllers; they are ' tough, relentless crusaders against crime' (*ibid.*: 24). The final stage of the progression ends with *The Bill* in which there is a synthesis of care and control in the police image. Here the police provide the 'service of protecting the public by the appropriate use of legitimate force' (*ibid.*: 27). The movement towards a synthesis of care and control was to see the development of female leads such as those in *The Gentle Touch*, *Juliet Bravo* and *Prime Suspect*. Despite the balance between care and control, there is much to suggest that scripts for *The Bill* in recent years have emphasised and fuelled the dangerous and glamorous elements of police work which are paramount to police identity and imagery.

In addition to providing illuminating and illustrative material on the changing politics of police legitimation, Reiner's analysis provides vital information on the gendered and discriminatory nature of policing, more broadly, and offers interesting insights into some of the more specific debates about the changing forms of masculinity within British policing. Such characterisations preserve the image of the police and policing as ultimately male and masculine. It is the crime-fighting model, with its attendant imagery of danger and an emphasis on the need for physical strength, that has taken ascendancy in the police organisation both in terms of fictional and factual accounts.

Academic research also continues to emphasise the fact that, despite the knowledge that most policing revolves around providing service and maintaining order, the cultural image of the masculine crime-fighter defined through physicality endures. It is not my intention here to suggest that the powerful significance engendered by *Dixon of Dock Green* is absent; far from it. So powerful is the significance of this image that Reiner notes that debates about the police continue to evoke nostalgic calls for a return to the '*Dixon*' style of policing, as if he had been a real person not a fictional character (*ibid.*: 21). There is little doubt, however, that these calls are more likely to come from external bodies and the public; the lower ranks in policing still stress 'real' police work in control terms (Stephens and Becker 1994).

Police work continues to be presented in its mythological form where masculine identities continue to be constructed, negotiated, and reconstructed in routine social interactions. The police organisation continues to encourage the imagery and mythology of 'street cop' masculinity to pervade organisational processes. The cult of masculinity offers an opportunity within which a core aspect of the police role – the willingness and the ability to use force – can be celebrated. The glorification of violence and a crime-fighting mission provide the ideological justifications for the authority that is exercised against fellow citizens, 'for the exercise of coercive authority is not something that just anybody can do, it is traditionally the preserve of real men, who are willing and able to fight' (Waddington 1999b: 297).

In line with Acker's ideas about the structuring of organisations, tasks and jobs within policing are gendered, representing defining features of police work which can be seen as distinct and indeed as oppositional: 'paper work vs real police work' or 'social service vs crime fighting' (Hunt 1990: 15). It is through such implicit cultural codes mediated by masculine and feminine symbols that meanings of police work are constructed and confirmed. Female officers belong to the feminine world of administration and emotion while their male counterparts inhabit the world of action and danger (*ibid.*). More importantly, the gendered significance of tasks holds serious implications for the career progression of officers, in particular that of women officers. The implicit cultural and unconscious meanings that mediate the police construction of reality assume significance in relation to each officer's place in the organisational hierarchy. Distinctions serve to construct hierarchies of workers where men remain at the top. Women's lack of success is often justified on the grounds of their unsuitability to the demands of the job, and their contributions are presented in terms of 'deficits' (Heidensohn 1994b).

33

The importance of physicality to police identity is evident from the very early stages of a police career. The physical fitness entry tests that officers face continue to inhibit women's entry and progress in policing. The way in which such tests disproportionately affect women remains high on the agenda of those campaigning for greater equality. The British Association of Policewomen (BAWP), the European Network of Policewomen (ENP), the National Centre for Women and Policing (NCWP) and the Australasian Council of Women and Policing (ACWAP) have all emphasised the gendered and discriminatory nature of such physical tests. Findings from BAWP indicate that current tests show a disproportionate failure among women candidates. In focusing on upper body strength and speed, current fitness tests are designed 'for men and focus on men's ability ... [and as a result] men pass. Over 90 per cent of men can pass the current test, thus they are only actually a "test" for women, who have failure rates of 40–50 per cent' (BAWP 2002: 2).

Women's perceived lack of physical presence, of tough physique and, above all, of masculinity is used as rational and legitimate reasons for their exclusion. Assertions that the work of policing is too dangerous for women or that the situations they may encounter in their daily work are too physically demanding for them to handle contribute to a discourse in which the hegemonic model of masculinity is one in which to be masculine is to be strong and physically aggressive (Connell 1987). The lack of physical strength and the ensuing problems in violent situations remain a consistent justification offered by policemen for women's continued differential deployment and their negative view of policewomen.

A number of studies have, however, consistently shown that much routine policing does not involve violence or physical danger. There appears to be a consensus about the disparity between the realities of police work and the perceptions of it held by the police themselves (Jones and Newburn 1997). Punch and Naylor's (1973) now frequently cited study continues to hold significance. Their study of calls made to the police in three Essex towns over a two-week period led them to note that the police constructed not so much a crime-fighting force as a 'secret social service'. Hough's (1985: 11) analysis of the workload of uniformed patrol officers provided further confirmation of this view. His analysis of 1,944 incidents attended by patrol revealed that only about a third (36 per cent) involved crime incidents; 14 per cent related to accidents; 19 per cent to public order; and the remainder, 31 per cent, to social service tasks. Research conducted by the Audit Commission (1990) gives further validity to such findings.[1] In noting the level of physicality and danger involved in policing, Balkin (1988) claims that incidents involving physical force were rare, estimating that 80–90 per cent of police officers' time was spent on non-criminal or service functions. When comparing occupational risk statistics, Jermier *et al.* (1989, cited in Coffey *et al.* 1992) argue that policing is less risky than mining, construction, agriculture or transport work, and that while policing is more physically dangerous than some occupations, it is far from the top of the list. There is little doubt, then, that the occupational self-image of the police as crime-fighters is not just a 'distortion of what they do, it is virtually a collective delusion' (Waddington 1999a: 117).

In understanding more fully the processes that have helped shape such gendered meanings, no discussion is complete without a historical appreciation. The binary, and at times, opposing worlds of 'care and control' and 'service and force' that characterise police work today can be traced to the historical underpinnings of women's entry and struggle for acceptance. Women's journey into policing was one that began in the domain of 'care', their work firmly grounded in an ethic of moral rescue work (Schulz 1995, Segrave 1995, Carrier 1988).

A recurrent theme that runs throughout the history of women in policing is their purported unsuitability (physically or otherwise) for the work of policing. This view was echoed in policing and societal circles alike. Typical of male hostility was an article by an anonymous writer in 1931 in the *Saturday Review of Politics*, which stated that 'a policewoman is, in short, a contradiction in terms. I object to those amateur guardians of morality being made members of the "force". I protest against the public support of this amiable but useless absurdity, the she policeman' (cited in Segrave 1995: 100). For decades, the belief in the natural association between women and social work tasks, and their lack of physical ability, underpinned their limited role in policing. An article published in the *Police Journal* in 1929 (cited in Miller 1999: 95) captures neatly the essence of what was to govern much of the twentieth-century thought on gender and policing:

> There is now almost universal agreement that policewomen should not attempt to do general patrol work. Police work of this type is rather exacting in its physical demands, and men as a sex have greater physical strength and endurance than women as a sex. The police officer doing patrol work, moreover, is engaged in the main protection of property and the prevention of crime-types of work for which women have no peculiar or unique qualifications. In view of the general and specific nature of patrol work, the requirements as to strength alone are sufficient to be a determining fact.

Drawing on historical accounts of policing, it becomes clear that although 'pioneer' policewomen were able to secure some space and place in policing, they did so while working outside the realm of male policing. In this way, occupying the sphere of crime prevention was firmly established as women's domain. Despite the creation of a separate sphere that did not threaten male police officers' jobs or their scope for exerting control, there is much to suggest that early policewomen experienced enormous resistance to their presence in policing (Carrier 1988, Schulz 1995, Miller 1999).

Modern policewomen are no longer confined to the world of social service tasks, yet they continue to be branded with the legacy left to them by their pioneering forerunners. The gendered nature of these binary worlds continues to attract support in debates about gender and policing today. If we examine attempts by police organisations across the world to move away from a crime-fighting model of policing to a more 'service' type style through re-inventing 'community style' policing strategies, we may begin to fully appreciate the powerful nature of the gendered meanings that police officers attach to their work, their image, and their identity.

Miller's (1999) study of gender and community policing offers an insight into the continued resistance of police officers to engage with social service type tasks. Officers in her study were involved in resisting the potential changes in image and identity that community policing may bring. Miller explores how stereotypically feminine traits, once used to exclude women's participation from patrol and to separate the 'real' crime-fighters from the 'office or social work cops', have now been resurrected and elevated in community policing agendas and practice under the guise of a gender-neutral discourse of caring.

At first glance it may appear that the enactment of a 'caring' philosophy is no longer solely in the hands and minds of women. On closer inspection, however, it becomes clear that, despite this language of gender neutrality, the association of community policing with what was traditionally women's work lives on and remains at the forefront of officers' minds. Miller points to the persistence of a 'subterranean effect of gendered expectations and task divisions' (*ibid.*: 95). In accepting the less macho role inherent in community policing, police-men found ways to re-establish their masculinity. Regardless of the type of neighbourhood, the kinds of activities that were organised and performed afforded officers opportunities to confirm their gender, to *do* masculinity. Men pointed to earlier and current crime-fighting activ-ities, selected tougher neighbourhoods, and favoured a more visible law enforcement stance in their version of work. Even those men who excelled in interpersonal skills continued to emphasise law enforcement. Female officers were also concerned about their image, reluctant to be essentialised as 'perfect' for neighbourhood policing, since, as women, they were already seen as nurturers and stereotyped as more emotional and intimacy oriented. Miller notes that women's response as community officers took several different paths. Some exaggerated their masculinity, following the more male career advancement model, others emphasised their femininity as a means to an end, allowing them to connect more easily with residents. Others adapted both masculine and feminine dimensions assuming a more androgynous style. Regardless of officers' adaptation, the continued practice of marking out the differences between men and women is clear.

The resistance towards community policing is also borne out in the British case. It has been widely noted that community policing initiatives have had to contend with subversion and opposition by the lower ranks in particular (Irving 1986, Dixon and Stanko 1995, Fielding 1994b). In some ways, this can be expressed as a generalised 'culture of resistance' on the part of the lower ranks who are hostile to the assault on the 'shibboleths' of policing (Dixon and Stanko 1995). Fielding (1994b) found that, despite organisational claims to the contrary, community constables were marginalised and despised by patrol officers and suffered conflicting and confusing role expectations. In more specific terms, Waddington (1999a: 214) highlights the gendered nature of resistance to community policing, when he notes that 'Traditional "macho" police sub-cultural values are directly assaulted by the implicit, but strong, emphasis on "care" rather than "control"'.

The idea that policing has successfully shifted from a 'force' to 'service' orientation, or claims that the crime-fighter has been replaced by a peace-keeper, have been over exaggerated. They remain optimistic readings of organisational change within policing. A more realistic reading of the changes is offered by Morgan and Newburn (1997) in which they argue that, since the *White Paper on Police Reform* (1993) and the *Police and Magistrates' Courts Act* (PMCA) (1994), the role of crime-fighting has been emphasised above that of peace-keeping. Crowther (2000) also points to the significance of focused policing strategies such as Zero Tolerance Policing. The recent implementation of such a strategy in a number of British towns and cities is further evidence of a process of redefinition of community forms of policing.

In the same way that early policewomen's participation in the police project marked a threat to men's roles, so too is women's integration into policing today symbolising a threat to men's definition of their work, their occupational culture, their social status, and their self-image as 'real' men. Hunt (1990) argues that women's presence in policing serves to expose the myths that have shaped police work. In opposition to the public image of the crime-fighter, she argues that the work of policing is largely composed of 'social service' and 'street cleaning' tasks. Symbolically, then, the female police officer reminds her male colleague that:

> ... he can only achieve manhood by denying and repressing the essential feminine dimensions of police work, [so] male resistance to women can therefore be viewed as an attempt to preserve the myth which not only legitimates police work in the public's eyes but also affirms the policeman's identity as a man. (*Ibid.*: 15)

If women can *do* policing, the value of the practices as a means of exhibiting masculinity is open to question (Messerschmidt 1993: 175).

The issues raised by such studies fit well into the larger literature on the gendering of skill. In her study of gender and technology, Cockburn (1991) emphasised the way in which skill is gendered, with boundaries redrawn and maintained between male and female, skilled and unskilled. Given the changing nature of organisations, studies of women's positions will need to take account of the fluidity of the category of skill or merit. Definitions of what is meritorious can undergo change depending on the power of particular groups to define it, and women pursuing expertise might find it being 'redefined' as they reach for it (Kessler *et al.* 1985). If police organisations are successfully to make the transition from 'control' to 'caring' police models, it might be that the 'feminine' traits that characterise the objectives of the new approach will need to be masculinised in order to fit into traditional policing frameworks. Achieving this 'redefinition' of what constitutes a 'man's job' may be necessary for male officers to successfully manage the previously stigmatised identity of doing 'women's work' as community police officers (Miller 1999). Recasting 'feminine' virtues associated with 'women's work' and imbuing them with honour may also be a strategy to ensure change. Without such a recasting, Miller argues, 'neighbourhood officers will continue to be seen by others as "pansy police" ... The success of this however, depends on reshaping unacceptable traits, associated with femininity, into acceptable ones associated with masculinity, or "real" police work' (*ibid.*: 70).

To recap briefly, I began this chapter by emphasising the way in which the cult of masculinity has been held responsible for negatively impacting on women's experiences of policing. I also argued that the cult of masculinity is better understood through its association with lower ranks and through themes of physicality. Moreover, I questioned the explanatory power of the cult of masculinity for making sense of the experiences of policing for those in more senior positions. My intention in the final part of this chapter is to outline my arguments regarding the potential differences that might arise when the issue of rank is positioned at the centre of such debates.

Doing gender in policing has involved the creation of distinct differences between men and women – such difference has been strongly grounded in a discourse of women's physical 'unsuitability' for police work. Using women's physical unsuitability as a justification for their continued exclusion, however, becomes less tenable as women move upwards in the police hierarchy, with police managers the least likely to be called upon to exhibit physical displays of strength and prowess. In turn it could be argued that, on achieving rank, women will no longer face hostility, discrimination, and exclusion. This presumption, however, is a naïve one. There are multiple cultures operating in the police organisation, and in some cases these are shaped by rank position. My argument is a simple one: the cult of masculinity, so often used to explain women's negative experiences and lack of progression in policing, does not possess sufficient explanatory power for making sense of the experiences of police-women who hold rank. Senior policewomen continue to face a gendered environment where masculinity persists, and yet they are confronted with a different kind of masculinity – one where physicality is less obvious, but where traits associated with 'managerial masculin-ity' dominate. It is to this issue that I now turn.

A multiplicity of police cultures and identities

Handy's (1991) *Gods of Management* provides an interesting starting point for an appreciation of the multiplicity of organisational cultures across and within organisations. Drawing on Greek mythology, he outlines four basic types of organisational culture and allies them to various Greek gods: the 'club culture' (Zeus); the 'role culture' (Apollo); the 'task culture' (Athena); and the 'existential culture' (Dionysus). Each type of culture and god works on quite different assumptions about the basis of power and influence, about what motivates people, how they think and learn, and how things can be changed. The 'club culture' tends to involve groups of like-minded people introduced by like-minded people, working on empathetic initiative with personal contact rather than formal liaison. This culture depends on networks of friendships, 'old boys' and comrades. The 'role culture' is best typified by a bureaucracy, resting on the assumption that everything can be organised in a logical fashion and everything is held together by a set of rules and procedures. As a result of its bureaucratic nature it is strongly imbued by the concept of hierarchy, and power is held by those at the top. The 'task culture' is organised around a network of loosely linked 'commando units', each unit being largely self-contained but with a specific responsibility within an overall strategy. It places a strong emphasis on group talent and its leadership takes the form of teams of mutual respect, recognising expertise as the base of power or influence. The 'existential culture' is the culture of the professionals; here individuals can preserve their own identity and freedom in an environment where the talents or skills of individuals are valued.

It is important to stress here that such conceptualisations of culture are neither static nor monolithic. In most cases, Handy (*ibid.*) argues, organisations will find they have progressed through the 'club' culture to the 'role' culture, to which they have subsequently added elements of the 'task' and 'existential' cultures. Through the process of organisational change and restructuring comes a reordering of the gods, which in turn brings a reordering of organisations that will make a difference to the way in which that organisation works and its participants experience their daily lives. In applying Handy's conceptualisation to policing, it is the culture of Apollo – the 'role culture' – that best characterises the police organisation. Chapter 4 will demonstrate that, despite calls for change to allow the realisation of a more Athenian landscape with its attendant emphasis on teamwork and culture of consultation, the police organisation in Britain remains firmly rooted in an Apollonian landscape, characterised by a strict hierarchical linear career ladder. As a result, it remains firmly rooted to the concept that authority is distributed according to position in that hierarchy. Above all, Apollonian cultures are 'efficient when life is predictable, [but] they hate the obverse – change' (*ibid.*: 25).

Reiner (1992: 109) points to the potential differences in organisational styles and cultures of police forces which occur between different places and periods, highlighting the differences that might result according to individual variables such as 'personality, generation, or career trajectory ... rank, assignment and specialisation'. Fielding (1995) points to intra-rank differences, noting the distinct subcultures among officers engaged in 'routine patrol' and 'community constables'.

Young (1991) details the distinction between uniformed and non-uniformed officers who each possess their own variations and characteristics. Other studies have already pointed to the diversity of culture between ranks. Manning (1977), for example, cites a threefold hierarchical structure in policing comprising 'command', 'middle-management', and 'lower participants'. Reuss-Ianni and Ianni (1983) and Punch (1985) have also pointed to the fundamental division and difference between 'street cops' and 'management cops'.

Mapping gender onto rank, Hunt (1984) and Fielding and Fielding (1992) stress that in police imagery, 'management cop' culture and high rank is inversely correlated with masculinity. Fielding and Fielding (*ibid*.) note that the oppositional attributes associated with gender also relate to issues of status. In particular, the feminine characteristics that correspond to 'inside work' and the formal order are associated with 'management cop' culture. In contrast, the masculine attributes that relate to 'outside work' and the informal world are associated with 'street cop' culture. Hunt's (1984) work emphasises the way in which 'management cop' culture is tied to gender in an unequivocally negative way, with rank being inversely correlated with masculinity in the policeman's view of the world. Here, rank-and-file officers perceived that administrators were engaged in:

> 'Feminine labor' such as public relations and secretarial work. These 'pencil pushing bureaucrats' were not involved in the 'masculine' physical labor which characterized 'real policework' on the street. High ranking administrators were also viewed as 'inside tit men', 'asskissers' and 'whores' who gained their positions through political patronage rather than through superior performance in the rescue and crime fighting activities associated with 'real police work'. (*Ibid*.: 288)

Forms of 'street cop' masculinity are being posited against 'management cop' masculinity, with the latter being constructed through themes of femininity. Such perceptions, however, are still concerned with men's occupation of territory – that is, both rank-and-file and management terrain. The more pressing question to address, perhaps, is what happens when women begin to occupy this territory?

Many of the policewomen interviewed in this study pointed to the emergence of a new managerial culture in policing, highly performance driven and preoccupied with meeting performance indicators and targets. This new management style encourages a form of 'competitive masculinity' that encourages, 'a way of relating to the world wherein everything becomes an object of, and for, control'. This in turn 'generates and sustains a hierarchy imbued with instrumentalist careerism, and the language of success, emulates competition linked to decisive action, productivism and risk taking' (Kerfoot and Knights 1993: 67). There is much to suggest that, following the organisational restructuring that commenced in the mid 1980s, managerial masculinity in policing today holds much in common with the 'smart macho' culture identified earlier by Maddock and Parkin (1993). The social construction of police management is one in which managerial competence is intrinsically linked to qualities attached to 'corporate' men. The following narratives are drawn from senior policewomen's own characterisations of police leadership. The police leader of the twenty-first century described below is a tough and forceful leader, symbolised by aggressive, competitive and performance traits:

> Success is in part a matter of personal determination, but to get to the top you have to have an element of ruthlessness, selfishness, drive, and determination. There aren't very many heads of empires that are Mr and Mrs nice guys; you have to be prepared to push yourself.

> Those women who are reaching the high ranks at the moment are the ones who can fit into part of this drive and current aggressive system. The last women to have got in have been very strategic, very ruthless go-getters, very ambitious women.

> The move to superintendent is huge. I am not going to rush into it until I am ready. I think I have all the skills; it's just the hunger for power – you are using power and not influence at that level – it's the hunger for it that you need, which I don't have at the moment.

> To get further I knew I would have to do things that I wasn't willing to do, in that you had to become a bully very nearly in the way that you had to assert authority and do things, and it was against my principles.

These senior policewomen's observations are in direct contrast to the management worlds described by Hunt (1984) and Fielding and Fielding (1992). For them, management is the very antithesis of 'real' policing; those working in such spheres are better characterised through their association with feminine tasks and, as such, are not 'real' men. In highlighting the multiplicity of cultures that exist in policing, such conceptualisations continue to be stranded in the dichotomous world of the female and male. Consequently, their potential to explain the experiences of women in management is limited. In positing femininity against masculinity, it is all too easy to miss the variations within each, ignoring the complexity of officers' lives. The masculinity that characterises management culture is simply a variant on the more traditional form of masculinity associated with policing. The various processes of organisational change within policing that have encouraged such a construction will be explored more fully in the next chapter.

Notes

1 The Audit Commission (1990) demonstrated that 22 per cent of police activity was spent on preventative control; 16 per cent on report writing; 11 per cent on station duties; 10 per cent on crime incidents; 10 per cent on traffic control; 8 per cent on other incidents; 5 per cent on traffic duties; and 18 per cent on other duties.

Chapter 3

Rethinking organisational change

The search for how best to achieve change in organisations has long been the focus of study for organisational theorists (Bate 1996, Schein 1985). The same can be said of policing, with the concept of change dominating official police and academic discourses alike. The idea that things *can* and *might* be changing in the police organisation is a central tenet of this book. All of the policewomen interviewed in this study felt that they 'had lived' and were 'continuing to live' through a period of major organisational change. I have urged a reading of change in which individuals play an active role – in this case, women as police leaders. This chapter will draw out some of the debates about change that hold significance for the study of gender and policing. In particular, I will focus more closely on some of the issues that stem from the discourses of enacting 'change through equality' and 'change through quality'. Although distinct, by their very nature these discourses are inextricably linked, with the police organisation focusing its attention on demonstrating 'quality through equality' and 'equality through quality'. It is through these two doctrines that we can witness the development of a substantially altered agenda and identity for police officers.

In their work on the *Futures of Policing*, Bayley and Shearing (1996) point to the radical change that has occurred in policing systems across developed economies. In arguing their case, they use the police service's search for a new identity as evidence of this change. In searching for possible sites for achieving a new identity for police officers, the movement towards developing diversity through equal opportunities seems an obvious site for exploring a changing police identity. This chapter has two main parts: first, it reflects on the concept of change within the police organisation through a consideration of the development of equal opportunities. Second, it outlines the impact that such change might have on the identity of police officers.

Change through equality

By tracing women's involvement and experiences of policing before their formal integration into mainstream policing in the 1970s, we are able to gain a more accurate historical reading of the development of equality in policing. Policewomen's low numbers, together with their relatively low status, have rendered them nearly invisible to historians, with historical accounts focusing almost exclusively on the male police organisation (Critchley 1978, Emsley 1996, Rawlings 1995). In Britain, much of the early work on women in policing either stems from policewomen's own memoirs (Allen 1925, Wyles 1951) or from official sources such as the *Baird Committee Report* (1920), the *Bridgeman Committee Report* (1924) and the *Royal Commission* (1929). While informative in detailing events, such sources do not situate the gendered significance of women in policing.

In the past decade or so, there have been some texts that have provided a more academic interpretation of women's entry into policing. Carrier's (1988) work remains a useful initial reference point for detailing events in Britain. His work meticulously describes the campaign for the employment of women as police officers from 1914 to 1931. Bland (1985) and Radford and Stanko (1989) also offer an insight into the introduction of women police, focusing on the social control aspects of their development. Heidensohn's (2000) *Sexual Politics and Social Control* develops these ideas further by situating women's social control within broader debates about risk and globalisation. Her work also focuses more closely on the historical development of global networks of women in policing. There is also a range of texts that interpret events in America (Schulz 1995, Feinman 1986, Segrave 1995, Appier 1998, Miller 1999). Much less is known about events in New Zealand and Australia but a good account of the latter can be found in the work of Prenzler (1994).

These texts demonstrate a consensus about the context of women's increased presence in policing, documenting clearly the role that external crises have played in establishing women as police officers. Tracing women's early entry into policing in Britain, for example, Brown (1996) argues that while women's entry into policing was often preceded by lobbying activity, successes were probably due to the concessions made on pragmatic grounds in response to some contemporary crisis. It was the First World War in Britain that provided the impetus for women's entry into policing and the Second World War that secured a degree of expansion rather than the efforts of suffrage campaigners (Woodson 1993, cited in Brown 1996).

In further support of this, Heidensohn (1989) notes that the 1960s and 1970s were a critical time for the police organisation in the US. Following a series of urban riots and numerous corruption scandals, the recruiting of women was seen as one solution to rebalance a police organisation in crisis. The entry of women in policing at times where 'desperate remedies' are needed is characterised by Heidensohn (1996b) as indicative of the way in which women are sometimes used to provide a 'cloak of virtue' to a project or agency.

In a comparative approach of policing, Brown (1997a) offers a litany of nations who have utilised the increased recruitment of women as a strategy by which to regain a degree of public acceptance and legitimacy for policing. Brown (1995) points to a speech given by the Commander of the Belgian Gendarmerie, which had recently admitted women, noting that the integration of women was held to be especially important as this created a reflection of society more appropriate to a gendarmerie breaking with its military past. The expansion of the numbers of women police officers in Asian countries has also been associated closely with an influx of refugees and an increase in illegal immigration (Alleem 1989, Calderwood 1974, both cited in Brown 1997a).

Outlining the impetus for police reform in Australia, Prenzler and Wimshurst (1996) argue that increasing women's presence forms a crucial strategy in professionialising the police. In these cases:

> reformers portray attempts to 'feminise' law enforcement as a progressive move, usually designed to provide a 'human face' for organisational practices, a 'civilising' influence. Seen in this light, women are 'allowed in' at particular historical points when agencies wish to (re)legitimise their practices. (*Ibid.*: 16)

The idea of 'allowing women in' continues to be a feature in the growth of policewomen's roles today. It is not my intention here to underestimate the role played by women themselves in fighting for a permanent place in policing, but simply to think more critically about the occasions when calls for more women are made. Women, without doubt, have exercised their own agency and exploited advantages offered to them. The upheaval of the First World War, with its manpower shortage and increased sexual fears and tensions, afforded policewomen the opportunity to be involved in the function of policing more fully and to demonstrate publicly the need for their existence. It was to be an opportunity that women involved in policing would seize and exploit. In her memoirs, Allen (1925: 11) notes that one of the most significant developments of the first months of the war was the 'swiftness with which momentous decisions were made and acted upon. Many women accepted their responsibilities with astonishing readiness, electrifying their followers into instant activity.'

The mid-1970s was to bring about the end of the separation between women and men in policing and push forward a new era of integration for police officers in Britain. The symbolic significance of integration as a restructuring moment was clear in the accounts of senior police-women I interviewed. Underlying their recollections was a tacit understanding that things were going to change. The majority of women who had joined pre-integration were happy at the prospect of joining forces with men, reflecting that being part of the separate policewomen's department ensured their existence as 'tokens' in policing and prevented them from engaging with 'real' police work. One officer notes:

> I was quite content in those days [pre-integration] but a lot of people weren't. A lot of women saw the move towards an integrated service as a step backwards. There were old, entrenched attitudes and I think a lot of women at that time were single, career women from after the war and it was before a lot of women had started working, so there were not that many women in the organisation at the time. When we integrated and went on to relief I felt happy . . . but for a lot of women it was very difficult to come to terms with what was in fact a new job. A lot left at that time and a lot retired; it then really became a new breed of women who joined the organisation, a different type.

However, the idea that integration would automatically improve women's situation and bring about equality for police officers did not materialise. Relatively little was done to prepare the police service to become a gender-integrated organisation in the aftermath of the *Sex Discrimination Act* (SDA) 1975. Brown (1998) argues that almost no effort was expended to develop procedures for equality of opportunity in promotion, training or other developmental aspects of career advancement. In a review of career advancement of British men and women officers selected for fast track promotion from 1962 to 1991, Adler (1990, cited in Brown 1998: 274) notes that in the aftermath of the

47

SDA 1975, women officers actually did worse in achieving promotion when compared to men. She suggests that this was because women were now competing against the total number of eligible officers instead of being considered in terms of the number of appropriately qualified women from the previously separate Police Women's Department. One of my respondents recalls her thoughts on her own as well as other women's potential promotion prospects as a result of integration:

> I was so glad when they said you're going to mix with the boys; I thought, at last. Then I remember thinking, but what about promotion? I remember thinking, well that's it, I'm never going to get up ... I never thought it was unfair though, it was the days when equal opportunities wasn't what it is now. There were demands on organisations for fairness and you just hoped and prayed you got a good Gov. who would dish it all out in a fair way.

Another officer notes the loss of expertise that had been developed over the years as a result of integration:

> The policewomen's unit under went a metamorphosis, transforming itself and then allying itself to the CID, which I got posted to ... But when you think about all that knowledge – I remember that they had files of it, logs and maps, all their work charted out – all that specialist knowledge gone forever. I don't think we have ever been able to regain that kind of expertise since.

Schulz (1995) and Miller (1999) both note the double-edged impact that integration and the move to patrol in the late 1960s was to bring to policewomen in America. For some, undertaking patrol assignments meant a loss of prestige, a step down on the career ladder. For others, the move to patrol was to begin a journey that would lead women out of a specialised, gender-based role into a genderless one, that of general assignment policing. In securing the successful transition into mainstream policing, many women were to turn their backs on their traditional roles. In the movement towards equality, policewomen were 'forced to reject their history ... [and] repudiate their past' (Schulz 1995: 1).

The price for achieving formal integration was a costly one. Women who had reached senior positions in the separate policewomen's service were forced to relinquish them as they joined forces with men.

Many of those who had joined the women's police service to undertake the associated duties saw their original mission and purpose change. Brown and Heidensohn (2000: 4) describe the move towards integration as

> ... the striking of a somewhat Faustian bargain. The price for admittance was a loss of a radical agenda and the acceptance of male definitions and methods of control, for their continued presence women accepted lower status and restricted roles whilst integration has been marked by overt hostility and harassment.

In 1986, a study by Sandra Jones proved critical for its observation that official policy statements enshrining equal opportunities in the police organisation still remained absent. Calls were made for an equal opportunities policy, that such a policy should spell out the intended consequences for recruitment, training, deployment, and careers, including promotion (Jones 1986). The push towards equal opportunities has increased considerably since Jones's recommendations and the past decade has been characterised by an organisational discourse in which change has been distinguished by an embracement of equal opportunities.

A comprehensive document *Equal Opportunities Guidelines for Police Managers* was distributed to all officers of the rank inspector and above. This work provided the basis for the Home Office Circular 87/1989 *Equal Opportunities Policies in the Police Service* issued to all police forces in England and Wales in November 1989 (Home Office 1989). This marked a significant shift for equality at a policy level, firmly stating government commitment to the concept of equal opportunities. It is important to note that, though rarely ignored by senior officers, Home Office circulars do not dictate local force policy but act as necessary guidelines on the basis of which local policies may be formulated. As a result, McKenzie (1993) notes that progress towards an agenda of equality was very much a feature of the energy and commitment of the individual chief constable. He states: 'even in the equal opportunities area, this autonomy has an impact, for Chief officers may decide the nature of their initiatives and the extent of their intervention with total freedom' (*ibid*.: 160). Home Office Circular 87/1989 clearly stated that force policies

> should ensure the best use is made of the abilities of every member of the force ... [and that it] should show that all members of the service are firmly opposed to discrimination within the service

and in their professional dealings with members of the public. (Home Office 1989: 1)

It recommended that forces use the codes of practice issued by the Equal Opportunities Commission and the Commission for Racial Equality guidelines in formulating their own policies and practices.

By 1993, it was clear that all forces had put in place a written equal opportunities policy (Anderson *et al.* 1993). To further demonstrate a commitment to increasing the number of women in policing, in October 1991 the Metropolitan Police Service publicly committed itself to the aims and objectives of *Opportunity 2000* (renamed *Opportunity Now* in 1999). Despite a slow and slovenly start, the police organisation now offers an impressive array of equal opportunity initiatives, including the development of career breaks, part-time working, and job sharing. On a policy level, at least, it appears that structures are now firmly in place to ensure an agenda of equality of opportunity. However, the picture presented by research so far, and the evidence that unfolds in this book, suggests a different reality for members of the police organisation. The process and nature of change is complex, often resulting in contradictory, unexpected, and at times unintended effects.

Although I am deciphering the language of equality in terms of gender for the purpose of this book, the past decade has demonstrated the complexity of the meaning of equality, with policing discourse on equality being shaped by a number of elements. In recent years, the issues of 'race' and 'racism' in relation to policing have come to dominate both public and police debate. It has been well documented that the police exercise their powers disproportionately and discriminatorily against black people (Bowling and Phillips 2002, Crawford *et al.* 1990, Jefferson 1988, Jefferson and Walker 1992, Jones *et al.* 1994, Macpherson 1999, Reiner 1989, 1993, Smith and Gray 1983, Stevens and Willis 1989, Willis 1983).

Research also indicates that Asian and black officers experience discrimination and harassment, encountering difficulties of racial prejudice exhibited by both the public and their fellow police officers (Holdaway 1991, 1996). A *Thematic Inspection on Equal Opportunities* (HMIC 1993) described a police force that had fallen short on a proportionate representation of officers from ethnic minority communities and drew attention to the persistence of racist banter that turned officers away from careers in the police. Reviewing the position of ethnic minorities and policing in 1996, Holdaway notes that virtually no constabulary in the UK had taken a positive stance regarding policies that address the processes of racialisation. In tracing the positions and roles of ethnic minority officers, Brown and Funelle (1993) argue that while figures do show a small increase in the percentage of ethnic minority officers, there still remain anomalies in their deployment. While providing valuable material on the experiences of ethnic minority officers, the small but growing work remains male centred (Holdaway 1996, Holdaway and Barron 1997, Bland *et al.* 1999). The lack of knowledge about the experiences of ethnic minority policewomen remains a serious omission in our understanding of the interactive effects of race, ethnicity, and gender.

Another defining element of the discourse of equality has been an attempt to address the question of sexuality. July 2001 saw attempts by North Yorkshire Police to validate its claims to have embraced 'diversity' through the celebration of two 'good, effective – and transsexual officers' (*Guardian* 21/7/01). Burke's (1993) study on the experiences of homosexuality in the police service provides grounds for scepticism in relation to the police position on the issue of sexuality. Officers in his study accepted that while statements on equal opportunities were a step in the right direction, they did little to enhance the realities of the working life of gay officers, who experience difficulties in negotiating their place and identity in an organisation grounded in the norms of heterosexuality.

More recently, the controversy surrounding Commander Brian Paddick, the highest-ranking publicly gay policeman, gives further evidence to those who argue that little has changed. Paddick attracted controversy by launching a pilot project to downgrade the prosecution of cannabis users to concentrate on dealers in harder drugs. Following revelations about his private life, Paddick became the subject of vilification by the tabloid press. The Metropolitan Police quickly followed suit by recommending that he be moved to a much less high-profile administrative position at Scotland Yard. While some claimed to back Paddick in public, a catalogue of leading police figures have repeatedly undermined him. Ben Summerskill of *The Observer* notes that one of the Metropolitan Police Commissioner's senior colleagues reassured a gathering of journalists that 'only the best officers are nowadays involved in investigating police corruption. They're not chosen on the basis of equal opportunities.' The implication was clear. Officers from minority groups, such as Paddick, had won their positions on the basis of tokenism (*The Observer* 24/3/02). Inspector Stephen Warwick, spokesman for the Lesbian and Gay Police Association (LAGPA) noted that:

What has happened to Brian Paddick on lots of levels is a result of homophobia. It's still institutional in the police. As with institutional racism, you're made to feel less part of the organisation and less valued as an officer. (*Ibid.*)

Brown (1996: 201) also notes the problematic nature of addressing sexuality in police organisations when she states that, unlike sexual and racial discrimination, the question of sexual orientation has been the 'most invisible and consequently the least debated'.

Despite the noteworthy achievements of the police service regarding the promotion of equal opportunities, it might be prudent to withhold such praise at this stage and offer a few words of caution. As the police organisation begins to tackle a variety of oppressed groups, there is always the risk of a hierarchy of oppressions emerging. This might be particularly true in Britain, given the recent high-profile cases of police malpractice regarding racism. Arguably, in light of the Macpherson Inquiry (Macpherson 1999), racialisation processes have become more pivotal than gendered processes. Racism has become regarded as the main form of oppression with gender slowly becoming subsidiary. I will return to such debates in Chapter 6 where I outline the potentially competitive nature that may result between minority groups. Policewomen's own reflections on the development of equal opportunities are central to our understanding of the 'lived' experiences of change. The following section begins to draw out some of these perceptions.

One of the strongest features that bind senior policewomen together (regardless of their service length and rank) is the belief that they 'have lived' and continue 'to live' with the permanence of change. In asking senior policewomen to reflect about their careers, women were able to recall dates, times, and moments with a high degree of clarity. Those with longer service histories were able to vividly reflect and demarcate the nature of change through what can be described as a series of restructuring moments. Closer scrutiny of these moments allows us to ascertain the way in which women themselves have defined and understood change within the police organisation.

In reflecting on the development of equal opportunities, the majority of policewomen asserted that things had improved. There was a consensus that things had become fairer both for those working inside policing and for citizens on the receiving end of policing. The praise awarded to equality measures was simultaneously accompanied by strong criticism. A fairly common complaint among women was that the police service had simply gone 'too far' in its pursuit of equal opportunities, reaching a state in which policing was being held hostage to the demands of an equality agenda.

Coyle (1995) notes that alongside every workplace equality initiative there is always a strongly 'competing discourse' that constructs equality measures as privileging women at the expense of men. Analysing a model developed for women's entry into policing, Brown (1997a) notes that one of the key stages of development is marked by the assembly of hard facts through research which might paint a picture that highlights problems such as sexual harassment on a generalised basis. In turn, she argues that this research is greeted by disbelief and that strategies are enacted to try to neutralise the impact of such results. However, 'as equal opportunities policies begin to bite, there is some evidence of a backlash effect within the informal culture' (*ibid.*: 15). The following senior policewomen's reflections provide visible manifestations of both the 'competing discourse' and of the 'backlash effect' which Coyle (1995) and Brown (1997a) predict:

I am a little cynical about it. I sometimes think we over promote equal opportunities ... I think this is a danger you can create. There is a cynicism among the police force in general about equal opportunities, because for them [men] they feel if you are white and male and heterosexual then you are being discriminated [against] as opposed to all the other minority groups.

One of the problems is that equal opportunities was hyped up to such a degree where people have now reacted against it and now, in fact, if anything are making more jokes about it.

The equal opportunities pendulum seems to have swung very far in the police, with men seeming to feel insecure.

There is nothing worse than something which alienates people. I think, to a certain degree, this is what equal opportunities does. There it was meant to be helping all, but in effect, because the police went in all gung ho and said, 'you will do this now', you know 'you will operate equal opportunities', it was just thrust on the police, there was no real cultural change. The result is that people get resentful towards things they feel they are being forced to be part of and that includes men and women ... It should have been about changing the hearts and minds of individuals, not thrusting it on us.

It's all about balance I suppose. Equal opportunities just came at a time when of course we severely needed it, but the police wasn't ready for it. It was all too much in one go [and] as a result the progression of policy has suffered I think. People think things have gone too far and that's not just those lower down, but those up here. That's a shame I think.

It's completely a different beat now. The police language regarding individuals is unrecognisable; equal opportunities just rolls off the tongue now for all. All officers are at least aware of it. That doesn't necessarily mean that everyone is using it the way it was intended. Often, with these kinds of changes, women get blamed for all its negative sides. I get the impression from my colleagues that they think things are out of control now, that we have to bow down to everyone in the name of equal opportunities.

Susan Harwood's current research into the Western Australian Police Service suggests a strong backlash against the current Commissioner's progressive attitudes towards redressing gendered inequalities. She notes that lowering the wall that officers face as part of their physical fitness testing is perceived by both men and women as a 'lowering of the standard' (personal communication, April 2003). The idea that redressing gendered inequalities results in substandard policing is a strong theme in the following senior women's narratives. Alongside the general praise for developments in equal opportunities was the perception that policing had 'gone soft'. One officer notes:

We can very much see a service ethic being espoused. It's about equal opportunities and political correctness, but the pendulum has swung too far. Too many grievances these days, too many moaners which are women. We have to be a disciplined service to be successful. I really do fear we have lost this. Before the changes, no one would have said boo to a goose; it's not like that anymore.

Another officer points to the negative effects that 'going soft' has had on police discipline and standards:

We have gone a bit soft and I don't agree with it. I'm afraid what has actually happened is that what was called a disciplined force which the police were considered to be is no longer so disciplined, it is more lax. Standards have fallen, certain standards of behaviour, respect for rank, appearance, quality of work, pride in work, all of that has slipped and a lot of that is down to the fact that supervisors are not supervising in a firm enough manner. I view it as a general slackening of the general structure which leads to falling standards. While there are positive sides to the changes, the downside is that managers seemed to have abrogated a lot of their responsibilities in the form of a responsibility to the organisation and the responsibility to provide a public service and that's the only reason we are here for. Interpreting the softer regime as not having to drive people on as much as they used to and not demand results and not provide the accountability we used to have, that's where I think we are falling down.

Such views echo Reiner's (1991) findings on chief constables' views about police discipline in which many of them expressed concern about the relaxation of militaristic principles and disciplinary standards. The notion of 'going soft' was also reiterated in policewomen's reflections on the changing nature of police leadership and leaders. Given their length of service, many of the women interviewed had witnessed enormous changes in the styles of policing. Even those with the shortest length of service were able to reflect on a changing form of leadership. All of the women stressed that police leadership had become 'less autocratic' and much 'softer' in approach. The following comments were characteristic of the majority of responses:

I find that senior management operates a much more open door policy and is less rank conscious than before.

In the past, they [Leaders] held more distance and probably ruled with a rod of iron, now it's all very pally pally, open and friendly.

While appearing a positive step in the movement towards governing internal police relationships, this move was not always welcome. Bayley (1994) notes the significance of rank in the police hierarchy when he argues that deference to authority is mandatory in the police organisation. Higher ranks give orders to lower ranks and lower ranks obey. Lower-ranking officers commonly address superiors as 'Sir' or 'Ma'am'; superior officers address subordinates by their first names. Overall, policewomen's perceptions were that the police organisation had become 'less rank conscious' and 'less hierarchical' in nature with the emergence of a 'questioning culture', as the following officer observes:

The organisation has become less confrontational. When I first joined there was much more of a sense of discipline, you knew your place. When the Governor spoke to you, you just did it. Then in the 1980s, the police just reflected society – individuals became much more open and ready to challenge – so PCs were less daunted about challenging their sergeants and inspectors. But this has led to other serious problems, this has led to the organisation being ineffective in managing its own people. As soon as you try to be firm in your management and leadership style, you are preparing ground for confrontation and now there are mechanisms for individuals to resort to: the grievance procedure, complaints. While the changes have been good in getting rid of some old dinosaurs, it has almost gone too far the other way with managers not managing.

Here the ability to achieve authority becomes problematic with senior officers less able and likely to pull rank. In addition, it was emphasised that such a situation may hold specific difficulties for women leaders in policing.

Things have changed; we are much more caring. Leadership is much more about needs, but we have in turn become really frightened of confrontation. Some managers are fearful of asking their subordinates to do things, frightened even of their own shadow. We are less autocratic now, more communicative, and consultative, but this has left us with huge problems in the police. It would happen just as women are getting in and up, all of a sudden you've got these women in who can't use the same tools as men have had at their disposal to get results – you know, no shouting, no demanding. I luckily don't feel I have to resort to this to get results but I know of many women who are really finding this change hard, even blamed as playing a contributory role in this softening up.

Through its various processes, restructuring brings with it degrees of uncertainty. As individuals begin to take their place in this new order, it might be that they will feel unfamiliar and uncertain about their surroundings. It should perhaps come as no surprise, then, that some officers are nostalgic and hark back to a past in policing where they were governed by a clear power structure. In spite of what might seem numerous and grave organisational shortcomings, it was a time when officers knew what was expected of them. Officers 'knew their place' in relation to both those above and below them and so were able to draw upon and enact appropriate scripts and behaviour. The following officer recalls her disappointment on achieving rank only to find that it had become less acceptable to use the title 'Ma'am':

> In the old days, if an inspector came into the briefing room at the beginning of the shift you all stood, it's a simple thing but you stood. It's respect, and [for] anyone inspector [or] above, you stood and then, even in a day-to-day regime and office, if a senior officer walked in you would acknowledge it by rising and then they would say 'no, that's all right'. It's a mark of respect and they were always referred to as Sir or Ma'am, no question about title. When I arrived here there were several people that would walk past you in the corridor and not acknowledge you. Now I would never have thought of doing that even if it's a nod or a 'Sir', 'Ma'am'. Some were even coming up to me and saying is it OK if I still call you [her first name]. You can also walk into a room and no one takes a blind bit of notice and you have to cough and say excuse me. In some ways I felt cheated, I had finally got to inspector and, I know it sounds very superficial but when you first take on the rank and someone calls you Ma'am, Boss or Gov. it's a nice feeling. I felt cheated because I had always accorded that amount of respect to others and it's sad that people don't feel like that anymore.

The powerful meanings attached to hierarchy and rank serve as strong clues to understanding the failure of attempts to fracture police identity. The ability to hold and maintain rank, using and drawing on the associated leadership scripts, is a key and potent feature of police leaders.

In summing up briefly, the development of equal opportunities has gone some way since Jones's (1986) recommendations. Structurally, the police organisation has responded to calls for change with all officers having access to procedures that claim to ensure equality of opportunity. Nonetheless, women remain unconvinced of their effectiveness and are cautious of their potential. There remains a fundamental difficulty in the approach that has been adopted by the police organisation – that is, a liberal, gender-neutral position (Brown 1998). This approach seeks to neither deconstruct nor question the meaning of policing; nor does it seek to reappraise the skills required to do police work. Instead, the concern of those adopting a liberal approach is how well individuals fit within the existing organisation and its structures. In this case, it focuses on the extent of women's ability to adapt to policing. It proposes that women who can do a job equivalent to men should be given the opportunity to do so but implicitly accepts that the norm for the job is still based on a male model. Any difficulties that may arise in this process are inevitably constructed as problems residing with individual women. As a result, we should not be surprised if women become characterised as being inadequate and men become resentful of the 'special treatment' that may follow (Liff and Cameron 1997).

Change through quality

At the same time as meeting the demands for the development of equal opportunities, the police service has been subject to a new managerialist order based on economy, efficiency, and effectiveness (McLaughlin and Murji 1995, 1997, Morgan and Newburn 1997, Leisham, Cope and Starie 1996, Waters 1996, Charman *et al.* 1999). The 1980s and 1990s witnessed a considerably changed agenda for policing, leading to a service-wide approach to 'quality of service'. There has been a clear attempt by the police to become more 'responsive', 'customer oriented' and more 'businesslike' in its approach. The ongoing reform of the police organisation is best understood as part of the ongoing managerialisation of the public sector, of which managerialism is fast becoming a permanent feature (McLaughlin and Murji 1995).

A significant shift underlying this movement has been a deliberate attempt to transform the policing paradigm from a narrow conception of the police as a law enforcement agency to a broader conception of the police as a service. Inherent within this shift has been the movement towards a greater emphasis on the 'quality' of service in police organisations. The visible manifestations of this shift can be traced to a number of key documents published by the police organisation. The *Plus Programme* launched in April 1989 by Sir Peter Imbert, then Commissioner of the Metropolitan Police, was to be the mission statement for professional policing in the 1990s. The Metropolitan Police had committed itself to a major programme of change, with a fundamental review of the command structure, the organisation of specialist support systems, together with an examination of the effectiveness of rewards, sanctions, and communication systems (Walker 1994). Considerable emphasis was placed on open management and meaningful consultation with all ranks of officers, with a view to affecting the culture of the organisation.

In 1990, the Association of Chief Police Officers (ACPO) in conjunction with the Police Federation and the Superintendents' Association launched the national *Quality of Service* initiative. At the heart of the national *Quality of Service* initiative was the *Operational Policing Review* (Joint Consultative Committee of the Police Staff Associations 1990), a survey conducted by representatives of the three police staff associations. It proposed that drives for greater efficiency within the police service had led to an erosion of service styles of policing, that the public expressed a preference for a community-oriented service style of policing rather than an enforcement-based approach. The document reported that public dissatisfaction with the police stemmed largely from inappropriate and outdated policing styles and poor service delivery. The *Strategic Policy Document* (ACPO 1990) then went on to consider the findings of the *Operational Policing Review* and made recommendations. The report noted that insufficient effort had gone into monitoring service delivery and assessing the quality with which the service was delivered to the public (Waters 1996).

Perhaps one of the most observable links of the interconnectedness of the discourses of 'quality' and 'equality' can be seen in the significant shifts that have taken place with regard to the treatment of victims of sexual offences and domestic violence (Plotnikoff and Woolfson 1998, Hanmer *et al.* 1999). Subjected to heavy criticism[1] for their inadequate treatment of women as victims of violence throughout the 1980s, the 1990s saw the Home Office, together with the police service, respond to such criticisms with a package of reforms. Home Office Circular's 69/1986, 60/1990 and 19/2000[2] have all worked towards shifting the issue of domestic violence and the treatment of its victims to a more central position in the policing remit. Many forces in Britain now have Sexual Offence Squads, Family Protection Units and Domestic Violence Units (DVUs) staffed by specialist officers (Bourlet 1990, Edwards 1994). Reports of the effect of such changes remain mixed,[3] but the resounding message from such changes is that policing priorities have shifted or at least become redefined (Edwards 1994, Jones *et al.* 1994). In this instance, the drive for greater 'quality' is strongly underpinned by a concern for achieving greater 'equality' through a gendered agenda.

Reform of the police organisation continued to be a key issue in 1992 with the new Home Secretary, Kenneth Clarke, embarking on a catalogue of inspections subjecting the police even further to the rigours of managerialism. He announced the establishment of an inquiry under the chairmanship of Sir Patrick Sheehy to review the rank structure, the remuneration framework, and the terms and conditions of service of police. This was then followed by an internal Home Office review of the tripartite structure of police governance in July 1992, and a Home Office survey of core and ancillary tasks in December 1992.

The various facets of managerialism in policing have already been well rehearsed elsewhere (McLaughlin and Murji 1995, 1997, Morgan and Newburn 1997, Leisham, Loveday and Savage 1996, Waters 1996). My aim is simply to draw out the significance that some of the changes may hold for understanding a changing identity for the police organisation and its officers. Commentators have noted that despite the far-reaching changes to local police authorities, it was the Sheehy proposals that dominated discussion (McLaughlin and Murji 1997, Morgan and Newburn 1997, Rawlings 1999). The Sheehy Inquiry (Sheehy 1993) posed one of the most radical challenges to the police organisation. Its proposals for organisational change offered the potential to substantially remodel policing, both at an administrative and cultural level.

Armed with the task of realising more efficient and cost-effective management of existing resources, the Inquiry team set about addressing a variety of issues. These included an examination of: the structure of forces, to ensure that they met the management needs of a modern police service; roles and responsibilities of the various ranks; salaries of police officers; rewards and sanctions for good and bad behaviour; and conditions of service, work practices, and professional standards (*ibid.*). The Inquiry team produced a radical and wide-ranging report in June 1993, which made 272 recommendations. Of particular significance were the recommendations to simplify and streamline the rank structure through a reduction of managerial ranks, and the intention to introduce new conditions of service for officers, including tenure of post, fixed-term appointments for new recruits and those promoted to higher ranks as a way to end the 'jobs for life' culture. Both of these recommendations signify substantial organisational restructuring, the effects of which are deeply gendered and hold important ramifications for both women and men in policing.

Despite the radical proposals put forward by Sheehy, the report's significance goes beyond its recommendations. The police response to Sheehy that was to follow its publication provides an interesting example of the potential power of individual agency through the power of resistance. Sheehy's vision of organisational change for policing was strongly resisted and the campaign against it was vociferous. The proposals led to the biggest mass rally held at any point since the introduction of the new police in 1829 (Morgan and Newburn 1997). In response to the Sheehy recommendations, the *Guardian* ran a full-page advertisement sponsored by the Police Federation on 14 July 1993, calling for a Royal Commission that would make a detailed examination of the requirements and the nature of modern policing. Such was the strength of the response that by 16 July *The Observer* headlined 'Howard set for U-turn on police' (cited in Walklate 1993a).

McLaughlin and Murji (1995) note that as a response to Sheehy, a variety of apocalyptic warnings were made to back up the claim that Sheehy had no place in the future of policing. Police officers maintained that reducing the ranks was a 'retrograde, unwarranted and unproductive step' because rank conferred prestige and status and was organisationally important as a motivator and a necessary component of effective supervision. Consequently, following the successful lobbying campaign by the police and, to a lesser extent, local authorities against the Sheehy and White Paper proposals, McLaughlin and Murji (1997) note that the Police Magistrates' Courts Act (PMCA) (1994) contained less than the full reform package. While Sheehy recommended that the number of ranks should be reduced from nine to six, in the event only two were abolished – those of deputy chief constable (at least in name) and chief superintendent. Fixed-term contracts were also introduced for chief officer positions with the possibility of these being extended to superintendent ranks in the future (Leisham, Cope and Starie 1996).

While many of Sheehy's recommendations were eventually successfully averted, Morgan and Newburn (1997) assert that the very existence of the Inquiry reinforced the view that, as far as the government was concerned, the police service was increasingly to be run along business lines. They note that the developments in policing in the 1980s and 1990s should be sufficient to indicate that the role and responsibilities of the police are a contested issue. Despite resistance, it has been argued that police reform is significantly changing the nature of policing in Britain towards a 'new policing order' (Leisham, Cope and Starie 1996). There appears to be a strong consensus among commentators that, despite the resistance and often diluted outcomes of proposals, taking all the developments together, the ideological framework within which the police operate has been transformed (*ibid.*, Savage and Charman 1996, Waters 1996, Butler 1996, Morgan and Newburn 1997, McLaughlin and Murji 1995, 1997, Charman *et al.* 1999). More significantly, perhaps, it is predicted that the effect of such changes will continue to have a profound impact upon the police and that this in turn will play through to the cultural 'mind set' of the police (McLaughlin and Murji 1997).

Changing identities

Researchers have all too often ignored the gendered effects of organisational change. In the same way that organisations have been viewed in gender-neutral terms, so too have the processes of organisational change and restructuring. Halford *et al.* (1997) argue that by primarily perceiving organisations as rational instruments in the implementation of economically driven strategies for change, the processes of restructuring have become perceived purely in terms of their effects in reducing costs and raising productivity. Such a position ultimately results in an inaccurate and partial explanation of the effects of restructuring. For Halford *et al.* (*ibid.*: 65), restructuring is tied up with 'redefining and contesting the sorts of personal *identities* and *qualities* which are seen as desirable or undesirable for organisational members to possess' (original emphasis).

Some writers on women and management have been optimistic in their predictions of the potential changes that organisational restructuring may bring. Itzen and Newman (1995), for example, argue that organisational restructuring towards less hierarchy, more team functioning, and greater flexibility might in principle work towards reducing some of the disadvantages that women face. Other commentators remain less convinced by such suggestions of change, holding that, when analysed critically, the new discourses of organisational change might appear to offer a radical departure from traditional approaches but the traditional values of masculism are clearly discernible. Hopton (1999), for example, argues that when considered from the perspective of critical studies in masculinity it can be inferred that these 'new' management ideologies reflect values that are typical of traditional masculinist behaviour such as competitiveness (Brittan 1989), risk taking (Harris 1995), and the domination of territory and other individuals (Stollenberg 1990, Hearn 1992). Drawing parallels between contemporary management philosophies and the masculinism of militarism, Hopton (1999) argues that as the significance of militarism is waning in society, managerialism is developing into an alternative paradigm of idealised masculinity.

The movement towards increased quality of service has resulted in the significant restructuring of organisations, bringing modifications to the nature of work and working patterns. Coyle (1995), for instance, has argued that the 'downsizing', 'delayering', and 'decentralising' of organisations has given way to a demand for a highly flexible workforce. Handy (1994) has proclaimed the arrival of the 'portfolio worker' and Bridges (1995) predicts the end of 'the job'. Following Sheehy, the police organisation has been affected by such modifications, with the processes of restructuring leading to the downsizing and removal of levels of management in policing. The police organisation is one with fewer police officers at senior ranks. Senior policewomen interviewed demonstrated an acute awareness of the potential implications of reducing the number of ranks for their future role in policing as women. The following narratives demonstrate vividly the reality of such a situation. Far from creating more opportunities, flatter organisational structures are leading to an increased rivalry and competitiveness between women and men (and in many cases between women) over a reduced number of higher-level management jobs:

> Less ranks, more competition, that's all I see before me and you know women won't go for it, they don't know how to compete.

> There is no doubt [about] the impact of losing some of the ranks. The whole nature of what's going on will bring about huge implications for those coming through. There is no doubt about that; we are all set up against one another now. It's quite strange really, we used to pride ourselves on teamwork, even if we were rife with sexism and racism and all that stuff, but we saw ourselves as united. Whereas now it's each to their own – you make your own way here, you mark out your own territory.

The following observation is worth quoting at length for it sets out a picture of some of the gendered effects of restructuring and offers some thoughts about the way in which women and men negotiate this new landscape of increasing competition:

> I think [senior policewomen] find it difficult. Being a woman is hard, they find they have to step out of the police role. Because we are such a performance culture there is a lot of rivalry within a team, such that women get pushed to the back, in terms of the calls, arrests, operationally. Men tend to take the attitude that their careers are more important, their career aspirations are more important, they have to get performance targets to prove to their managers that they are worth being recommended to the CID, and women are being pushed to the back of the queue. When there are [so] few jobs to go for, and this is a new thing that has crept in the last few years, as streamlining of jobs, those good ones are like gold dust. This performance culture is relatively new, a subtle shift where you find men arguing that women don't need the performance figures as much as your male counterparts, because you will probably leave and have kids, women will get pushed out, that's a sad reality. It's a fight between the enemy within, and this you know has been organisationally driven and not individually driven, this whole performance culture has spin-off effects.

Such concerns may be particularly pertinent if we consider that the effects of downsizing has specifically led to a reduction of posts in the middle managerial layer, a layer that frequently represents the final stage to be reached before women hit the glass ceiling. Together with the changing structure of the police organisation, policewomen pointed to a change in the nature of their work. In line with Tienari's (1999) finding of 'artificial reclassifications and shifting content and status' of managerial positions, women in policing may be entering positions that are coinciding with a dissemination of managerial titles to positions without significant status or authority.

> I am a bit disillusioned with the next rank. I do most of the job now anyway with the devolving of work but I just don't get any of the credit.

> I look at what I am doing now in this role, and then I think of what my predecessor did in this role and it's not comparable. That's not just because he was a bit uninspiring but also that workloads have changed; we are now doing much more, doing the work of the ranks that have gone.

> I sometimes ask myself, why bother, why bother to keep going? I'm only doing some of the work that my old chief used to do, just he got paid for it and got the recognition. It really is too much pressure and for what? We certainly don't do it for the salary.

> Ironically, the job I am doing now is one that is done or was done by a chief officer, an ACC [Assistant Chief Constable] but as we downsized the ranks we passed off a lot of the jobs.

In these cases, it is apparent that managerial responsibility has been pushed downwards to lower grades. This devolved responsibility has not been accompanied by a devolved authority nor has there been a recognition of this extra responsibility, either in terms of financial reward or in terms of occupational kudos.

Flatter organisations do not necessarily create an opportunity for women's career development or for their greater participation in the decision-making process. More usually it means more work. Many of the policewomen recounted the increased pressure to work longer hours. This stems not only from increased workloads and reduced staffing levels but also from a growing managerial culture that places a high premium on doing so. The intensification of a management culture characterised by the ability 'to get things done' has become a key feature of organisational life since the late 1990s. Visibly working long hours has come to be an indicator of commitment and stamina. Maile's (1995) work suggests that employees who want to retain employment in the new organisational structures have to demonstrate qualities that are often at odds with personal or familial considerations, such as 'risk taking' and extensive geographic mobility. Individuals who are prepared to move around the country, gaining experience in a variety of organisations, are considered more worldly and at the centre of 'cut and thrust' decision making. In the context of increased competition and the intensification of work, excessively long working hours for managers have become the norm. The stark choice that policewomen often have to make between pursuing promotion and addressing the needs of family life will be explored in more detail in the following chapter.

With reference to local government management, Coyle (1988: 48) points to the emergence of an alternative masculinity. She suggests the arrival of a 'creeping "hard" managerialism' characterised by a 'workaholic "macho" ethos', which increasingly associates managerial competence with masculinity. In response to the fact that policing had become more policy driven, Reiner (1991) characterised the new generation of senior police officers in his study as 'bureaucrats'. In a more recent appraisal of changes since then, Reiner (1998: 89) observes that the 'bureaucrat' is being replaced by the 'business man':

> Sadly the post-Sheehy and Police and Magistrates' Courts Act 'reforms' are threatening the Scarmanesque diplomatic type of Chief constable. Current Home Office pressure is leaning towards a new type: the business man, cynical yuppies who know the performance measures for everything and the meaning of nothing.

The 'business man' shares much in common with the inhabitants of the 'smart macho' culture to which I referred in Chapter 2.

Despite organisational talk of a new breed of police leader grounded in the language of equality and quality of service, senior policewomen noted the rise of a new form of male dominance characterised by an increased sense of competitiveness and individualism. The cult of masculinity, then, 'slides seamlessly into the performance culture' (Brown 2003: 183). Despite a different emphasis and a different language, 'performance culture has the same underlying principles of competition and the condoning of rule bending and rule breaking in order to achieve targets' (*ibid.*). In *doing* leadership, women were acutely aware that the police organisation continues to value and reward the transactional approach underlined by competitiveness and individualism. The effect that such traits might have on women's own strategies of doing leadership will be explored more fully in Chapter 5.

Analyses of organisational restructuring have traditionally had a tendency to treat change separately from gendering processes. As a result, the gendered effects of such change have been noticeably absent. A significant number of initiatives have been undertaken by the police organisation to ensure both 'equality' and 'quality'. There is also evidence to suggest that police leaders have become fluent in what were once foreign languages in policing. They have become bilingual in the languages of 'quality' and 'equality'. A strong commitment to equal opportunities and to quality of service are the hallmarks of the modern, managerial chief constable (Leisham, Cope and Starie 1996). The managerialist approach has brought with it a fundamental appraisal of the role of leaders within the organisation and subsequently, a rethinking of the nature and characteristics of appropriate leadership. It is to this issue that the next chapter turns.

Notes

1 The domestic violence literature has documented at length the ways in which domestic cases are treated as 'rubbish' work by the police who avoid arresting assaultive partners. Common criticisms were that incidents were not being taken seriously and were seen as civil rather than criminal matters and that inadequate recording practices obscured a true picture of the extent of domestic violence (Hanmer and Maynard 1987, Radford and Stanko 1989, Stanko 1989, 1995, Edwards 1989, McConville et al. 1991).

2 While Home Office (HO) Circular 69/1986 was advisory in nature, reminding officers of the seriousness of domestic violence and of existing legislation, Circular 60/1990 was more forceful in its approach. It encouraged the development of: policy documents and clear strategies for dealing with domestic violence incidents; an interventionist approach based on the presumption of arrest when an offence has been committed; a recording for domestic incidents which reflects procedures for other violent crimes; and the establishment of dedicated units or specialist officers to deal with domestic violence incidents. HO Circular 19/2000 further reinforced the seriousness of domestic violence to police organisations but more specifically bound the quality of policing of domestic violence to the measurement of Best Value performance indicators.

3 In some areas, there is evidence of improvements in police practice. Hanmer and Saunders (1990), for example, reported greater satisfaction with police treatment after the introduction of Domestic Violence Units

(DVUs) in West Yorkshire, and Morley and Mullender (1994) found that women generally preferred dealing with non-uniformed DVU officers. In her Islington study, Mooney (1993) found that women who had sought help from the police since the implementation of the new policies were more satisfied with the treatment they received than were women who had been to the police prior to the policy changes. However, an evaluation of domestic violence units by Cromack (1995), based on research in Hull, found little evidence of improvement in police practice since new policies had been introduced. Grace (1995) adds to this pessimism arguing that, although most forces had introduced polices to deal with the needs of women, the translation of policy into practice had been less successful.

Chapter 4

The making of police leaders

The existence of the glass ceiling within organisations has for some time now provided organisational theorists sufficient explanatory power to account for women's absence from leadership positions. Given that the glass ceiling within many organisations has now been cracked, how can we reconcile and make sense of the fact that women are still under-represented at the top? In Chapter 2 I stressed the importance of going beyond a gender-neutral logic if we are to fully understand the way in which organisations work. It is worth restating here Acker's (1992) notion of the gendered substructure, in which the spatial and temporal arrangements of work assume significance. It is within such spatial and temporal arrangements that the gendered nature of work becomes most apparent and that subtle cultural forms of discrimination manifest themselves. Ideas about femininity and masculinity are embedded in such organisational arrangements and gendered identities are created and sustained.

I have also argued that, despite the fact that the glass ceiling within the police organisation has been broken, it continues to successfully achieve social closure for female police officers. This chapter focuses its attention on exploring in more detail the spatial and temporal arrangements that govern police work and the identity of the police leader. To suggest that the career ladder is being climbed by a universal and disembodied worker is a myth. Progression within policing is premised on an 'ideal' type of worker. Through women's own narratives of their journeys to the top, the characteristics of this 'ideal' worker become clearly visible. Reflecting on their careers through temporal (time) and spatial (place) dimensions, senior policewomen emphasise the importance of achieving credibility and commitment. Not only are such competencies informal (inasmuch as they are not enshrined in official job specification), they are, by their very nature, deeply gendered, both in definition and in accomplishment.

I have also stressed elsewhere the importance of individual agency. The extent to which senior policewomen are in possession of some kind of 'career strategy' is central to our understanding of their journeys to the top. While the concept of strategy remains a contested one, it still forms a useful means through which to explore forms of human agency. In their analysis of career pathways in a range of occupations, Halford *et al.* (1997) note that one of the central ways in which agency can be registered is by exploring the salience of strategy. They suggest that in doing so it is helpful to conceptualise career narratives as a continuum ranging from 'contingent to strategic' – 'contingent' careers consist of changing responses to unfolding opportunity, whereas 'strategic' careers approximate a notion of planful development (*ibid.*). I will be drawing on this continuum to explore senior policewomen's careers. In making sense of women's own experiences of the journey to the top, it may be instructive to outline some of the structural tenets that govern the police career.

There's only one way up – from the bottom and within

An understanding of the way in which officers are recruited at the outset, together with an investigation of the promotion process they face once inside the police, are essential in making sense of the ways in which police identity is formed. The way in which 'time' is experienced, constructed, and manipulated is a central feature of women's experiences of getting to the top. The significance of 'time' is grounded within the very structure of the police career. *Doing* and *managing* 'time' becomes a key resource for developing and maintaining a police identity, and even more significant for the construction of a police leader identity.

The police organisation in Britain is a good example of a strict linear organisational career with all entrants beginning at the bottom and working their way up through a highly structured series of ranks. Prior to the Sheehy Inquiry (Sheehy 1993), the police service's organisational structure was characterised by nine ranks. Since then, the Police Magistrates' Courts Act (PMCA) (1994) went on to compact the rank structure by reducing the overall numbers of police ranks to seven. Although the number of ranks throughout Britain is not consistent, Britain remains firmly rooted to the concept that authority is distributed according to rank. The highly structured career path in policing is not peculiar to Britain; the majority of modern police forces throughout the world posses some degree of structure, although the form of that structure varies considerably. From a comparative perspective, Bayley (1994) notes that Australia has the most elaborate with eleven and sometimes twelve ranks; Japan has eight and Canada, seven. He also stresses the important consequences that organising in terms of ranks holds. Having a flat-based pyramid that quickly tapers to an elongated top effectively means that the chances of promotion are severely limited. With the exception of Japan,[1] about 75 per cent of police throughout the world are at the lowest rank (Bayley 1991). In 2002, Britain's police organisations were made up of: 0.17 per cent chief and assistant chief constables; 1.05 per cent superintendents; 1.3 per cent chief inspectors; 4.94 per cent inspectors; 14.68 per cent sergeants; and 77.86 per cent constables (Smith *et al.* 2002).

Unlike some of their counterparts elsewhere in Europe and the rest of the world, Britain operates a single entry system of recruitment with all officers without exception beginning their careers as constables. Both female and male officers experience the effects of such a system but, by its very nature, there is a high degree of predictability about male promotion prospects built into a linear organisational career structure (Halford *et al.* 1997). Though all officers may begin on an equal footing, there are a number of measures taken by the police service to identify potential high-flyers, with systems in place to ensure the 'fast streaming' of officers who demonstrate high management potential via the Special Course and the Accelerated Promotion Scheme (APS) (the Special Course was a forerunner of the APS), followed by structured progress throughout the various command courses (Charman *et al.* 1999). More recently, with the advent of the National Police Leadership Faculty, we can see the emergence of an array of senior leadership development programmes aimed at pushing forward those who display a potential for high office. Following the Home Secretary David Blunkett's recent proposals on reforming the police, Brown (2003) notes that fast tracking could see movement from constable to Basic Command Unit (BCU) commander in five years. I will return to the gendered implications of such structuring later in the chapter, but for now I want to emphasise the importance that starting at the bottom and recruiting from within has for carving out an appropriate police identity for the police leader.

Concern over the selection, appointment, and training of chief officers is not new. The idea that police chiefs should be drawn from within their own ranks has been the subject of debate throughout the past century. Such concerns can be traced back to debates conducted during the 1920s and 1930s, when a number of proposals by Sir William Nott-Bower, Sir Arthur Dixon and Lord Trenchard were put forward in an attempt to enhance the quality of senior management.[2] In short, the result of these debates was a firm commitment to the continued sanctioning of the ideology of internal recruitment. The extent to which the police organisation can continue to cling to this ideology of internal recruitment, however, remains a matter for conjecture.

Coupled with the concern over the selection and appointment of chief officers is a concern over the inadequacy of preparing recruits for their roles. The educational standard of entrants into the British police service has long since been a subject of intense commentary by academics, police practitioners, and policy-makers alike. In 1992, Reiner claimed that the poor educational standards of recruits and in particular the shortage of graduates were key in accounting for the demise of the image of the police as an efficient disciplined bureaucracy. An important recommendation of the *Scarman Report* (1981) was the encouragement of further training and higher education for police officers. Over a decade later, Adlam and Villier's (2003) collection of papers on police leadership point to the continued shortcomings of police education, focusing in particular on the inadequacies of the Police Leadership Development Curriculum.

A strong educational profile is often seen to be a useful indication of an individual's career potential. In his work on chief constables, Reiner (1991) notes that chief officers were more likely to have higher qualifications, either on entry to the service or as a result of study undertaken during their careers, with a clear trend towards it being the norm for chief constables to hold degrees. The women I interviewed also evidence this trend. Seventeen of the women were in possession of a university degree, and one was in the final stages of completing a doctorate. However, unlike traditional areas of study such as Law, which characterised many of Reiner's Chief Constables, degree subjects of senior women included a range of areas including Sociology, Chemistry, Psychology, and Zoology. It is also worth reminding ourselves here that, historically, it was early policewomen and not policemen who placed a considerable amount of effort into their quest for greater professionalism through increased education, training, and specialism (Carrier 1988, Heidensohn 1992). By the 1920s, policewomen themselves were actively working to create a more credentialised profession. It was Lieutenant Mina C. Van Winkle, president of the International Association of Women Police (IAWP) and director of the Women's Bureau of the Metropolitan Police Department, who criticised the use of untrained police matrons and volunteers claiming that '... vulgar, uneducated, untrained, policewomen degrade the service in the eyes of both the public and the policemen. They are a bad influence with clients in the community and a menace to the police service in general' (cited in Owings 1925: xi). Interestingly, women in policing have historically possessed a higher level of academic qualification than their male counterparts (Heidensohn 1992, 2000). It seems that the same is true of modern policewomen (Hartley *et al.* 2002, McGuigan *et al.* 2002).

The increased emphasis and importance on the possession of a degree, together with the growing number of degree courses in Policing, Criminology, and Criminal Justice Studies, attest to the movement towards credentialising the work of policing even further. This theme is echoed in the work of Leisham, Loveday and Savage (1996) who argue that the nature and extent of change in the development and expansion of new higher educational courses and training opportunities for officers reflect the continuing aspirations of the public police towards truly professional status. Bayley (1994) demonstrates that in Los Angeles, most officers of the rank of captain and above hold an advanced degree. By contractual obligation, several officers are sent each year from the New York State Police and the New York City Police for post-graduate degrees at local universities. The value of possessing a higher educational qualification is reinforced by Vickers (2000: 512) when she notes that 'Higher education ... can engender the ability to handle difficult or ambiguous situations with greater creativity or innovation, as well as pointing to an ability to adapt to change more readily.'

While the general education requirements of police officers have risen, they remain some way behind the education level of the general population (Panzarella 2003). Despite the growing importance of external qualifications, in-house training continues to take precedence in achieving police competence. The recent development of Centrex[3] as a centre of excellence for police training looks set to revolutionise and drive forward higher standards in police training in England and Wales.

The majority of senior policewomen perceived higher educational qualifications to be an important attribute for promotion but not necessarily grounded in any practical use for the work of policing. Studies of police training have concluded that for the most part police training is not geared to meet the actual 'on the job' requirements of police officers (Norris 1992, Fielding 1988). It was the *Scarman Report* (1981) that provided an early call for a review of training for supervisory and managerial ranks. Subsequently, the new training course for the promotion of sergeants and inspectors – the Objective Structured Performance Related Examination (OSPRE®) – was introduced in 1992. Through its focus on job-related exercises, OSPRE® underlines the importance of good interpersonal managerial skills. The basis of promotion became strongly attached and dependent upon the ability to display predefined areas of competency.[4] Made up of two parts,[5] recent research by Hartley *et al.* (2002) and McGuigan *et al.* (2002) has demonstrated that for the past eight years women have consistently been more successful than their male counterparts in Part II.

At a more senior level, the late 1980s and early 1990s saw the selection and appointment of chief constables come under review. Emphasis on the training and career development needs of senior command officers can be found in a Home Office Affairs Committee Enquiry into *Higher Police Training* (Symposium on Higher Police Training 1990). Home Office Circular 98/1991 went on to require those wishing to achieve Association of Chief Police Officers (ACPO) rank to undertake the Strategic Command Course (SCC) at the Police Staff College, Bramshill.

Attendance at Bramshill has in itself been hailed as a crucial rite of passage for senior officers, marking a 'key point in the career development of police officers'. More significantly, such attendance 'plays a crucial role in selecting, socialising, and in an informal sense controlling, all future police managers' (Wall 1998: 225, 235). Entry into and movement within the final tier of the police hierarchy requires the ability to jump a series of mini-hurdles. In order to be offered a place on the SCC candidates must first be selected through the Extended Interview (EI), an annual round of selections for suitably qualified superintendents (formerly chief superintendents before the rank was abolished in the wake of Sheehy). Charman *et al.* (1999) note that the EI method has been used since 1962 and originates from practice elsewhere such as the military and civil service. However, new procedures have actively discouraged the practice of informal interviewing and focus instead upon the objective appraisal of the candidates' professional competencies. It is held at residential assessment centres and involves three days of high-pressured interviews, written exercises, 'objective' tests of ability, and a variety of group discussions and simulations. Through these, candidates are closely observed and assessed against a range of criteria including: strategic perspective; confidence as a leader; judgement; achievement focus; communication; information search; team building; negotiating; and influencing. The significance of the EI is emphasised by Wall (1998: 201) when he notes that it serves as 'an important, if not the most important, tool in the selection process'.

A brief note about selectors is also deserved. All appointments to ranks below the level of assistant chief constable are made internally; appointments above that rank are made by an external committee of the Local Police Authority (LPA), although typically such committees are chaired by the chief constable. Forces other than the Metropolitan Police are governed by the constitutional arrangements under the 'tripartite system', consisting of an LPA, the chief officer, and the Home Office (Jones and Newburn 1997). However, following the recent changes to the membership of the LPA, brought about as a result of the PMCA (1994), Charman *et al.* (1999) note the potential 'professionalisation' of the appointments process, given the business backgrounds of newly appointed 'independent members'. The creation of a new independent Metropolitan Police Authority on 3 July 2000 also marked a radical change in the policing arrangements for London. The Authority is made up of twenty-three members, twelve drawn from the new Greater London Assembly, four magistrates and seven independent members. One of its key roles lies in the appointment, discipline, and removal of senior Metropolitan Police officers. The need for closer scrutiny of the machinery for the selection, appointment, and management training of senior police officers remains clear. Until then, we might have to be content with Tomkins and Brunstrom's (1995) finding that the process of appointment and selection of ACPO ranks is riddled with inconsistency and arbitrariness, with the whole system being described as an 'unprofessional lottery'. In mapping out women's journey to the top, I want to begin firstly by drawing out the significance of the temporal dimension in achieving credibility and commitment. The latter part of this chapter will then go on to consider the spatial dimension of officers' routes with a consideration of 'place'.

Doing and managing 'time'

If we examine 'time' in its most literal form, we can see that the route travelled by police officers in their quest for higher rank is a long one with the upper limit of a police officer's length of service normally being thirty years (Bland *et al.* 1999). On first glance, the potential length of a career in policing suggests ample time for new recruits to plan and develop a strategy for reaching the top. On closer inspection, however, it might be the case that this long career path might not work in favour of all officers, holding particular significance for women. In his study of chief constables, Reiner (1991) notes that after the initial hurdle of promotion (from constable to sergeant), those who realistically want to have a chance of becoming chief constable must move fairly rapidly through the middle management ranks. He notes that this follows 'from the simple arithmetic fact that most prospective chiefs reach sergeant rank in their late twenties so they have just over twenty years to achieve seven further promotions before they reach their early fifties, after which age few chief constables are appointed' (*ibid.*: 78).

Given the potential length of a police career, I wanted to explore the extent to which women were consciously involved in any strategic calculation about the timing of their careers. Drawing on Halford *et al.*'s (1997) continuum, very few of the policewomen describe their career progression as 'strategic', with most of their journeys best described as 'contingent'. In reflecting on their own careers, the majority of the policewomen commented on their lack of strategy. This is particularly true of their first ten years of service. Most of the women emphasised a lack of choice or strategic intent with regard to their occupational journeys, characterising their career paths as 'haphazard'. The following observation is typical of women's reflections of their careers:

> I have always certainly had ambitions for this job. From an early stage I always had a vision, but I honestly can't say to you that I planned every move. I don't think it was very strategic; when I look back, it was a case of where there were opportunities, I went for them.

Another officer states:

> I can say there was no strategy at all in my career, I took promotion very early on I suppose. It almost seems like things just turn up, its like waiting for a bus, you wait ages for one and then all three turn up together. I have never looked and said, 'I'm going to spend thirty years in this job and by the time I have six years' service, I will do this and this'. It just wasn't like that. I suppose now with only eight years left, I do look and say well where do I want to be in the next few years?

Gaston and Alexander's (1997) findings add further support here, particularly their revelation that one in three policewomen, compared to one in seven policemen, remained undecided about their future. The accounts offered by the more senior women in my study stressed the importance of external influences. Some noted the influence of both male and female colleagues, line managers, and/or mentor figures who had encouraged their potential by urging them to take on additional work and projects created by vacancies where work needed to be covered. Many had been encouraged to take opportunities afforded by chance and circumstance, thereby 'acting up' into more senior positions on a temporary basis.

Who would have thought it, me where I am? Sometimes I still can't believe it. I am married with kids and so sometimes I have to blink to make sure I'm still here, you know, pinch myself. I suppose it's all been a bit of chance and a huge stroke of luck . . . Of course, I have worked hard, damn hard at everything I do, moved up steadily but I have also had some good support around me . . . men and women, in and out of the service, who have kept me going.

I am just not ambitious, and people just can't believe that, because of my position and I am still fairly young. I tend to just do my job and when I want a fresh challenge I just look around for something new, so what happens has come along in spurts in my career. I don't think, 'Oh, I want to be a chief constable therefore I had better do this and this and that.' I just tend to go for things as and when. If I see an opportunity that I think will suit me then I'll go for it . . . When I say I am not ambitious I don't want you to think that I don't want things, I work very hard and I am very demanding on other people as well, therefore they may think I am aiming at promotion but I just think you should do your job.

I have tried to do all the things I like, to be involved in the areas I enjoy – that just happened to be operational, which of course has stood me in good stead in getting here. I have tried to be as broad as I can in gaining my experience base. I have been lucky though that I have enjoyed what I was doing, be it in personnel, training or whatever. I have had lots of stints at 'acting', this has certainly helped my progression. I haven't mapped it out this way, it just sort of happened that way. I suppose I was in the right place at the right time.

Having joined in 1978, all I can say is that I have worked at every promotion over that past 19 years or so. I have had a variety of roles, some of which I have really enjoyed but I wouldn't say I am ambitious by nature. The organisation to a certain degree instils that philosophy into you I suppose: you know to drive hard, to work hard if you want to get where you're going. I didn't always know I was going to get this far, I think it dawned on me when I reached superintendent rank. I really thought, well, I've got bags of time, why not go for it?

In the late 1970s, Kanter (1977: 92) observed that 'if sponsors are important for the success of men in organisations, they seem absolutely essential for women'. The influence of mentoring on career advancement here is depicted as a positive experience. Chief constables in Reiner's (1991) study also emphasised the importance of patronage and the support of an informal mentor or sponsor in determining their progression. There were some instances when women were able to recall the presence of an informal mentor, but for the most part senior policewomen put their career progression down to their own determination, hard work, and vigour. Many were able to articulate the benefits of a mentoring system and felt that they had missed out on the kind of 'informal mentoring that goes on between men'.

I have never had any kind of mentor, not in my career . . . not even informally. It's been all on my own. Although this mentoring stuff is quite new to the police, men have always done this among one another. There have always been givers and receivers; you know of the informal mentoring that goes on between men.

No one has ever encouraged me or helped me, you just do it yourself. My boss in my old job used me, he used my skills but he also helped me, it was reciprocal.

Although I have not had guided career progression throughout my career, I suppose this has come more into focus now . . . I started to notice and became aware of my potential and I started to have input from other people.

While the official system of mentoring is a relatively recent phenomenon in policing, informal mentoring has always played a part in the selection of those deemed appropriate for the heady heights of police leadership. 'Getting noticed' and being 'in the frame for leadership' holds significant benefits. It is here where the identity of officers is potentially transformed and where officers might begin to perceive themselves as destined for 'the top'. As the following woman notes, both are crucial in the formation and development of the appropriate self:

77

> I have never had a formal mentor or anything like that, but there were of course people who encouraged me. All the people who have encouraged my somewhat rapid rise through the ranks have actually been men, partly because there weren't very many women around and those that were around were not necessarily that way disposed to supporting other women ... My senior officer has provided help and encouragement. It wasn't even a case of saying, 'Will you consider going for this?', he would say, 'Why aren't you going for this? You really should be.' So, he was crucial. He really believed in me. He didn't help me make decisions, but reminded me that things out there did exist.

The limited number of black officers with rank who could assist in the promotional process makes the lack of sponsorship even more relevant for black female officers (Pogrebin *et al.* 1999).

In claiming 'no strategy', women provide an overly pessimistic view of being strategic. It might be the case that these women are reflecting on the entire length of their careers rather than on some of their specific movements. Women's professed lack of strategy was not always grounded in their narratives. Evidence from those women who are involved in managing the conflict between home and family, for example, demonstrates a strikingly different picture of women assiduously planning their time in and out of policing. Women are also in clear possession of some kind of strategy in their responses on managing 'place'. Both are subjects to which I will return in the latter part of this chapter.

Scott's findings in the late 1990s suggest that while rank aspirations at the beginning of police careers were the same for men and women, more men aspired to higher rank compared to women when asked about their current promotion target, with men making twice as many applications as women for higher rank (Scott 1997, cited in Brown and Heidensohn 2000). Equality legislation may have served to increase women's aspirations for higher rank, but Brown and Heidensohn (2000: 87) note the continued gap between men and women in terms of 'activating their promotion trajectories', with women not activating theirs. The lack of a careerist outlook is not unique to women. Of Reiner's (1991) chief constables, only two articulated a strong careerist outlook, admitting that they had joined with the ambition of being a chief constable and in both cases had carefully planned their careers. In seeking to make sense of police officers' aspirations for success, Bland *et al.*'s (1999) study on ethnic minority officers found that aspirations for rank tended to manifest themselves only after officers had achieved their first promotion; each promotion encouraged officers to focus on the next move. Reiner (1991) also found that it was early success and encouragement that tended to raise officers' expectations for promotion.

The importance of movement in the early years is telling. The early success for Reiner's chief constables was inextricably linked to what he terms the 'first to' syndrome, classifying officers as innovators rather than adaptors (*ibid.*: 97). As a result of the 'first to' syndrome, Reiner notes that officers were able to build on the momentum created to make further innovations, drawing them to the attention of the powers that be who determine the career paths of senior officers, including figures from the Home Office, Her Majesty's Inspectorate of Constabulary (HMIC) and prominent chief constables. The concept of being the 'first' is echoed strongly in Heidensohn's (1992) work on British and American policewomen. She observes the concept of pioneering as a recurrent theme in policewomen's narratives and notes, among British women, the phenomenon of 'perpetual pioneering' (*ibid.*: 180). This is also true of the majority of senior policewomen in this study and is encapsulated neatly by one policewoman's response:

I think my biggest difficulty is the fact that I have always felt that at times everything I do has been pioneering.

All of the senior policewomen in this study had some kind of pioneering story to tell and were able to give dramatic instances of being pioneers, being the 'first' at something, be it rank, specialisation, position or area. For senior policewomen, however, the 'first to' syndrome is compounded by the 'only' syndrome insofar as women often experienced being the 'first and only to'. The significance of this can be understood more fully through Kanter's (1977) analysis of tokenism. She describes the way in which the proportion of women in a particular workplace affects women's lives and notes that tokenised women feel highly visible and isolated from their peers. Their differences are exaggerated and their token attributes are distorted to fit pre-existing generalisations and stereotypes based on their gender. In an attempt to avoid being identified with other tokens by the male majority, women distance themselves from each other, resulting in feelings of segregation and loneliness. Many women in Heidensohn's (1992) study described their situation as close to 'lonesome pioneers'.

While being the 'first' provided chief constables in Reiner's (1991) study with an added impetus in their journey to the top, being the 'first' for senior women had the reverse effect. Senior women often experience an increased sense of visibility as a result of being the 'first and only', and this extra visibility in turn creates a state of increased isolation for women, working against rather than in favour of their career profiles. Also, in direct contrast to Reiner's (*ibid.*) findings that chief constables received encouragement in their early years, many of the women I spoke to conceptualise their experiences more in terms of a continued pressure to go for promotion than encouragement. The following experiences not only detail this sense of pressure, they also point to a degree of agency exercised by women themselves in resisting that pressure:

> I certainly received a lot of pressure to move beyond the ranks . . . I think that's because of the need to produce a profile of women coming through the system . . . I have resisted that to a certain extent.

> I could have been promoted a lot earlier because of the pressure, the corporate pressure was on me much earlier because I was a woman. I have resisted pressure from my senior officers to get promoted quicker because I wanted to do things to my liking.

> If you reach a certain standard, there is a certain amount of pressure on you to go for promotion to the next rank and that still exists, rightly or wrongly . . . Maybe there is more pressure for women . . . I was pressurised, maybe that's too strong an expression. I actually had a senior officer come to see me who questioned me quite closely as to why I wasn't going for that specific promotional board and he made it quite plain to me that when the next opportunity came around I would be expected to apply.

A recurring theme of women's narratives of their career was the significance of 'time' as a key resource for achieving a successful career, not only in terms of *doing* time but also in terms of *managing* it. The high degree of predictability about male promotion prospects within policing unfolds in the following women's narratives. The work of policing, and by implication the lives of police officers, is structured to accommodate a male chronology of continuous and uninterrupted employment. The importance of time-serving is a critical ingredient in demonstrating commitment and credibility. Getting to the top involves achieving an identity that has been cultivated through a full-time, long, and uninterrupted career pattern.

The importance of achieving commitment through a full-time status and identity was particularly evident for those women who are involved in managing the balance of work and home. Family commitments remain one of the major stumbling blocks to career progression. Women found it difficult to reconcile work, career, and promotion requirements of the police organisation with the demands of family life. Given existing organisational arrangements, senior policewomen emphasised the power of an 'irresolvable conflict' between being a police officer and being a mother.

> There are barriers for women . . . I think at the end of the day a lot of it comes down to families. It is the biggest barrier to women and while this is apparent in all organisations, there is something about policing that doesn't sit well with the existence of families, maybe this is masculinity at its worst.

> You have people like me who want to have a family and this is the most difficult job to do and have a family. I get home, I sort out the washing, the cleaning, the ironing, the cooking, I then drop into bed, and then two hours later I get woken up because I am on call. It's bloody difficult, and the men don't face that, they have a partner, a wife, who has cooked the dinner, washed and ironed their shirts, [ensured] that the birthday cards are sent to Aunty Flo. You have to be very single minded and women have domestic commitments, it's very difficult to balance.

The majority of women articulated a strong awareness about the consequences of combining work and home, with many citing the deliberate trade-offs that form part of their daily existence. From their accounts, it seems that the conflict between work and home is as intense for those officers without children. The policewoman below recounts her decision not to apply for higher rank as a result of this irresolvable conflict.

> I made a decision two years ago not to apply for any more operational posts. The reason is that the superintendent rank makes so many demands on your personal life that I don't want to give any more of my time, my life, to the job. Superintendents are on call twenty-four hours a day, I could be posted anywhere in London, twenty-four hours a day, being called at two or three in the morning. There are many demands. Somewhere in all of this I have a life. I work on average ten hours a day, I commute for three hours Monday to Friday, I want to keep my marriage, I feel if I go for one more rank, the sacrifice is too great.

Kirkcaldy *et al.* (1998) make a pertinent observation when they note that while police officers' wives may offset the occupational stress experienced by their partners, there is little to suggest that the reverse is true for senior women. The work of senior officers is not simply about demonstrating the ability to work long hours but also about being prepared to move around for the work of policing. Indeed, one of the key features in marking the transition to the ACPO ranks is the demonstration of the ability and commitment to *do* policing 'anytime' and 'anywhere'.

> It's a race, you know, to take part, to move around living in odd-bod accommodation throughout England. It's very competitive . . . Sometimes you feel it is almost a surreal experience, you are numbed by it.

The Home Office will not approve the appointment of a chief constable to a force if they have already served both as an assistant chief constable and deputy chief constable in that same force. Thus, anyone appointed to chief constable will have to have worked in at least one other force previously. Reiner's (1991: 80) study indicated that most chief constables would have moved between forces in their careers, noting that this 'is sufficient for them not to be regarded as locals, but as "cosmopolitans" part of a national pool of mobile senior officers'. Given the extra familial responsibilities that women often bear, the ability to be perceived as or to become 'cosmopolitan' becomes limited.

The importance of the 'time' in relation to achieving credibility and commitment becomes even more significant when trying to make sense of the possibilities offered by recent police initiatives such as the introduction of flexible working practices. The current push towards flexible working patterns emerged over a decade ago. In 1990, the Police Advisory Board agreed to the establishment of an experimental scheme to introduce part-time working and job sharing for police officers across six forces. Studies have speculated about the potential benefits that such changes could bring. These have included improvements in sickness records, retention, productivity, morale, and commitment, together with an improved ability to attract potential new recruits. With respect to women, evidence from a study by Tuffin and Baladi (2001) demonstrates that such developments have in many cases retained the contribution of women officers who would otherwise have left the service if they had not been able to reduce their hours in order to meet childcare commitments. They go on to note that each officer retained with more than five years' service saves the force a minimum of £23,000 (to replace the costs of recruitment, probationer, and ongoing training for an operational officer). Indeed, the sum is conceptually far greater when we begin to take into account the loss of experience that has been invested in officers.

However, a 1995 HMIC report on *Developing Diversity in the Police Service*, found a poor take up of these schemes and pointed to the resistance of middle management in terms of understanding the benefits of flexible working practices. Six years later, Tuffin and Baladi's (2001) work confirms HMIC findings by demonstrating an increase of 1 per cent for those officially classified as involved in flexible working practices (rising from 1 per cent in 1995 to just over 2 per cent in 2000). The issue was revisited in 1999 when the ACPO created a working group to develop guidelines for the service on flexible working practices. Reinvigorated by the launch of the Gender Agenda in 2001, we can see a renewed interest in the development of greater flexibility in the working practices of police officers. Given that this book is concerned with progression and leadership, it is important here to note that there are some important exclusions to the operation of flexible working practices. In particular, there remain restrictions in police regulation for the provision of part-time work for those in higher ranks. The changes to the restrictions on part-time work have allowed part-time work for probationers and inspector ranks. It is at more senior levels, however, that the opportunity for flexible working practices all but disappears. For more senior ranks, the requirements for 'on call' decision making, under the *Police and Criminal Evidence Act* (1984), serve as a continuing barrier and justification against the development of flexibility. Research conducted by the Superintendents Association has, however, questioned the need for 'on call' decisions to be taken by superintendents and suggested that many chief inspectors felt that such requirements were archaic and did not fit with the strategic role of superintendents in modern policing (Davies 1998).

Despite the advancement of more flexible working practices, the majority of senior policewomen remain sceptical of such arrangements. Women not only stressed their fears about their own abilities to re-engage with their work, given the perpetual and ongoing state of organisational change in policing; they also reflected a fear that the police organisation might not allow them to return as full and committed participants. One officer notes her unease at her forthcoming decision to embark on a career break:

> After my career break I intend to come back. I love my job and have worked too hard not to return. Everyone thinks I won't come

back ... This is a very worrying time, this is probably the worst time in my career to be leaving. It was a very difficult decision.

Such concerns are mirrored in Halford et al.'s (1997) work on the adoption of flexible career patterns in local government and nursing, in which they found that women become more strategic once they return to work after a career break to have children. They go on to suggest that this might be linked to a heightened sense of responsibility or to a practical need to become more efficient and organised once overall levels of responsibility rise.

Despite earlier protestations from policewomen regarding their lack of career strategy, there was evidence of an awareness of the importance of 'time' in relation to their careers. The majority of women cited specific key moments when the notion of planning a strategic career became heightened. The need to become strategic for police-women was evident through the various stages of planning a family, including before conception, throughout pregnancy, and on return from maternity leave. For these women, the need to become more strategic derives not only from the need to become more efficient and organised but from a tacit understanding of the need to demonstrate commitment to the career and not to be 'left behind'. Some, for instance, spoke of the haste in which they returned to their positions after maternity leave:

I went off on maternity leave a week before I had my daughter and then came back twenty weeks later. I could have taken a career break, but if I had taken five years off and then come back, you will never catch up. There are many young people who would overtake me. If I want to stay in the service and do well I have got to bite the bullet, you need to stick it out.

At that time [mid-1970s] if you got married you left, and I think I was one of the first, one of the very few who actually got married had children, took maternity leave for three months and then came straight back to work full-time. It was almost unheard of when I did it; people said to me, 'Oh, you won't come back' and of course I did, I have done it twice.

Part-time working represents a significant step forward in the develop-ment of working practices in the police service. Part-timers are a potentially valuable addition to police resources, in many cases retaining the contribution of officers who would otherwise be lost to the service. However, it becomes clear that part-time working does not count towards demonstrating credibility or commitment. If women in management choose to limit their working hours, they do so in the knowledge that they might also be limiting their career opportunities. All of the women who had engaged with flexible working arrangements considered that their promotion prospects had been affected by doing so. Such a pattern is reflected in a number of studies. Stone *et al.* (1994), for example, demonstrate the resistance within the police service to acknowledge the possibility of performing anything less than the full range of duties associated with a given post. In terms of career progression, they note that 28 per cent of respondents considered their promotion prospects to have been affected by working part-time, a situation in which they felt their commitment was doubted. Adams's (2001) work on senior management in Australia also notes the way in which the commitment of those officers who engage with family friendly policies is brought into question, with officers being perceived and constructed as not really taking the job 'seriously'. Hochschild's (1997) study of a large 'family friendly' corporation in the US further emphasises this when she argues that, despite the availability of 'family friendly' policies, neither men nor women use the flexible working practices available to them. Conscious of management's lack of support for such policies, employees posses a strong awareness that their career prospects will be ruined should they choose to engage with flexible working practices.

Only one of the women I interviewed was currently working on a flexible basis. Her case is an interesting one, firstly, for the clandestine nature of her arrangement and, secondly, on account of the fact that she illustrates a clear understanding of the value that the police organisation attaches to a full-time, uninterrupted career profile, mapping out her strategic movement in and out of part-time work in the hope of securing future promotion.

> I did resume full-time working just before my promotions and just after promotions because I knew that no one would want me if I had worked part-time; these were most definitely conscious decisions on my part to do this. The police service is great at coming out with guidelines, good practice and policies and supports all these different ways of working but when it comes to the workplace none of them do it, none of them respect part-time working. Most people talk about other part-timers not knowing I am a part-timer, because I don't tell anybody apart from my manager. They don't make full use of part-timers, they are useless, they simply pigeonhole them.

Overall, senior policewomen were generally supportive of part-time working, but all identified supervisory posts in their current structural form as being ill suited to part-time working. Only two officers felt that there was room for structural manoeuvring given the demands of managerial roles. For senior policewomen, achieving leadership is characterised by those who demonstrate a 'total commitment' to the job, underlined by a sense of 'single-mindedness', 'ruthlessness', 'determination', 'ambition with a hunger and thirst for the power' that high office may bring. But such a commitment remains incompatible with flexible ways of working. One officer notes that:

> I think there is a glass ceiling which can be put in by some women. I could say to myself now, because of some of the attitudes I have experienced, 'I'm not going any further because having a baby is the end of my career', which is a view I have had expressed by almost everyone. But I know that there is not in reality a glass ceiling. When I return from maternity leave I will be able to prove myself again and will still be able to get there. I think it's unreasonable that roles should accommodate women. I would of course like to be a chief constable one day, to be an ACPO officer, ACC [Assistant Chief Constable] or above and I know that that is a twenty-four hour a day commitment and that is what is required of being a police officer and I want to be a police officer. I think that as women, if you try and say I want to change my job description, then that is what encourages problems with equal opportunities, and I can understand that. Why should a man have a different job to a woman? If I am going to have children there is no difference, I wouldn't expect him to take time off excessively to look after the child, I don't intend to either.

Another states:

> As a woman, you have to pull your weight, if you want to do this job you have to take the rough that comes with it, which is the shift work and the rest of it that comes at this level.

These views serve to sustain the male-dominated managerial structure reinforcing and reproducing a masculine organisational logic of work and culture. These findings are echoed in the work of Holdaway and Parker (1998: 55), which found that 27 per cent of men (compared to 7 per cent of women) agreed that 'part-time working should be discouraged by senior officers to avoid the organisational problems it might create'. Indeed, many of the officers in their study perceived a lack of 'on the ground' support together with an active discouragement for policies such as part-time working. They argue that both home and work roles are relevant to women's decisions to seek promotion, with 17 per cent of women (compared to 5 per cent of men) indicating a potential conflict with domestic commitments as a factor in why they had not applied for promotion. A total of 13 per cent of women (but just two per cent of men) had indicated difficulties in working the hours required of them. Above all 'ideas about motherhood, parenting, commitment to a career and so on were enacted within the constabulary, to sustain a police framework of constraints around women officers' experiences of employment and opportunities for advancement' (*ibid.*: 56).

Career ladders have become an important tool in managing the social relations of organisations and in constructing particular forms of dominance. In particular, Halford *et al.* (1997: 112) point to a new form of division emerging among workers, more generally, and among women, more specifically. They point to an increased divisiveness between 'encumbered' and 'unencumbered' workers – that is, those women with children and those without – suggesting that an individual's family responsibilities play a key role in defining an employee's 'career worthiness'. In short, 'women appear to have as much chance as men of moving rapidly through clerical grades, as long as they do not have children, if they do, their prospects immediately worsen' (*ibid.*). Recent government findings, in which women are forgoing substantial earnings due to both the 'Female Forfeit' (the difference between the earnings of childless women and men) and the 'Mother Gap' (the difference between the earnings of childless women and women with children), further reinforce such views (CEDAW 1999). Even in countries such as Sweden, where state regulations strongly protect the rights of individuals (both female and male in the form of maternity and paternity rights) to do both work and caring, research indicates that employers will sort out both jobs and employees in terms of their expectations about who will use such rights, reinforcing gender segregation in the process (Widerberg 1991).

Attention to the broader management of time was a fundamental element of women's narratives in explaining their successes and their failures. Many of the policewomen articulated a growing awareness of the timeframe that governs the police career, albeit too late an awareness for their own careers in which they claimed to be 'running out of time'.

I see myself achieving the next rank but I very much doubt I will get to ACPO rank, simply because I would probably run out of time.

I think there is still some kind of glass ceiling in operation . . . It's probably the ACPO ranks where it becomes most difficult. Only in the last five years is it that you will have had women with the right experience and level of service coming through. Realistically, how much service does a man have before getting to ACPO, superintendent, normally twenty years? So, for women coming through the new system, we are ready now. I think the next five years will be interesting, they have now got the level of service where they should be pushing up to the higher ranks. When I joined, the average length of service for women was under four years, so realistically how could you expect women to come through with so few years' service?

Women, and not just in the police service, are still trying to make it to the top. I think one has to be quite realistic about this. The timeframe is just being reached where women who are now married and have children can actually get to become senior officers, because up to thirty years ago – either as soon as you got married or definitely if you had children – you would have to leave. So it's only now that you can start to get through and yet now it may be too late.

In their study of senior police in the Berlin Metropolitan Police, Kirkcaldy and Cooper (1992: 227) also assign importance to the variable of age, finding that older personnel experience more 'threat from impending redundancy or early retirement, an absence of any potential career advancement and opportunities for personal development and feel the adverse impact of demands on the home–work interface more than younger personnel'. Such findings are in direct contrast to those of Kirkcaldy et al. (1998) who report that senior officers in Britain showed less signs of job stress than their younger, more junior counterparts. They are quick, however, to acknowledge that the timing of their study coincided with the investigation into the structure, pay, and conditions of British policing by Sheehy (1993). They state: 'it may be that officers at this rank positively welcomed retirement, given the organisational upheavals likely in the aftermath of the proposed changes' (Kirkcaldy et al. 1998). Rather than easing the sense of stress, the agenda proposed by Sheehy (1993) served to augment and intensify senior policewomen's stress about their future.

Itzen and Phillipson (1995) also highlight the issue of 'gendered ageism' as a double jeopardy for women in organisations. In their study of women in local government and in the private sector, they describe the discriminatory impact of the combined effects of ageism and sexism on women's conditions of employment and career opportunities. A consideration of both age and gender may prove critical in giving greater context for explanations about why women are not reaching the top in policing.

The police career continues to be remarkably resilient to change. Utilising flexible working patterns does not count towards the profile of earning or demonstrating either credibility or commitment. On the contrary, the police career is one that tends to define itself as being at odds with domestic responsibilities. Moreover, while it may be true that new paths are being opened up in the journey to police leadership, these new paths continue to rely on well-worn and trodden routes, with the traditional male career model remaining the normative standard for judging career progression. Through adhering to such a model, the police organisation continues to successfully achieve social closure for women in policing. As a result of men's lack of primary responsibility at home, men have more access to the resource of time and thus are more likely to be able to comply with and work the long hours that are required for most senior jobs (Rutherford 2001). The police organisation continues to pay homage to the concept of 'time'. Time-serving is a core constituent of the 'smart macho' management culture and is fundamental to the identity of the police leader, with senior management demonstrating both long hours and a continuous uninterrupted full-time career profile.

The project towards developing alternative working practices for police officers goes beyond simply offering different working patterns. It provides an important strategy for bringing about real organisational change, potentially fracturing the police identity. Challenging the single entry scheme together with a full-time status may serve to loosen the stronghold that men retain in policing. The notion of dual (or multiple) entry, with senior officers recruited separately, occurs in a number of countries including the Netherlands, Sweden, France, and Hong Kong (Punch 1985, Bayley 1994, Mawby 1990, 1999). In the quest to recruit skilled managers to policing, for example, the Japanese police system does this through a process of lateral entry at senior levels. Through a system of stratified recruitment, highly qualified people are employed directly to middle rank (inspectors) to be trained for promotion to senior managerial positions (Bayley 1991). In proposing a blueprint for the future of policing, Bayley (1994) notes the limitations of an organisation stratified by ranks. In police organisations authority flows from the possession of rank yet ranks are not necessarily connected to organisational needs. He argues that police organisations of the future would be better served if each of the levels of the police organisation were distinguished by their responsibilities and functions and not simply by the authority they have to make decisions. In his vision of the future, an entirely new kind of police institution could be created with the abandonment of ranks in policing, to be replaced by levels of organisation distinguished by function. In so doing he argues that at each level there will be a police officer who can think, decide, and act, for where authority attaches to function, formal rank is not necessary (ibid.).

In further support of this position, Charman et al. (1999) note that the single entry system places particular pressures on selection and training processes. In dual or multiple entry systems, where candidates can begin at inspector or even superintendent level, police staff can be recruited from the outset on the basis of possession of management potential and all subsequent training can be oriented in that direction. In doing so, they question the efficacy of continuing with a single entry system of police appointments, arguing that the adoption of more flexible career entrance points within the police could enhance both the process of appointing senior police managers and provision for the great majority of officers who will remain in the lower ranks (ibid.). They also question the necessity for ACPO post holders to have been, in every case, a sworn in police officer. They note the emergence of the senior 'civilian' police manager appointed with professional expertise in personnel management, finance, and administration. Such a situation is not unknown in other parts of the world. Police chiefs in the US, for example, are elected – that is, politically or internally appointed and thus we can see a number of civilian police chiefs in the US (Mawby 1999: 50). The opening up of the ACPO to non-sworn officers could provide a more flexible environment for the appointment of even the most senior police and it is anticipated that more flexible forms of entry will serve to enhance women's progression through the ranks as has occurred in Sweden.[6]

The significance of hierarchy for senior police officers' sense of identity is emphasised by Adlam (2002) who argues that the strict hierarchical ordering that characterises the police career serves to create and sustain officers' perception of themselves as different. Already 'separated off' from the public at large, police officers 'experience a relatively steep and clearly symbolised status hierarchy'. In turn, the police organisation simultaneously practises 'the sacralisation of the most senior officers and the infantilisation of junior'. In short, the police organisation 'serves to cultivate a pervasive socio-biological elitist rationality – a rationality that is consolidated as individual police officers ascend the rank hierarchy' (*ibid.*: 27). This 'superiorist outlook' is embedded in one of his respondents (*ibid.*: 29) who notes that:

> I've spent most of my professional life climbing the ladder of promotion – trying to get away from the mass – getting out of the mass.

The significance of rethinking the way in which the police service is organised should not be underestimated. Indeed, any attempt to break down the hierarchical nature and rank mentality of the police is a project worth pursuing. Securing a place at the top, however, goes beyond the ability to *do* and *manage* 'time'; it also involves *doing* and *managing* 'place'.

Doing and managing 'place'

Debates about what counts in terms of career profiles are decisive and the areas of work undertaken throughout one's career have implications for officers' promotion prospects. In Chapter 2 I argued that the meaning of police identity and work is demarcated and constructed along gender lines. The police organisation has been characterised by the opposing worlds of 'care and control', with women belonging to the former and men to the latter. The idea that progression and promotion is simply characterised by upward movement is misleading. Progression in the police service is not only accomplished through the achievement of rank, it can also be accomplished through lateral movement into specialist departments and positions.

Attention to the gendering of certain jobs reveals the persistence of structural segregation between workers; not all workers are equal, and nor are all tasks. Research by Halford *et al.* (1997) has demonstrated the way in which certain jobs in organisations are considered 'dead zones'. For example, they cite cashiers' work in banking, night working in nursing, and benefits work in local government as examples of working in 'dead zones'. Given what we already know about what is valued as real work in police culture, we should not be surprised to learn that the same is true of policing. While the effects of entering specialist areas in policing, such as domestic violence work, might be seen as a potentially useful experience in maximising an officer's competitiveness when applying for promotion, such decisions might also prove to have a longer lasting discriminatory effect on officers' progression. This is ultimately bound up with, and dependent on, what the specialism is and on who is doing it.

A number of studies have suggested that certain roles in policing have been designated as best suited to women and some to men. Anderson *et al.* (1993), Jones (1986), Young (1991), and Walklate (2001) all point to the fact that policewomen tend to be assigned and to occupy positions that are regarded in policing circles as 'low status', including work with women and children. Young (1991: 24) points out that policewomen often tend to get 'hived off into the feminine caring posts or into the "soft" areas of community involvement or juvenile liaison [and] they subsequently fail to acquire the necessary career pattern of action postings'.

Westmarland's (2001: 184) study offers a serious challenge to such works, arguing that women in her study are

> not being differentially deployed on general patrol, that work with young people and domestic violence was not seen as 'women's work' and there is little evidence female officers were not being promoted because they lack the general experience and 'arrest portfolio'.

For officers in Westmarland's study, working on domestic violence incidents, although unpopular, afforded them the opportunity to achieve a 'good pinch'. In direct contrast to these findings, senior policewomen articulate a position which suggests that involvement with such work might serve as a 'good pinch' for some officers, namely men, but occupying such roles as women does not have the same desired effect. Women's contribution to such areas is diluted; their skills constructed as natural extensions of their own abilities as women. In contrast men's lack of natural association with such tasks allows them to reap the benefits of such involvement. Note the following officer's reflections about working in the field of domestic violence:

> Working in domestic violence was great, but for me . . . when I actually look at it in terms of my promotion, it actually hindered me. I like to get a balance in my life of things to get involved in. I am very interested in women's issues but I also need to get on with the rest of the job, a balance. I will always take this with me I feel that strongly about it, but am involved in other issues. Operationally I know I am OK, so I feel the credibility is OK.

Not only does she cite the hindering effects of such involvement, she simultaneously gives greater supremacy to operational work. Another officer further emphasises this when she revealed her intention to:

Be at the front end of policing where the action is, you know, where the rough is and not in some backwater support role.

Such a view is reminiscent of a typical response given by one of Heidensohn's (1992: 176) American policewomen, who stated: 'one shooting, two stabbings, and hauling bums, I love it'. Contrary to Westmarland's (2001) findings, the following senior women's observations illustrate the consequences of possessing a career without an operational base:

I know why I have been unsuccessful, it has nothing to do with unfairness or discrimination, but I do feel it is because of the way in which I got my experience. I think it is my career base. I have been disadvantaged because of the way the job was at the time, in terms of what women couldn't do. I didn't get really stuck into operational work, so while I am competing with male officers with the same service as me, I know they will have done things that were closed to me.

If you want to get promoted you have to show you have overall experience throughout the service, that has to have an operational arm. There are some women whose personal circumstances would preclude them from getting that experience, because of the working arrangements. For example, if you want experience of intelligence and following targets you can't say I can only manage between 2 p.m. and 6 p.m., it does not fit in with what is required. So if you are a woman with a family you may well have gaps in your experience and therefore go for jobs which are more conducive to personal requirements, rather than what will progress you.

Demonstrations of credibility in the police organisation are enacted through the association with operational work and crime fighting. The gendering of police work prizes the concept of action and physical strength; nowhere is this more obvious than in operational roles, more particularly within the work of public order specialists. Many of the women interviewed spoke at length about the need to achieve an operational profile if they were to stand any realistic chance of achieving higher rank. The following narratives plainly express the importance attached to the skills that such operational profiles offer potential career climbers.

> The public order credentials I have, I feel, gives you a certain charisma, and leadership abilities. People are aware that when the chips are down that you can actually stand there and be a port in a storm, that you are not going to crack up, no matter what. I think it helps to have charisma, there is a problem in the organisation at the moment that some of those in higher ranks have not got that experience.

> It is very important to me to have a hands-on approach, I suppose that's why I have worked in some of the busiest stations and areas. It is very important where you have worked, for the organisation. I don't know whether that is right or wrong but it is important, and the fact that you can work in the worst areas. It adds a certain credibility to your CV. Also that (1) I can do the job, (2) I can do it very well, and (3) for my own peace of mind I can cope with some of the worst areas.

> In terms of credibility, the public order status has sometimes helped. In terms of the way in which I was seen by Area, that I was taking a risk, it was impressive. I felt they had a lot of confidence in me to deal with public order situations.

Others, opting for a strong operational profile, did so in many cases simply to show that they, as women, could.

> I was determined not to be seen as a stereotypical woman, and that's why I have always been keen to get involved in the operational issues.

> So far, I have managed to gain a number of really high-profile jobs for a woman . . . I think this is really important to raise women's profile. I have tried to demonstrate that operationally in a very macho world of public order, women can do it. But I don't do it men's way, I am a woman first and I make no apologies for that.

Doing operational work not only gives officers the accompanying skills, its impact has far-reaching consequences. Embedded within such roles is the potential to acquire and accomplish 'charisma' – an essential yet unwritten component of good leadership. Achieving the position of chief constable is infused with notions of joining a special, almost mystical, elite. In extracting their own characterisations and ideas of good leadership, many of the more senior women interviewed assigned a heroic character to the job, describing their conception of good leadership through themes of 'strength', 'heroism', and 'mysticism' – the police leader is constructed as a mystical hero. The majority of these women still adhere to the idealised romantic idea of the charismatic leader as necessary for the police organisation.

> Leaders are different, not just different in gender terms but they are different people . . . Leadership should be inspiring and quite romantic really.

> You need to be some kind of hero to be a chief constable. You have to have it, that indefinable specialness, that aura, that thing that takes people with you, that vision, that awe-inspiring thing that some leaders have and some don't. The ones that don't are the ones that go unnoticed and unremembered.

> You have to be a very strong character to get into the senior ranks. If you are a wilting flower you cannot be a senior officer, it just doesn't work in this organisation. This can be very hard, very isolating, you need great charisma in this job.

While not the exclusive preserve of men, the concept of the 'hero' is predicated on being male.

> For me, it's all about the idea that people will follow you, whatever you do or say . . . It's that special thing, very brave, very smart, the heroes of policing, or should I also say heroines, now that we have some women up there, but it doesn't quite sit well in those terms.

Reiner (1997: 1007) suggests that modern societies exhibit what might be termed 'police fetishism' – that is, 'the ideological assumption that the police are a functional prerequisite of social order, the thin blue line defending against chaos'. Evident within the following respondent's views is clarification that this fetishism remains male in base and orientation:

> To really change things you would have to get loads more women in to make a difference, maybe 40 per cent across the ranks. This would change things radically. But imagine it, I don't know how

the public would feel about 40 per cent of women patrolling our streets. I know that male officers couldn't fathom it, but probably if I am honest I don't think women officers could fathom this either, I don't know if we could run law and order like this.

As a result, some female officers voiced the concern that women may not be able to demonstrate the charisma necessary for leadership:

I worry that there are not that many visual and impactive charismatic women. I worry that we may be suppressing it but not developing people. Whereas men tend to come through because it's acceptable, for women you have to drag it out of them. If you ask men and women candidates to tell you about their strengths and weaknesses, men will always tell you about how good they are first, women will always tell you their weaknesses first. This is a real issue, women need to learn to sell themselves in the same way that men do, of crucial importance for policing is to be dynamic, you know, out there in your face.

Some women do have it. I've seen a few glimpses of it sometimes, but not very often, they just don't know how to dress their ideas up, how to sell it, how to really drive people on. It's just not easy for us to be like this, you know talking the talk of real leaders.

Initial job allocation also achieves its importance through the way it feeds into other forms of discrimination (Newman 1982, Rosenbaum 1980, 1985). Burton's (1992) work suggests that the allocator may well know that a particular area is a 'dead end' with women being more likely to be streamed in those directions. Women end up receiving what Rosenbaum calls a 'custodial socialisation' (1975: 237) rather than a challenging one, affecting self-assessment and others' assessment of capacity for advancement. The evidence suggests that initial assignment to challenging positions is more significant for subsequent advancement than later events, that assessments in an employee's first few years have a profound and enduring effect on later career outcomes. There is also work which suggests that even where career ladders are more fragmented (offering a number of ladders), the specific route taken to seniority is gendered. In a study of engineering, for example, Evetts (1998) notes that women engineers were encouraged to choose the professional rather than the managerial route. These women were thereby becoming highly skilled technical specialists but not the managers of other engineers; hence they played little part in the managerial decision making of the organisation. This gendered structural division of technical labour into professional and managerial positions is also apparent in the work of Savage and Witz (1992) on banking careers.

The policewomen in Westmarland's (2001) study demonstrate the power of individual agency clearly. She argues that 'In some areas of police work, women officers are more able to choose, have autonomy, and use their "femininity" to achieve control of their careers than has been claimed previously' (*ibid*.: 30). The senior policewomen I interviewed did not use their femininity in this way, but there is some evidence to suggest the power of individual agency. In much the same way that senior policewomen are employing a degree of strategy in managing time, there is some evidence that they are fighting back in terms of managing place. In some instances, women talked about consciously resisting or turning down potential promotions in areas they deemed 'dead zones', areas that might prove detrimental to their future career advancement.

> Over the years, I watched people being promoted and the only way females got promoted was through training. I decided I didn't want to do that, if I was going to be promoted I wanted to be promoted because I was capable of carrying the rank. I wanted to prove myself as a patrol sergeant so I turned that down, which caused a bit of a furore in personnel, and HQ, because you weren't supposed to turn promotions down but you were supposed to kiss the hand and say thank you very much.

> You really do notice that women are shoved into training, there's loads of them there. This is not a route I am prepared to go down.

> I always remember when I did my stint in personnel, now I look back and think this in some way helped to broaden my profile but at the time, well five years after I left it, I knew that I had to shake that label otherwise I never would. I had to get straight back into operational duties.

The following respondent's experience is worth including in its entirety for she details the importance of making the right decisions in managing 'place'.

> I went into training early on in my career, which I thoroughly enjoyed, but I was keen to get more operational experience so I became a patrol sergeant. An opportunity was then presented to

me to join the computer unit. I knew nothing about computers, and I was stunned to be asked, it seemed a totally ridiculous thing to do. I don't know, but I believe that the person who wanted me on that unit was trying to make a statement about equal opportunities. It was offered to me as a sergeant and I didn't want it, I said no, I am waiting for promotion. They interviewed me and I got it a week later, but they offered it to me as an inspector. I wasn't aware when this kind of opportunity would arise as a patrol inspector, so I took it. I was there for a couple of years, which was normal to spend in HQ otherwise you get a bit remote from reality. I then took the opportunity to go out as a patrol inspector . . . I then became pregnant a year later, came back after six months and intended to come back as a patrol inspector. I had firmed up a vacancy but I was persuaded by the same person who had employed me at the computer unit that a move to a new dept called the Inspectorate would be more beneficial to the CV than being a patrol inspector. I was very reluctant to take the post once again because it was not operational. I was told to discuss it with the then chief superintendent, he basically said to me, 'in your case you don't need that operational experience, you should take this job, it's a new dept, you'll learn lots', and I did. It was a very interesting role; however, it's been like a millstone round my neck that I have had these periods of non-operations in my career. You see, it seems more focused for women, that one period out and somehow they think women are always at HQ. It's all about street cred. That took me to 1993 when I went for promotion. Assessment centres had just been introduced, I was absolutely totally relieved, pleased, ecstatic, because at last they would judge me on what I could do and not on the old boy network, and therefore I was very pleased to succeed in getting through that assessment board. They then said I needed more operational experience, which I found absolutely infuriating, given that I had wished to go on patrol in previous years, yet had been persuaded by senior officers that this was inappropriate. So here we were a few years later being told, sorry you haven't got this mix of operational experience.

Holdaway and Parker (1998) also found that women were more likely than men to indicate that their lack of experience deterred them from applying for specialist posts. The issue of 'forced postings' is also apparent in the occupational stories of another minority group in policing. In a study of ethnic minority officers, Bland *et al.* (1999) noted that most officers accepted that postings driven by the requirements of the force would not necessarily coincide with the preferences of individual officers. While some officers were able to interpret this experience to their benefit, presenting the forced posting as an opportunity to gain experience in different types of policing, others remained unhappy with the impact this had on the direction of their career. In either case, officers expressed a reluctance to challenge the basis of the posting, because they ran the risk of being seen as difficult and experiencing possible negative consequences on their career. The management of 'place' becomes even more problematic for those women who had used flexible working practices during their careers. Many pointed to the simultaneous use of 'forced postings' by their supervisors, postings where the opportunity to achieve credibility through an operational profile is severely limited, proving detrimental to their career advancement. Women who undertake flexible ways of working might find themselves marginalised into areas deemed 'suitable' by their managers (Rose 2002). Here the use of flexible working practices has serious repercussions for place.

While Westmarland's (2001: 94) proposition that women's deployment to certain policing tasks cannot be explained simply by virtue of a 'male power' operating in 'some conspiratorial way' is legitimate and useful – in that, it challenges existing simplistic characterisations of power in policing – her analysis fails to take account of the more complex and subtle operation of male power. The differential deployment of tasks that officers might encounter in their police careers is achieved through gendered processes that have much to do with the problematic relationship that exists between the (male) structure and organisation of the police career and the reality and nature of many women's lives. Through the embeddedness of gendered structures, 'male power' does not operate so much in a conspiratorial way, but rather operates in a much more legitimate and routinised way.

This chapter has explored some of the gendered implications of the journey 'to the top'. Not surprisingly, being in the right place on the hierarchical ladder at the right time in one's career trajectory are important considerations in the move upwards. Despite a reduction in the number of police ranks, the police career remains remarkably resilient to change and continues to be driven by hierarchical considerations. The ability to *do* and *manage* 'time' and 'place' has been paramount in securing both a police identity and a place at the top in policing. The implications of not managing 'time' and 'place' have had the effect of ensuring that some policewomen are unable to display the right amount or type of commitment and credibility, never seeming quite right for the job, lacking in experience or lacking in service length.

The senior policewomen in this study are at a variety of stages in their careers. On the one hand there are women who are fulfilling the criteria of length of service but are not fulfilling the appropriate career profiles required of the charismatic police leader. These women felt they had occupied too many positions in 'dead zones' to warrant a place in the higher ranks. Much of their work was not grounded in operations, which is necessary for being put in the frame for leadership roles. On the other hand there are a small group of women emerging who are sufficiently competent in their operational skills but have not yet accumulated sufficient length in service to warrant a place at the top. So, to what extent is it possible to talk of the glass ceiling as a thing of the past in the police organisation? Theoretically, the glass ceiling has been broken – there are no legitimate reasons why women cannot achieve the same positions as their male counterparts. At the same time, there is much to suggest that the glass ceiling in policing remains intact, albeit taking on a different form. Evidence from Simpson and Altman (2000) on young women managers suggests that the glass ceiling has been relocated and is now positioned at a higher level so that young women, through hard work and effort, break through lesser barriers lower down the hierarchy but encounter the glass ceiling at, or beyond, senior management. The same is true for women in policing.

Notes

1   Japan's figure stands at 44 per cent.
2   For a full review of their proposals, see Wall's (1998) analysis.
3   Centrex is the working name of the Central Police Training and Development Authority.
4   The competency areas for sergeants and inspectors are as follows: professional and ethical standards; communication; self-motivation; decision making; creativity and innovation; managing and developing staff; leadership; operational planning and strategic planning. Strategic planning is only appropriate for officers of the rank of inspector.
5   The OSPRE® system is based on two interrelated parts. OSPRE® Part I is a two-hour multiple choice paper, which tests underpinning knowledge, understanding, and the application of legal principles to given problems. Success in Part I qualifies candidates to attend OSPRE® Part II some six months later. The OSPRE® Part II examination comprises seven role-acted work simulation exercises. Rank-specific work simulations are developed following critical scenario interviews with job-holders. The exercises take place in a series of rooms, with candidates starting at any one of the exercises and moving around an examination carousel. The carousel

consists of fourteen exercises, seven preparation periods, and seven interactive work simulation exercises. A preprogrammed timer governs the timing for each exercise. For a fuller description, see McGuigan *et al.* (2002).

6 Figures from the European Network of Policewomen (ENP) in 1998 show that Sweden has one of the highest percentages of women in management positions in Europe, standing at 14 per cent.

Chapter 5

Doing leadership

In stressing the potential of individuals to transform organisational agendas, I have been keen not to construct this potential around the idea that by increasing the number of minority groups in organisations, change will inevitably follow. On the contrary, my position is a simple one. Increasing the number of women in policing (in any organisation) will not in and of itself result in change. Such a position is encapsulated concisely by Jan Jordan's (2002) work on the policing of rape, in which she asks, 'Will any women do?' Her answer is, irrefutably, no. Much of the work on women in leadership and women and policing has focused on researching the differences that women and men bring to organisations. The first part of this chapter, then, will review some of this material and assess its significance for the police organisation. The second part goes on to provide an insight into how senior policewomen in this study have adapted, coped, and carried out their leadership roles – in effect, to explore how women *do* police leadership.

Women in leadership

As women have entered organisations in increased numbers and begun occupying positions of authority, we can witness a burgeoning interest in women as leaders. Since the early 1980s the extent to which women *do* leadership differently from their male counterparts has dogged organisational analysis. Despite this fascination, it is worth remembering that 'sex' as a difference of consequence in the study of leadership was neither discussed in Stogdill's review of leadership in 1948, nor in the first edition of the handbook of leadership in 1974 (both cited in Brandser 1996). Historically, the gaze of leadership theorists has remained firmly fixed on men.

Early studies of women in management aimed at drawing out an assessment of the differences between women and men, both in terms of their leadership styles and in terms of their effectiveness. Focused on areas such as personality, motivation, personal attributes, skill, and leadership styles, the emphasis of studies was on comparative research where women managers were to be understood in opposition to their male counterparts (Marshall 1984, Rosener 1990, Grant 1988, White 1995). Much of this early research concentrated on whether women possessed the qualities commonly associated with 'management' and 'leadership'. Traditional conceptions of leadership are bound up with the classic and scientific approaches to management, characterised by highly rigid, formalised, and hierarchical organisations resembling military hierarchies. The common characteristics that formed the 'ideal manager' were described in terms of the traditional male managerial model that was typically characterised by aggression, competition, and rationality (White 1995).

Within conventional leadership research there appears to be a persistent answer of 'no difference', with the differences between women and men's leadership styles presented as minimal. In general, the research on women managers argued that women were as effective as men as managerial leaders, with women demonstrating an ability to display the common characteristics necessary for 'good' management (Powell 1990, Dobbins and Platz 1986, Donnell and Hall 1980). The few women who were 'successful' in management were portrayed as having adapted to typically 'masculine' styles of management and leadership, finding individualised means of survival. Such means have in turn given rise to both the myth and the reality of the 'Queen Bee', 'Dragon Lady', 'Bitch', or 'Female Barracuda' (Nicolson 1996, Kanter 1977, Ussher 1990, Morris 1994). The subtext of these studies, however, is that women in fact 'fit the pre-established organisational situations through a pervasive theme of no difference, meaning women are "as good as" men – but without questioning who had defined this "goodness"' (Brandser 1996: 6). Moreover, without questioning the meaning of this so-called 'goodness', traditional conceptualisations of 'leadership' and 'success' remain static. With the influence of gender diminished, such studies serve to verify the idea that organisations and leadership are gender-neutral structures that provide equal opportunities for both men and women.

Much of the research into women's roles in policing has also been taken up with an assessment of their abilities against men. This is particularly true of investigations into the abilities of pioneering policewomen at the turn of the twentieth century. In contrast to showing 'no difference', these early enquiries were heavily dominated by a discourse of 'difference'. In many ways, pioneer policewomen themselves cultivated this idea by stressing a distinction between their work and that of men. Evidence given to the *Baird Committee* (entrusted with the task of looking at the Employment of Women on Police Duties) in 1920 demonstrates this well. In response to being asked whether the character of the policewomen's work was different to men's, Margaret Damer Dawson, Head of the Women's Police Service, replied:

> Yes, it is a difference of temperament, of character, of physique, and of everything. It would do away with all those invidious distinctions between the men and the women if the two forces were absolutely separate . . . the women police are a sort of force apart . . . It is much more subtle work than ordinary male police work – the carrying out of the laws relating to bastardy, affiliation orders, the Licensing acts and so on. The men recognise it at once, and are keen to hand over to the women work which they have never cared for . . . the women are paid differently, taught differently, and organised differently, and I think they do different work. (Cited in Allen 1925: 166–7)

Throughout Britain, America, and Australia, policewomen were keen to emphasise the specialist nature of their skills and sought to establish the right of women to work with women and children. Schulz (1995) notes that 'pioneer' policewomen in the US used the concept of the 'women's sphere' to enter the world beyond their homes and to create positions for women in police departments in large and small cities. It is in these early years that women's association with crime prevention and social work oriented tasks came to be engraved in the psyche of the police organisation. Their work and positions were characterised by a strong dedication to service and nurturing following traditional gender roles. Crime prevention was firmly rooted and established as women's domain and women were to take an active role in becoming specialists in this kind of policing. These women marked a movement towards institutionalising a presence for the concern of women's issues. In working towards the securement of a women's agenda, Heidensohn (1992) notes that in some ways women were leading in certain kinds of social control:

while some women were fronting traditional activities, others had very much chosen their sphere, felt that they as women brought special qualities to it, and had in several areas invented or developed their own new roles and tasks ... Women set the agenda at various levels and undoubtedly ordered new priorities. (*Ibid.*: 24)

They sought to offer a different vision of policing and, though not in competition with men, there is evidence to suggest that they themselves were critical of men's abilities or at least aware of men's limitations. Carrier (1988) points to evidence from the *Women Police Service Report* of 1916–17 in which women took the Permanent Officials attached to the Home Office to task for their emphasis on physical force, claiming that moral force was as important. The Women Police Service (WPS) felt they had 'considerable evidence' to:

Prove that Policewomen were as able to control the unruly, whether men or women, as their male colleagues ... The Policewoman is as able to call for civilian assistance as the policeman. In our work we have noticed that the Policeman never runs physical risks if he can help it, and rightly so, for the maintenance of his authority. The Policewoman is in the same position, but we have recorded cases which show that the appeal of women police for a quiet arrest and the power of moral force which they use over attempted physical violence is more effective than overwhelming muscular demonstration. (Cited in Carrier 1988: 32)

Policewomen's formal integration into mainstream policing in the mid-1970s also spurred new questions concerning an assessment of their abilities. A key aspect of the integration of women into policing in the US, for example, involved a series of extensive evaluative studies of women's effectiveness on street patrol (Morash and Greene 1986). Generally, studies emphasised that there was little or no difference between men and women in policing. This shift in emphasis is perhaps better understood as an attempt to secure a permanent place for women in policing. In line with some of the broader debates surrounding women and management, the assessment of women's abilities continued to be measured against men, with men being routinely viewed as the embodiment of what policing is and should be.

More recently, in contrast to the 'no difference' studies, research within broader organisational discourse has begun to advance an acknowledgement of 'difference', demonstrating the different values and ways in which women and men manage people and assume leadership roles (Marshall 1984, Rosener 1990). This shift in discourse was consolidated by broader societal shifts in thinking about equality, in which 'sameness' was to be replaced by 'difference', with an acknowledgement of the value of differential experiences of the sexes. Marshall's (1984) construction of the dichotomous world of 'female' and 'male' values and ways of working is echoed in the majority of studies that acknowledge difference. In developing this binary construction of values, she posits that 'feminine' values can be characterised as being qualities that include interdependence, cooperation, receptivity, and acceptance; 'masculine' values, on the other hand, can be characterised as qualities that include self-assertion, separation, independence, control, aggression, and competition.

Perhaps one of the most cited studies on gender and leadership styles is Rosener's (1990) work on the differences in the way in which women and men describe themselves as leaders. Using their descriptions, Rosener goes on to develop gendered models of leadership in which she argues that women are less likely to adhere to the traditional command and control leadership style that men follow. As more women enter into management, she argues, they draw on their socialisation experiences as women, creating a different path to the top. That path is described as adopting a 'transformational' leadership style, a style in which the main aim is to motivate others by transforming their individual self-interest into the goals of the group. Unlike men, Rosener argued, women use 'transformational' styles by: encouraging others to participate so they feel they are part of the organisation; sharing power and information to reinforce open communication and create loyalty; enhancing individuals' appreciation of the worth of others by giving them praise and recognition; and energising others with enthusiasm and motivation (*ibid.*: 120). Moreover, they ascribe their power to personal characteristics such as charisma, interpersonal skills, hard work, or personal contacts rather than to organisational stature. By contrast, men are likely to characterise themselves as 'transactional' leaders – that is, they view job performance as a series of transactions with subordinates, exchanging rewards for services rendered or punishment for inadequate performance. Men are also more likely to use power that comes from organisational position and formal authority.

These findings are reflected in a number of studies on women and leadership (Loden 1985, Nichols 1993, Hegelson 1990, Grant 1988). Loden's (1985) work, for example, emphasises women's unique contribution to organisations as women. Feminine values (which she argues are natural to women) of empathy, attachment, nurture, and caring (among others) represent a complementary and important supplement to the traditional style of leadership. Hegelson (1990) also views women's values, or 'feminine principles', as strong and necessary parts of women's leadership, arguing that caring, being involved, and taking responsibility are all part of effective leadership. Both of these works rest on the notion that there are basic differences between the sexes. As a result, both are forced to define a dichotomous model of leadership in which 'feminine' behaviour is posited against 'masculine'. While making women visible, such studies contribute further to the gender essentialism that characterises such debates. Loden, for example, reduces the whole range of experiences into a simple, individual experience – a single category, the 'feminine'. She does not acknowledge the diversity between women, but rather essentialises the feminine, and hence those women who do not fall into her ideal, for example the so-called 'Queen Bee', are seen as pitiful examples of victims and not as valuable examples that will in fact enable us to better understand how women survive in organisations (Brandser 1996).

Rather than laying to rest many of the myths that have dominated discourses about women in leadership roles, such studies have further entrenched and sustained the often simplistic and sexist justifications for excluding women's participation in management. Nichols (1993: 62) warns against recreating a 'new maternal metaphor of management' in which elaborate extensions of prevailing sexual stereotypes and our traditional beliefs about the way women and men should behave are translated into an organisational context. Moreover, such works do not attempt to critically understand the structural arrangements of organisations that enable male managerial styles to dominate and flourish. Instead, they seek to make these so-called feminine qualities 'fit' the prevailing cultures and power structures of organisations, to integrate them as valuable assets in organisations as supplements and additions to existing models of leadership – that is, male models of leadership.

Bolder analyses of gender and leadership can be found in more radical feminist visions of the future, in which the values of a feminist and gender conscious leadership are proposed. Such visions, however, continue to essentialise women's nature through claims that women have something different to offer by virtue of their gender. The key point of departure for more radical contributions lies in their attempt to overthrow existing male conceptualisations of what leadership should be through pushing women's ways of working to the fore. The skills that are said to characterise women are not seen as something to be integrated into organisations but, more forcefully, as something that should replace existing models. As the workforce increasingly demands participation and the economic environment increasingly requires rapid change, Rosener (1990) argues that transformational leadership might emerge as the management style of choice for many. In speculating about the future of policing, Heidensohn (1992: 221) also argues that specifically masculine traits might no longer be particularly functional for much modern police work:

> if police officers need interpersonal skills, rather than tough physiques, if the job increasingly involves crime control of petty offenders and dealing with abuse and violence within the home, then not only is the macho crime fighter model obsolete as a model, he may actually be a liability.

The traits and transformational styles that have traditionally become associated with women are now being called upon as an alternative for organisations that want to overthrow and move beyond traditional command and control styles of management.

A feminist vision

The potential offered by more radical contributions has become known as 'feminist practice' (Bartlett 1990). The term has come to embody the employment of feminist methods and tactics to improve women's social, economic, and symbolic position. Feminist practice strives to promote core feminist values and goals, including the values of mutuality, interdependence, inclusion, cooperation, nurturance, support, participation, self-determination, empowerment, and personal and collective transformation (Ferguson 1984, Martin 1993). Such values are perceived to be in direct opposition to the practices that prevail in most corporations. Male forms of management, consistent with hegemonic forms of masculinity, attach emphasis to the core values of separativeness, competition, and individual success – values that feminist management rejects (England 1989, Jackall 1988, Martin 1993, Leidner 1991). In short, feminist practice is what feminists do and how they do it in the pursuit of feminist goals and aims (Acker 1989, Eisenstein 1985). The visions offered through feminist practice raise crucial debates concerning their essentialist nature, for the traits presented here might not simply reside in the hearts and minds of feminist women. There may be non-feminist women and men who strive for transformational outcomes for the benefit of their fellow workers. The key contribution of such theorisations is that, whereas in the past 'feminine' qualities were likely to be considered deficits, such qualities are now thought to be essential to productivity and the assessment of creative potential.

It is only through analysing policewomen's leadership styles that we can begin to assess the degree to which senior policewomen are involved in developing alternative styles of leadership – that is, those not traditionally associated with the command and control style of the police organisation. Only then will we be able to grasp the extent to which they as women leaders are working as active gendering agents.

The requirements necessary to act as a gendering agent encompass more than just the adoption of a more feminist driven leadership style. Bartlett's (1990) work in relation to the feminist challenge to *doing* law provides a useful framework for measuring and assessing senior policewomen's styles. If the feminist challenge to law is to have any realistic chance of success, Bartlett (*ibid.*: 831) argues that individuals need to be engaged in three broad areas: first, they must be involved in 'asking the woman question'; second, they should employ a degree of 'feminist practical reasoning'; and, lastly, be involved in 'consciousness-raising'.

Asking the 'woman question' consists of identifying and challenging those elements of existing doctrine that leave out or disadvantage women and members of other excluded groups. Such a position will serve to expose gender bias in ostensibly gender-neutral norms, practices, rules, and values. Thus, the 'woman question' challenges claims that male normative values and practices are necessary and correct. A feminist challenge of norms and expectations that favour masculinity and men in management positions can increase awareness of the ways in which women managers are devalued in, and excluded from, many management jobs (Hearn and Parkin 1987).

Using 'feminist practical reasoning' directs attention to the existence of multiple communities and the diverse circumstances within which people live. Women, it is argued, approach the reasoning process differently than men, resisting universal principles and generalisations, approaching 'problems not as dichotomised conflicts, but as dilemmas with multiple perspectives, contradictions and inconsistencies' (Bartlett 1990: 863). As a result of the wider contextualisation of issues, a greater understanding and exposure of injustice can occur. The value of feminist practical reasoning can be realised through the introduction and support of alternative conceptions of paid work, offering new ways of dealing with problems and dilemmas which affirm the concerns of women and members of other out-groups.

Lastly is an attempt to develop collaborative and interactive engagements with others based upon personal experience through 'consciousness-raising'. Feminists have long used consciousness-raising methods to validate their personal experiences and relate them to the experiences of others in similar conditions, exposing the multiple realities of organisational participants.

Looking for evidence of 'asking the woman question', the use of 'feminist practical reasoning', and the promotion of 'consciousness-raising' are central to my own analysis of policewomen's leadership styles. In order to give context to policewomen's leadership styles, it would be useful to consult some of the work that has contemplated the future of policing should women's presence in the service be increased.

(Re)constructing policing through a balance of gender

In her comparative analysis of American and British policewomen, Heidensohn (1992: 247) speculates about the nature and impact on the police and policing if the gender balance were reversed when she asks, 'what would happen if their [men's] "freehold" on policing ceased?' She postulates that an equality agenda has the potential to encourage a source of innovation and change into policy; a feminisation of policing through an increased focus on crimes such as rape, domestic violence, and child sex abuse; an undermining of police tradition and 'proper policing'; and the achievement of a representative organisation with increased opportunities for individual women. Brown (1997b: 36–44) also contemplates the future of policing should gender equity and cultural diversity within the police be achieved. Her vision shares much in common with Heidensohn, predicting a change in the emphasis of operational techniques, developing social rather than physical skills; a shift in style dominated by reactivity to one of proactivity; a radicalisation of policing priorities and an ability to influence the probity of police conduct; the development of new methods of cooperative management together with the development of new styles of communication both within the service itself and with the communities served.

The question of what an ideal police department would look like if it were designed by women in law enforcement was also the subject of a think-tank sponsored by the National Centre for Women and Policing (NCWP) in the US. Emerging from discussions was a police department that would be accountable to the community and one whose officers would be highly skilled in communication and problem solving. Adjectives such as 'brave', 'loyal', or 'strong', once used to describe the ideal officer, were replaced by 'ethical, people oriented, community oriented' (Feminist Majority Foundation 1997).

Following the beating of Rodney King, the Christopher Commission (1991) deplored the 'hard-nose' posturing of Los Angeles policemen, declaring in its report that male officers' aggressive style 'produces results at the risk of creating a siege mentality that alienates the officer from the community' (cited in Appier 1998: 168). The Commission urged the Los Angeles Police Department (LAPD) to develop a new style of policing based on communication rather than confrontation, noting that policewomen are less likely than policemen to 'abuse the public'. More specifically it pointed out that, despite the fact that women composed 13 per cent of LAPD's sworn personnel during the period 1986–90, none of the LAPD's worst offenders in cases of using excessive force was a woman. In an analysis that links the bias against policewomen with police brutality, the Commission claimed that 'the continued existence of discrimination against female officers can deprive the department of certain skills, and thereby, contribute to the problem of excessive force' (ibid.: 170). It found pervasive and deep-rooted sex discrimination and sexual harassment within the LAPD and argued that this discrimination aggravates the excessive force problem within the department by creating a disdain for women's less violent approach to policing by discouraging and preventing women from achieving equal numbers and reaching the highest ranks within the LAPD. The Commission concluded that hiring women police officers holds the key to substantially decreasing the incidence of police violence (report by the Women's Advisory Council to the Los Angeles Policy Commission 1993).

Since the beating of Rodney King, the Feminist Majority Foundation (FMF) has conducted extensive research on the relationship between gender and the excessive use of force by the police and has presented testimony during the public hearings and executive sessions of the Christopher Commission's investigations. In a report by the NCWP, Katherine Spillar, national coordinator of the FMF, notes that until now the integration of women into police agencies has been perceived in terms of creating potential problems and costs. Policemen feared more women would compromise the departments' toughness and competency, and thus lead to decreased morale. Following years of exhaustive research, however, she argues that a consensus of opinion now exists which suggests that women may be better suited to policing than their male counterparts:

> women not only can do the job of policing equally as well as men, but in fact hold the key for substantially decreasing police violence and its costs to the tax payer, while improving the ability of the police to respond to violence against women. (Spillar 1999)

In this instance, the full integration of women into policing has been transformed into an opportunity for a constructive solution to the costly problems of police violence. An increase in the numbers of women police officers at all ranks will serve to 'eliminate authoritarian personalities which thrive on violence ... [and will in turn] go a long way towards reducing police violence' (Feminist Majority Foundation 1995).

The same is true of policing in Australia. The potential to bring about change through an increased presence of women in policing lies at the heart of the *Fitzgerald Report* (1989). The report identified several main factors that contributed to the corruption, misconduct, and mismanagement exposed in the Queensland police force. They included: a rigid, over-centralised hierarchical structure; inequitable recruitment, training, and performance appraisal and promotion practices; and an insular organisational culture in which criticism of other police was seen as 'impermissible' (*ibid.*: 202). In response to such criticisms, women police were awarded the status of 'change agents', particularly charged with the task of reducing the level of corruption within policing. Women were perceived as important players in the movement to erode a 'police code' that protects officers guilty of misconduct or corruption. Drawing on the *Fitzgerald Report*, the *Wood Royal Commission Report* (1997) into the New South Wales police service made similar recommendations regarding the potential of women to achieve a greater diversity through the dismantling of 'inappropriate associations'.

In a paper presented at the British Criminology Conference, Hanmer and Saunders (1991) state that the employment of women is an issue, both in relation to requests by women and agencies in the community for women officers and the transformation of a masculine police culture in order to provide a more satisfactory service for women. The following studies all lend further support to the idea that a gender-balanced force has the potential to alter the ways in which the police respond to violence against women and violence in general. Homant and Kennedy (1985) concluded that women officers were significantly more involved than male officers in domestic disputes, and less tolerant of domestic violence including marital rape. Saunders and Size (1986) found that male officers endorsed traditional roles for women and held views that victims cause domestic violence and that arrests should not be made.

Studies by Bloch and Anderson (1973), Sherman (1975), Grennan (1987), Lunnenborg (1989), and Prenzler (1997) all conclude that women officers are less aggressive and more likely to reduce the potential for a violent situation to develop by relying on verbal skills and a communicative rather than an authoritative policing style. Grennan's (1987) study of civilian complaints made against the New York City Police Department also found that females neither use necessary force at the same rate nor are they as violent as their male colleagues. Neiderhoffer (1974) and Linden (1983) note how the superior verbal ability and conflict resolution skills of women police officers reduce the possibility that minor incidents between police and citizens will escalate into more violent ones. Belknap and Shelley (1992) concluded that increasing the number of women police officers would improve the relations between police departments and their communities. Women police are more likely to be perceived as 'friendly and service oriented' by members of their communities. This is echoed in Miller's (1999) more recent work on gender and community policing in which she argues that women's perceived skills are finally finding a legitimate place in police work and law enforcement.

The idea of reorienting service delivery to 'policing by women, with women and for women' (Walklate 1993b) is not new and can be traced to the work of early women in policing. Heidensohn (2000: 60) argues that it is possible to draw out the parallels between early pioneer women involved in social control in the last century and their modern-day counterparts in this century. A key feature of the pioneers' case was 'their universalising of the problems for which they saw policewomen as the solution: essentially these were "vice", trafficking in women and abuse of children'. She goes on to stress that contemporary organisations still stress a common, universal agenda; this time, however, it is 'domestic violence, trafficking and child abuse' (ibid.).

Research suggests that women have much to offer the police organisation. In some ways, they hold the potential to shift some of the more cumbersome obstacles that have made organisational change in policing impossible up to now. Working as active gendering agents, policewomen have the potential to shift some of the cultural meanings that have come to define police work as falling predominately within the domain of crime control. As a subsequent outcome, such a shift might serve to fracture the police identity both in terms of what it is they do and perhaps, more importantly, who they are, both of which are intrinsically bound up with notions of hegemonic masculinity. The experiences that senior policewomen have had in adapting to their new-found leadership roles tell us much about the significance of gender as a mediating element in the development of their own styles.

'Joining the club': adapting to police leadership

Much work that is concerned with detailing the strategies that women use in adapting to male-dominated organisations begins with Hochschild's (1973) study. Hochschild's starting point is that women are often 'tokens' and are initially marginalised. As a result, women face a number of dilemmas related to the conflict between the norms of behaviour appropriate for their sex and those appropriate for their occupational roles. Women react and adapt in a variety of ways; at the extremes of these adaptations, she suggests, processes involve women becoming either 'defeminised' or 'deprofessionalised'. The 'defeminised' woman seeks to overcome the limitations posed by socialisation, informal work structures, and men's attitudes in order to be appear professional. They see themselves as different from other women and become as good as or better than their male colleagues – their competence comes to mask their femininity. The 'deprofessionalised' woman, on the other hand, does not compete with male colleagues but accepts subordinate status and the concessions granted to her.

Perhaps the most widely cited study in detailing how women adapt to policing is Martin's (1980) observational account of women on patrol in Washington DC. Drawing on a sample of twenty-eight patrol officers, Martin describes women's adaptations to policing as falling along a continuum, which concurs with Hochschild's (1973), although for Martin the two adaptations are characterised by POLICEwomen (defeminised) and policeWOMEN (deprofessionalised). Martin notes that POLICEwomen who focus on law enforcement rather than service show a high commitment to the job, even criticising fellow female officers along with males. Their careers are more like males' in that they wish to do specialist work and to be promoted. PoliceWOMEN, on the other hand, emphasise the 'feminine'; they accept men's invitation to function as a normal equal while actually functioning as a junior partner or assistant and receiving treatment and exemptions from work, performing tasks appropriate for a 'lady' (Martin 1980: 185–203).

In appreciating the problematic nature of such typologies, Heidensohn (1992) warns against a misreading and misinterpretation of Martin's work. Although Martin states that the majority of the twenty-eight officers fell somewhere in between these two extreme positions, with only four being identified as policeWOMEN and three as POLICEwomen, successive work continues to focus on these two polar models of adaptation as the only forms of adaptation. Despite this, Martin's (1980) work has for the most part become a point of consultation for many studies on women in policing. Bryant *et al.* (1985) surveyed policewomen in two UK provincial forces, and by using Martin's typology in their analysis they conclude that many policewomen choose something approaching the POLICEwoman behaviour. They document some of the dilemmas and resulting frustrations experienced by policewomen as they attempt to negotiate a career in an organisation whose function the majority membership has sexually stereotyped as men's work. In addition they show how gender-based expectations of policewomen make it doubly hard for them to 'break and enter' into that world on equal terms. Drawing on this trajectory Heidensohn (1992) notes that officers in both the US and UK were POLICEwomen and policeWOMEN at once. They all wished to be part of the police, often had a sense of mission, accepted occupational values, practised 'street craft', defended and were loyal to their colleagues. At the same time, while they had wanted and tried to be 'one of the boys' they were debarred from entry or gained only conditional acceptance. Heidensohn notes that gender was made important to them, rather than by them, at the insistence of male colleagues.

Heidensohn maintains that much research on women in policing is 'basically about how women cope with police*men* rather than with polic*ing*' (*ibid.*: 84, original emphasis). Brewer's (1991) work on policewomen in the Royal Ulster Constabulary (RUC) interestingly draws on the legend of 'Hercules, Hippolyte and the Amazons' to characterise policewomen's adaptations to policing. The metaphor of Hercules is used to characterise the masculinity of policemen in the RUC. The respective gender features of Hippolyte and the Amazons are useful ways of describing the alternative ways in which female gender is managed. Some policewomen are Hippolyte-like in displaying femininity as much as the situation allows. They resist the adoption of all those traits associated with masculinity and do not attempt to become 'one of the boys'. As a result, these women tend to be 'loners' because they cannot 'give it back' (*ibid*.: 242). Other policewomen display the characteristics associated with the Amazons. The Amazon type do 'give it back', employing aggressive behaviour and humour in competing with their Herculean male counterparts. Brewer's incisive point is that whichever adaptation women choose, the 'all conquering Hercules policemen will win either way' (*ibid*.: 245).

Building on such works, Lanier's (1996) study of policewomen in the US attempts to go beyond bipolar distinctions by developing a more elaborate categorisation of women's adaptations to policing. His study includes both vertical and horizontal typologies that attempt to trace the differences between and within groups of policewomen. Officers are vertically categorised by years of service, motivation, and ambitions. Here he identifies three groups: Pioneers, Settlers, and Opportunists. A horizontal classification is presented based on their consciously selected clique group membership, which he classifies as 'Amazon, Hippolyte, Group acceptance and Lesbian/bi-sexual'. Both Amazon and Hippolyte classifications echo Brewer's (1991) characterisations of policewomen. Those in the third classification 'Group acceptance' were similar to Hippolytes, but at the same time strongly accepted and endorsed the police subculture. Scoring high on promotional exams and on the pistol range, these officers, he argues, were 'proud to be both female and police officers'. The final classification of women is differentiated by sexual preference, acknowledging that they were either lesbian or bi-sexual. In an attempt to negotiate her own identity as an officer, Hunt (1984: 243) argues that some women can *do* femaleness but only in masculinised categories, two dominant forms being the 'dyke' and the 'whore'. *Doing* gender by being 'aggressive, tough, hard and corrupt like a dyke' and 'sexually aloof, empathetic and vulnerable like a moral woman' enabled her to negotiate an identity that gave rise to her acceptance. The dynamics in the police organisation are strikingly similar to those identified by Williams (1989) in her discussion of the reaction of the military men to the integration of women. At one level, male officers argue that women are fundamentally unsuited to the job. However, if women perform effectively they are often labelled as 'masculine' or 'lesbian'; in any case, they are not seen as 'real' women. This designation allows men to maintain their sense of masculinity, while placing women in an impossible paradox.

The ways in which women *do* femaleness raises interesting points for this study, with many of the women interviewed involved in the cultivation and management of their image and identity. The process of getting to the top does not necessarily correlate with 'getting in'. One of the most commonly cited barriers experienced by women is that senior management is perceived to be a 'club', with its own distinctive set of rituals, symbols, and behavioural prescriptions that need to be learnt and enacted for the process of acceptance to take place. The need to achieve organisational belongingness was a central feature of senior women's narratives. Senior policewomen were characterised by a desire to 'fit in' with the prevailing cultures and power structures of the organisation, to integrate themselves within it and not look for visibility as women. What follows is an insight into some of the strategies that women have used in order to adapt and join the club of police leadership. The following officer speaks at length of the pervasive power and subtle operation of the male network of police leadership.

> If you look at how decisions are made you will find that there are a lot of things that go on that women are party to and others that women are not party to. If you play golf and you go around the golf course, an awful lot of decisions are taken here. Some women have taken up the game and can compete, others do not, they can't follow men into the men's locker room and an awful lot of, let's say, informal decisions are made there too. So as a woman you have to work out other ways to get to know people in as many different forums as is possible . . . You have to work out your own strategies, your own tolerance levels, this comes down to principles. I am not a drinker, so I may invite people round for dinner or go out for coffee. I think you have to understand the organisational dynamics in order to be successful. If you want to be a player, if you want to inform the process you have to make sure you are in a position to do that and you have to know how the organisation works, because for any lasting change it has to be well thought out.

Simpson (2002: 35) emphasises the power of 'insider knowledge' for women in management. Being 'in the know' was seen by women as important in terms of gaining insight into the politics of the organisation, and not knowing the politics could make one look 'naïve' and reduce credibility in formal situations such as meetings. The following officer also reflects on the male networks of police leadership. At its core she describes a group of men with a shared background who have worked with each other over many years. Men who have shared triumph and disappointment through their careers, who have come to know each other professionally and socially through their work and home lives. Above all, she points to a management culture in which there is a perceived sense of senior managers preferring to interact with members of their own sex:

> I first noticed it when I arrived, they didn't really want me here, they didn't know how to deal with me. I was almost alien to them, they had been for so long used to just male company. Yes, they had experienced working with women but not in this new capacity. I suppose for them they have spent years in the company of other men, at work, at conferences, at training, at promotion, they have shared all the ups and downs with these other men, it may be only natural they find women difficult to deal with.

Such findings are echoed in Roper's (1996: 24) concept of 'homosocial desire', where, intimacies between male managers are crucially import-ant because it is through them that 'exclusionary circles' are formed and maintained. As a result, bonds between men can lead them to prefer each other; male managers might support equality on a general level but, in specific cases involving them personally, they might favour a person of the same sex. Mindful of the diversity between men, however, it might also be the case that not all men are assured a place in the club. In her study of senior management of five multi-national companies, Wajcman (1996) observed that significantly more women than men perceived the prejudice of colleagues and the 'cliquiness' of senior management as an obstacle to their progress. As many as 76 per cent of women as against 43 per cent of men mention that senior management can be seen as a 'club'. Coe (1992) also cites the 'men's club' or the 'old boy network' as the greatest barrier encountered by senior women managers. This officer displays an awareness and acceptance of the reality that governs the journey to the top:

> I can only encapsulate it by saying it is very lonely at the top. You're going further and up all the time, and you're moving into an environment that has its own club. Another section for policing but at the highest level, but you're entering at the lowest point and like anywhere else it has a pecking order and has a way of fitting into things.

Women are not barred from police management cultures; they can enter, but they must accept the competitive traits that govern it. On arrival in their new posts, many of the women interviewed had tried to become part of the group, to 'join the club'. Some women felt they had succeeded by adopting male models of identity and behaviour:

Sometimes you don't do what being a woman you're supposed to do, sometimes you feel you have to be more assertive, but if this doesn't come naturally to you, you can make a complete hash of it. There is a danger of senior policewomen doing this, you can see it already with some, trying to be more aggressive than they need to be to try to prove a point.

You know you've got to prove yourself . . . I think you have to maintain your femininity and I think a lot of women don't because they think they will be accepted more readily if they are one of the boys, becoming clones of men.

Others had tried the strategy of 'being a man' for a short while, but on achieving further rank were able to realign back into their own styles. As a result, many felt they had given up on the processes involved in gaining admittance to the 'club':

It can be really difficult living in a male culture for so long as I have and you do either become one of the men or you go completely the opposite way. I suppose I did go through this phase, I did swear and do the things they do and then you regain your own identity again and you realise that you don't have to be like that, that you are your own person. Once you start getting more women through I think women will stop going through this thing of losing their identity.

I don't feel the need to be one of the boys. I don't feel the need to swear, swill beer down my throat because that's what men do, this is how it used to be. If you weren't one of the boys, you couldn't probably get on because you were a girlie.

Well, it's very macho, very male, you do cope with that, it's just the way it is, it's life. There is no question about it, I think I coped with a certain amount of acceptance I suppose. I just did my own thing really, kept my head down . . . I was very much, however, a part of the team; I wanted to be accepted and I never isolated myself. I suppose I put up with a lot of things which I really should have challenged. You don't want to be the one that stands out.

When I joined the police service, some of my female colleagues felt the only way they could be accepted into the police service was to be more masculine, hang around the boys, swear like them. I didn't feel like this, I felt very strongly that I wanted to maintain my femininity.

While some women had given up on the processes involved in gaining admittance to the 'club', others spoke about significant and rare moments when they knew their membership had been secured. When a woman is finally accepted as an equal in a male environment, she is frequently made the object of those displays of appreciation and intimacy that typify the community of men; achieving the emblematic 'slap on the back' signifies that acceptance (Gherardi 1995). To achieve the emblematic 'slap on the back', women must work harder and longer than men to justify their place, as the following women note:

> There is a constant need to have to justify yourself, to prove yourself. When women move to a station there is this idea that they [men] all sit back and wait to see if you can do it. I have, on numerous occasions, put my life on hold ... you know, worked longer hours, done things I really didn't need to do – be able to carry my shield for an inordinate amount of time, give the odd slap now and again, prove my worth – but I don't try to prove things anymore. I know I can do the job as well as my male colleagues so I have alleviated this pressure for myself.

> I always make sure I am rock solid, watertight in all my decisions. I am always aware that there are those who will scrutinise me more than my male colleagues, especially in my role in selections boards. If I selected too many women proportionally, I know they would be down on me like a ton of bricks so I am very prepared for this. I always remember the time when my chief officer said 'you're OK you are', it was like, finally. Then the word spreads among them, you know, that you're the right sort.

> As far as women are concerned, every man is good until he proves he's not and every woman is not good until she proves otherwise.

> Because I have been doing public order as a woman I have been able to push the boundaries for women, carrying all the equipment gives you the badge, I am actually seen in a macho world as being able compete in it.

> Women are not taken as seriously as men, women will always know the facts and will be assertive when challenged, they will be businesslike, they know all their stuff. Whereas men sit around the table more relaxed, not worrying, women are much more directed, more self-conscious. Women learn that people will always say you got there because of your skirt or because of the need to keep the numbers up, so I think that female officers, once they get on the

rank structures, are very direct and firm; you don't get many girlies. I think they have to compensate; women in these scenarios in action come ready and prepared.

Such experiences hold much in common with the 'transformation scenes' that policewomen in Heidensohn's (1992) study describe. Women in her study recounted pivotal events – some dramatic, others less so – that resulted not only in a confidence boost for women but also had the effect of granting them 'admission, of a kind, to the fraternity of real police' (*ibid.*: 142). Although men are also required to undergo rites of passage in order to confirm acceptance, she notes that the significance of such events are greater for women, in that:

> The problem for women is that they are initially defined as not belonging, not one of us, and as less than adequate officers. So they have both more to prove and are unable in essentials to prove themselves as 'men' because that is what they are precisely not. Transformation scenes are one way of dealing with the pioneer angle, and often, allied with professionalism, it is the way in which order is kept, both inside the police and in the world outside. (*ibid.*: 143)

In the long term, however, she notes such 'transformation scenes' have limited value for women. My own findings of such events suggest a much longer lasting effect for women. As a result of achieving the symbolic 'slap on the back', senior policewomen described being elevated to the position of being honorary men. Despite resulting in a disqualification of their gender, women accepted the symbolic significance attached and utilised such events to add further fuel to their journey up the career ladder.

'Just the right amount of lippy': managing body image

The concern with body image arising from women's narratives also raises important clues for unpacking and mapping out the cultural identity of the police leader. Given the significance of 'physicality' in defining the identity of officers, the lack of attention paid to the 'body' as an analytical concept remains a serious omission (Westmarland 2001). Gaining acceptance in any organisational environment involves the display of an appropriate body image, but the significance of body image might be even more telling in an organisation such as the police, where officers wear a uniform to ensure homogeneity. Indeed, the significance of the police uniform was as much alive in the thoughts of the historical pioneers as it is today. Commandant Mary Allen, for example, observed that:

> The question of a distinctive uniform for women employed in police duties was from the start a vexed one ... It was evident to all those closely concerned with the maintenance of order, that the uniform was in itself a deterrent, an actual weapon of defence, and that it had also a prompt moral effect. (Allen 1925: 24–5)

Such a position was in stark contrast to that exemplified by early American policewomen who did not see themselves as female versions of policemen but tried to separate themselves both physically and functionally. As a result, unlike British policewomen at this time, American women police were strongly opposed to the wearing of uniforms (Schulz 1995).

Officers' concern with body image also tells us much about the various ways in which the body is central in communicating messages of power and authority. In her work on policewomen doing public order duties, Heidensohn (1994b) notes the process by which police-women construct themselves as authoritative persons in order to manage disorder. Donning the police uniform does not automatically result in the achievement of authority; women have to learn how to make themselves authoritative (Heidensohn 1992). Unlike their Ameri-can counterparts who are armed, she argues, British women emphasise the symbolic expression of authority more through impression man-agement, relying heavily on what she describes as 'presence' and 'voice' in order to present themselves as convincing and calming officers of the peace.

A strong awareness of the principles that govern appropriate body image in policing was prevalent among senior policewomen inter-viewed in this study, with many of them actively involved in the management and cultivation of their body image. As one officer notes:

> I have always consciously thought about the degree of femininity
> I was going to expose.

Embedded within the following woman's narrative is the careful attention paid to displaying an appropriate balance of femininity and masculinity:

Everything matters, from your profile to what your name is, to the way you look. I used to be quite girlie, I suppose you would call it, really used to show off my femininity. I soon realised though that this wasn't the done thing. It's OK when you're down below but to move up, no, there is a set form, there is just the right amount of lippy to put on, just the right amount of hair to be dangling down, you soon learn to tone it all down.

While some of the senior women transgressed gender boundaries by rejecting the so-called trappings of femaleness in self-presentation, there were also those women who transgressed boundaries through emphasising their female appearance. The women cited below were all involved in displaying the attractions of their sex at work, clearly resisting what they felt were the appropriate images:

I arrived with very short hair, quite manly, look at me now [points to her long wavy hair]. I didn't think the butch look was getting me very far. I don't mean for it to sound that I sat down and planned all this, but I do remember a series of moments where I have reflected about what I look like. I am more successful this way, even a superintendent once said to me, 'grow your hair and see what happens'. Now he may have meant that in jest, but I did it.

I would be referred to as 'officer lippy' on account of my lipstick, it didn't bother me, it was in good humour. You need just the right amount of lippy though, I am not prepared to compromise my sex or my feminine attributes for anyone.

I feel that physical attraction has lots to do with influence. If female officers are quite masculine and not that attractive it is less of an issue, because people have a perception that they will behave in that way. The majority of ACPO [Association of Chief Police Officers] women, though, are all very feminine women. So there is an issue there about how they are perceived. You have to be very shrewd about what you say and what you do. For myself I like to wear make-up, to wear lipstick and to present myself in the form of my femininity, I feel this can be useful at times.

The cultivation of image is also visible in the management of some of the cultural artefacts of policing. Buildings, offices, furniture, and other material objects all carry significant cultural meanings for the *doing* of leadership. Some women were keen to overthrow and replace their predecessors' 'masculine office interiors' that gave a strict, impersonal impression signifying what they described as the suppression of emotion, feeling, and personal values. While the attention given to the presentation of the body and image is perhaps one of the most visible forms of doing gender, it is in the processes involved in the daily routine of doing policing that the significance of gender becomes most apparent.

Doing it differently: 'the organisational cuddle'

The extent to which women challenge and indeed transform leadership models in policing will be explored in this section. Alongside disagreement about the various ways in which women and men *do* police leadership, there was a strong consensus among senior women that gender plays a significant dimension in the way in which they, as women, exercise power and authority. Earlier in the chapter I outlined some of the elements necessary for the employment of feminist practice: to recap briefly, 'asking the woman question', the use of 'feminist practical reasoning', and 'consciousness-raising'. All of these elements have the potential to impact on the style of leadership employed, but it is perhaps the use of 'feminist practical reasoning' that can be traced most clearly in the following women's narratives. Many of the women *are* engaged in drawing on different ways of working not traditionally associated within the police organisation, characterised by a more holistic style of leadership. Many describe their styles in terms of a transformational approach to leading as opposed to a transactional approach traditionally associated with men in organisations:

> I don't manage in the same way as my male managers and yet I feel I am equally as effective by using different strategies. For me, I actually do care about my staff, from their development, their welfare, assisting them to get the maximum from them, but I see some of my male colleagues and they do it in a very different way, much more authoritarian.

> I allow people to manage but maintain control. I like to give people the freedom to get on and do and to be able to say this is yours, your project, but still maintain control. I don't like to interfere all the time, over their shoulder. I don't just leave them to get on with it, I give guidance.

I am the new breed: less autocratic, friendly, open and less power conscious than my male counterparts.

Senior policewomen in this study are using interactive styles by encouraging others to participate so that they feel they are part of the organisation, sharing power and information to reinforce open communication and create loyalty, enhancing individuals self-worth by giving praise and recognition, and energising others with enthusiasm and motivation.

I feel I'm very participative, I don't feel I compete in the same way as my male colleagues trying to outshine or out-do, I don't think I compete with my male or female colleagues.

I have developed a style I am happy with; I'm not an autocrat, I don't dictate, I am very participative, I like to give others the freedom to make decisions to develop in their roles, to be creative.

I am very much a believer of changing people's hearts and minds, it's all about mind shifts, to get people to start thinking. Lot's of people just accept things, they don't question anything because that's the way things have always been done around here. In order to change things you have to ask questions, pose problems; it is only through that type of interactive approach that they will be led down a path where they can justify the stances they have taken over years and that's beginning to happen with part-time working.

The significance of a transformational leadership style is noted by Densten (1999: 46) when he emphasises its potential to 'alter the higher order needs of followers by changing their attitudes, beliefs and values'. He goes on to stress that such behaviours are important to police leaders as they 'can directly influence rank and file officers and any process of change'. This ability to influence followers has been identified as a critical issue in the development of good police leadership (Tang and Hammontree 1992, Brown and Campbell 1991). The following officer offers a thoughtful appraisal of the change that may result by using transformational approaches:

I have enormous power but I never use it, I have enormous influence and I use it endlessly. I have my stripes, my salary and my position and this huge office. In law I have huge power to arrest people, close roads, stop processions, I can order people to do a number of things but I can honestly say I have never resorted to using my power. I hope personally my personality commands some respect and I will always use influence before power. I will try to take people on, if I ever had to say that's an order, I know I've lost the battle. I employ collaborative approaches in my dealings with people, it's far more successful. I suppose it's just a more covert form of leadership. My style may take longer to effect change, a much more incremental form of change but longer lasting I think. Some male colleagues are much more bustly and burly in their approach and may have a short-term impact, a short sharp shock effect but it really doesn't last long. If they move on, people are relieved so there's no structural or cultural change, it's just a style that lies with individuals. This is not good for the police service, to have an organisational style resting on individuals' shoulders.

We should be encouraged by the fact that some senior women are employing transformative approaches in their leadership. Such findings are in direct contrast to Densten's study of the leadership styles of senior officers in Australian law enforcement. His study found that in comparison to leaders in other organisations, senior police officers were more passive in orientation and were less likely to:

> . . . negotiate with their followers; be a role model able to influence and motivate their followers; create new understanding or persuade followers by using images or vision; provide experiential learning opportunities for followers; and solicit new ideas and creative solutions from followers. (Densten 1999: 54)

The lack of transformational leadership styles among police leaders is emphasised by Crank (1998) who suggests that law enforcement leaders respond directly to their unique environment by trying to control officers, giving direction using transactional approaches. Though they would not define their styles in such a way, it is clear that in *doing* leadership some of the senior women are also involved in a degree of feminist practice. Many felt that their advancement of greater participation, open discussion, and a more consultative and empowering approach to leadership had led to an increased sense of employee effectiveness and satisfaction with their jobs. In line with ideas on feminist practice, these women appear to exercise authority carefully by sharing rather than hoarding information resources and opportunities, and many are consciously involved in processes that promote cooperation, democracy, and participation while, reducing conflict, competition, and hierarchy, striving for transformational outcomes. These approaches were described as more effective in achieving good relations with colleagues and made for a more humane face in enacting the function of social control. The following officer notes her ability to:

> ... lead without leaving a trail of bloodshed like some of my male superiors both past and present.

Women's more holistic style of leadership can also be seen by the often rigorous and thoughtful analysis adopted in their decision making when taking account of police officers as individuals with obligations and lives that extend beyond their jobs.

> We all have to be aware that most of us are parents, most jobs are hard enough at the best of times, but policing, policing can be a nightmare when it comes to organising childcare. I do really try hard to be sympathetic to people's needs, and that includes fathers; now that's something that my male predecessor has never done.

> I suppose because I have kids of my own ... I know how difficult it is to sort them out when you're working. I do know that officers find it hard sometimes to do what is requested of them especially if we call them at short notice. If you say no you can't make it, it would have been a black mark against you in the past, but I don't see it like this. We all have a life outside policing, well most of us do anyway, and that should be respected as normal.

> Since I've been here I have found that men have been able to say things to me that they would never have talked about to a male boss, things that are important ... I have had conversations with some male officers about their babies not sleeping, or I have had male officers say 'I know you're stretched this week with a lack of staff but is there any chance of getting a couple of hours off', because it's their son's first day at school ... This is the way to change things, this is true evidence of change.

> I call it the 'organisational cuddle'. I'll say to my colleagues that there is space for an organisational cuddle. All people need to feel supported but it's the way you do it. It's not about being too overt, it's about having a gentle push and when people do drop you pick them up so they don't fall too far, you must remember people are our number one asset.

These views are in line with Ryan (1989) who argues that feminist practice as nurturance and caring requires corporate managers to view personnel as women and men with spouses and dependent children, with obligations and lives that extend beyond their jobs. Feminist managers affirm the multiple obligations and demands that employees have on their affections, energy, and time. The significance of such ways of working should not be underestimated; they might prove pivotal in any attempt to bring about change to an organisation that uses a full-time, uninterrupted, and long hours culture to help shape the identity of its officers.

There is evidence to suggest that policewomen are exercising their own agency working towards change; many women are involved in *doing* leadership differently. And while it may be the case that men are also employing such styles, women, by virtue of their sex, express the problematic nature of *doing* such leadership. Women stated that men who display such skills and abilities are perceived to be innovative and forward thinking, with such skills being positive attributes for their career profile. The display of such skills by women, however, is perceived to be an extension of their natural abilities and therefore less valued. How others perceive women presents an additional hurdle that women have to overcome in proving themselves capable of more senior positions (Gold 2000). In addition and with more disturbing consequences, utilising different ways of working raises real dilemmas for women who want to climb the career ladder. Senior policewomen noted both practical and symbolic difficulties in employing such empowering and interactive approaches.

A bit too soft

Working holistically by employing more participatory and consultative approaches requires a more time-consuming approach to project work. Women often experienced disapproval by management peers and senior management over the length of time taken to reach decisions. The experiences of the women below make clear some of the elements of the 'smart macho' culture of police management. The 'smart macho' culture demands quick decision making and makers – the transformational approach takes too long and is therefore perceived to be ineffective.

> They'd say I'm a bit soft, that I wait too long to make harsh decisions . . . I think they have an anticipation that I should be more autocratic, a harsher approach.

You need to acknowledge that you are working in an all male environment and men think and do speak in totally different ways, so if you are leading you actually have to know this. Men see a problem and tackle it straight on and sort out all the other bits after, whereas a woman's approach is to look at all the issues . . . so you may end up in the same timeframe but you will have gone about it differently. This may not be as attractive to men because they feel nothing is happening and in this organisation there is a requirement for action very early on; it can be difficult as they feel nothing is going on, although things are of course happening. I know that unless I constantly keep telling them that something is happening, battling on about it, they think nothing is happening.

It's all about difference, it's about understanding what it is that men are looking for and what you have to project to keep their confidence in you. The fact that you can do the job is irrelevant in a sense because they expect it to be done in a different way and unless you understand, unless you are able to key into their language, into their way of thinking, to key into certain words, you won't make it, they won't hear you. And they won't see you, they see what they want to see, they are blind to it.

At the heart of women's experience is a message that clearly spells out the difficulty of applying democratic principles to the work of policing without endangering the structure and hierarchy by which the police organisation is so strongly governed. Senior policewomen's observations demonstrate the way in which encouraging employee participation is perceived by colleagues as a situation in which there is no effective authority from leaders. Women were keen to stress that a focus on cooperation and participation does not mean an absence of difference, conflict, competition or hierarchy, nor does it result in a situation in which there is no effective authority from leaders. The full force of the 'smart macho' culture of police management can be seen most visibly in women's concerns about how their styles are perceived by others.

I think people perceive my style as weak, but what it really is, is that I won't take responsibility for others.

Sometimes I am concerned that my seniors think I am being too facilitative, too consultative.

I have been criticised for being too approachable. I do take an interest in the welfare aspects of the job perhaps more keenly than my male colleagues ... This may prove to my detriment, I may have to 'toughen up' in their eyes.

I am very open, a bit too open really, I am not very good at managing my time, I am too available for people, that is one of my faults.

I think I am perceived to be a bit over sensitive in their eyes.

Such perceptions are inextricably bound up with general discussions about the expression of emotion and more specifically with the gendered nature of emotion. In work that focuses on the legal profession, Pierce (1996) notes that litigators draw on a number of scripts in order to *do* gender. She argues that litigators make use of their emotions to persuade judges, juries, and witnesses. The use of 'intimidation', 'aggression', and 'strategic friendliness' not only serve the goals of the adversarial model, they also exemplify a masculine style of emotional labour (*ibid.*). Brazil (1978) refers to this style of lawyering as the 'professional combatant', others have used terms such as 'Rambo litigator' (Margolick 1988), 'legal terrorists' (Miner 1988), and 'barbarians of the bar' (Sayer 1988). Drodge and Murphy (2002: 425) emphasise that police officers are socialised against showing overt displays of emotion:

> The ideals of neutrality, objectivity, and impartiality are viewed as necessary antecedents of professionalism in the male dominated institution of policing. The emotional prescription for police work is tacitly understood: calm disengagement, affectless order, an unquestioning obeisance. There is a presumption that rational thinking can exist in a pure state devoid of emotional content, smoothing that is highly valued in police work where the phrase 'Just tell me the facts' belies a deep mistrust of emotions and a presumption that facts are untainted by emotional color.

Applying a gendered reading to the study of emotions offers the potential to achieve a more complex understanding of their meaning. The significance of emotion in *doing* gender in policing is exemplified in the work of McElhinny (1994) in which she describes how US officers highlight the way in which work identities may take priority over gender in identifying personhood. Female police officers in her study describe themselves as learning 'to be hard' and 'unemotional' as part of doing their job. She argues that one attribute of the gendering of police work can be seen through the non-projection of emotion;

masculinity is consistently associated with emotional distance. This allows female police officers to interpret behaviour that is normally and frequently understood as masculine (such as a lack of emotionality or displays of physical violence) as occupational.

The projection of emotion is a type of often uncompensated work shaped by the requirements of work structures within which individuals find themselves. Hochschild (1983) notes that jobs involving emotional labour (especially service jobs) comprise over a third of all jobs, but they form only one-quarter of the jobs men do, and over one-half of those women do. Emotional detachment is one way in which gender hierarchies are maintained. Expressing emotions signifies weakness and is devalued, whereas emotional detachment signifies strength and is valued (Cancian 1987: 125). It is during the routine interactions of policing that officers learn to act as 'tough cops', limiting their conversation to the formalities of their work. McElhinny's (1994: 94) study demonstrates clearly the lack of emphasis that officers place on personal lives, personal opinions, and personalities while on the job, with one of her respondents claiming, 'When I'm in uniform, I'm not a woman/man – I'm a police officer.' The relationship between showing emotion and demonstrating weakness is epitomised by the following senior policewoman who notes that:

> Showing emotion is not a good thing. I am quite an emotional person and to empathise with your colleagues is seen as a weakness.

Women were keen to stress that using different ways of working would bring untold benefits to the police organisation; at the same time, they were acutely aware that the police organisation continues to value and reward the transactional approach underlined by competitiveness and individualism, characterised by the ability to 'bite', as the following respondent notes:

> On two of the most recent promotion boards I was once asked 'can you bite?' It was felt I was too nice. In the other one, I was asked, 'how would you get into someone's face?' Nothing has changed you see, they still want a certain kind of leader, obviously one that can bite and get in your face.

Such a philosophy concurs strongly with Drodge and Murphy's (2002: 422) conceptualisation of leadership as a 'complex interplay of socially mediated processes occurring at the intersection of emotions and actions'. For them, leadership is not manifested through the emotions a leader displays nor by a leader's emotional intelligence, rather the significance lies in the 'emotional preferences or values of individuals underlying their thinking and acting that contribute to working towards a common goal. Emotions then are central to the pattern of values that emerge as leadership' (*ibid*.).

Being heard: achieving authority and obedience

So while it may be true that senior policewomen no longer have to demonstrate muscle on the streets as part of their jobs, the need for senior officers to display muscle in the offices of power is unequivocal. Women's ability to use the muscle required for police leadership has been seriously questioned by their fellow colleagues, with women in leadership routinely being conceived of as not being 'tough enough' for the demands of management.

Harlow *et al.*'s (1995) interesting work on the operation of 'silence' and 'din' in organisations provides a useful backdrop for exploring the process by which women in leadership come to be labelled as weak, passive, and over-sensitive. Using both the literal and metaphorical meanings of 'silence' and 'din' (with 'silence' signifying passivity and 'din' signifying action), Harlow *et al.* question who makes the most din and, in turn, who is silenced in organisations. In a gendered analysis, they argue that the din is between those who are most dominant in the organisation, usually the men who have the loudest voices. Those outside (or absent from) the din are silent and silenced; silence is achieved through the exclusion of others, in this case women. In this literal sense, then, women might be silent as a result of their oppression. That silence arises from being a subordinate group (Baker Miller 1988). Such a position is useful when trying to make sense of the extent to which policewomen are seen to be effective in the police organisation. I have already argued that 'getting to the top' in policing does not necessarily equate with 'getting in'; similarly, 'being there' does not necessarily equate with 'being heard'. Senior policewomen were accused by their colleagues of not displaying enough 'muscle', of not making enough 'din'. Women remain silent, being constructed as submissive, passive, docile, lacking in initiative, weak, and helpless. By implication, men are not silent; they are active, rational, scientific, and instrumental.

Senior police-women's ways of working were regularly challenged on the grounds of their effectiveness; they were repeatedly made to feel too sensitive and unable to withstand the rigours and demands required of police leaders. They experience difficulty in exerting managerial authority with peers and are often perceived to be the weak and soft link in the managerial chain. As a result, senior women experience difficulty in getting their voices heard and achievements made public. In the same way that some women might transgress gender by wearing badges of femininity (by wearing make-up and their hair long), there are also women who do not display the gendered behaviours expected of them in the workplace. On the rare occasions where women were recognised as making a 'din', they were quickly reprimanded for acting inappropriately. This is clearly the case for the following policewoman:

> I remember it, it was when all the Stephen Lawrence stuff was around, you know really sensitive stuff. We were at this meeting, which I was leading and one of my PCs said something. It was so race insensitive that I couldn't believe what I was hearing. I lost my temper very quickly and embarked upon a retort of its unacceptability. And yes, I swore as well. I was later hauled in by my chief who pulled me aside and said this wasn't what he expected of a chief officer, let alone a woman chief . . . That they had been looking forward so much to me coming, to it all being more civilised . . . I was gobsmacked. I have heard officers, male I may add, give a lot worse than that and more, and it wasn't even an issue.

In this instance the officer was clearly flouting gender behavioural prescriptions by losing her temper, being verbally aggressive and using foul language. There is a clear sense of imbalance between the sexes regarding the ethics and moral codes of professionalism. The effects of women not making 'enough din' or not exhibiting the 'right kind of din' might hold serious implications for them in their quest to be in the 'frame for leadership' as they climb the organisational ladder.

Some women also spoke of the problematic nature of enacting authority and receiving obedience where there is a reversal of authority in gender terms. It is worth reminding ourselves here that women are rarely employed to manage men in organisations (Reskin and Ross 1992). Interestingly in Wajcman's (1996: 273) study, most respondents (86 per cent) said that neither men nor women make better managers. In sharp contrast, when respondents were asked whether they would prefer to work for a manager of their own sex, a sizeable proportion

(21 per cent) of men stated they would prefer to work for male managers. Interestingly, 10 per cent of women also said that they prefer to work for male managers. However, neither men nor women expressed a preference for a woman manager.

Many of the women in this study experienced the problematic nature of exercising authority and receiving obedience. It was evident from their narratives that women are still far from being fully accepted in senior management. The following observations show clearly the difficulty that male police officers have in dealing with women who hold an equivalent or higher rank.

Men think they have to be in control of everything. If they see something that may be attacking their ability to control situations then they will attack it. It creates suspicion in their minds; a group of powerful women do this to men. Being the only man in an all-women environment would be very hard for men to comprehend, so where more women are coming through it starts to challenge their power and control.

The police are scared stiff of women, a lot of the men are. They can't bear to think of us in control, they don't know how to relate to us, more people than not have that problem.

Men don't know how to relate to us now as women that is, especially the older ones. They are used to women being beneath them in the rank structure, that's the natural and normal order of things for them, so we are a challenge.

I think people have a difficulty in accepting criticism from a woman. Women in authority may have an added problem.

Such sentiments are echoed in the work of Heidensohn (1992: 215) when she states that 'Men's resistance to women in policing is better understood as emanating from a struggle over the ownership of social control ... it may also reflect a deeper concern about who has a right to manage law and order.' Though some women do experience difficulties in enacting authority, others, particularly the more senior women in the study, spoke of the relative ease of enacting authority over subordinates. This was accomplished simply by virtue of their rank, and is summed up by one of my respondents who, while pointing to her stripes and various certificates, notes:

Come on ... who's going to harass me?

The ability to claim rank in this way adds further weight to the meaning that police officers attach to achieving power through rank. It also suggests that the relationship between the percentage of women and men and levels of sexist behaviour experienced might not be as straightforward as previously anticipated. Findings from Brown's (1998) study suggest that there might be other factors in operation that serve to override some sexist behaviour. For example, women who occupy a specialist division, involving a distinctive additional skill – women traffic patrol drivers, motorcyclists, dog handlers, or detective experts – do not appear to experience greater rates of harassment despite their minority position. In explaining this she argues that it could be due to the recognition that such officers have 'additional professional knowledge'. As a result, men are more likely to see her professional role as more important than her sex. The same may be true for senior policewomen. Despite their minority position, possessing and using rank can operate to minimise their harassment. Senior policewomen in this study did not speak of being overtly harassed as female police leaders. Rather, as their narratives throughout have shown, their experiences of discrimination are achieved through more subtle and intricate processes of exclusion. These findings are supported by Adams's (2001) study in which she claims that senior policewomen in Australia experience discrimination and harassment through a process of 'undermining'.

Citing material from the Command Course at Bramshill, Villiers (2003a: 33) equates good leadership with a transformational leadership style. He notes the secret ingredient of good leadership as the 'ability to convey a sense of vision and mission in a way that transforms and enhances the followers' sense of the possible'. In extolling the virtues and vices of police leaders, Miller and Palmer (2003: 113) argue that:

A good leader generates or stimulates others to generate new ideas; he or she questions, and at times seeks to replace, given rites and procedures; a good leader supports subordinates when they are in the right, even at personal cost; a good leader interprets the rules and the explicitly stated aims of the organization not only in the light of political realities, but especially in the light of fundamental ethical values that ought to guide the organization and its constitutive activities; and a good leader energises subordinates as members of a team in a collective enterprise to which all can contribute and from which all can derive kudos.

The majority of senior policewomen are involved in doing 'good' leadership; they are also involved in promoting a different kind of police leadership. In *doing* police leadership, women are enacting their own agency to develop more consultative, participatory, and holistic styles. Senior policewomen are also involved in doing both 'masculinity' and 'femininity' in order to achieve their goals. They have both adapted to and adopted new styles of doing things and exercising leadership, adding their own nuances to produce hybridised languages and styles of police leadership.

In many ways, their leadership styles are akin to some of the virtues of feminist practice. In exercising their styles, however, these women were careful to ensure that their practices were not constructed around the notion of 'feminist ways of working', but rather as alternative ways of working that are more humane than those displayed by their male counterparts. There is a tacit understanding among these women that working holistically using more participatory and consultative approaches does not necessarily count towards earning the profile needed to be a police leader. There is little incentive to encourage leaders to use other leadership styles (Densten 1999). As a result, in an attempt to reject extreme individualism, competition, and dominance in order to employ different ways of working, these women often face tensions and contradictions. There is a perceived sense of increased competitiveness between leaders, with women suggesting that women could succeed if they just kept at it and worked harder to do better. In adapting to the police occupational culture, the findings of Brown and Heidensohn (2000) suggest that women officers are the least likely to use resources such as union or staff associations; they are also unlikely to make use of formal mechanisms that address organisational inequality. Rather, women's coping strategies are characterised by working harder and achieving additional qualifications. Not surprisingly, in trying to cope with their increased sense of visibility, women affiliate themselves more closely with members of their rank than with other women. Building on Martin's (1980) continuum of POLICEwomen and policeWOMEN, the majority of policewomen in my study are better characterised as SENIOR POLICEwomen. Those women who have successfully climbed the career ladder are highly rank conscious, they are senior police officers first and foremost and adopt strategies to minimise their increased visibility and in many ways suppress their consciousness as women. The steadfast attachment to hierarchy with its attendant 'rank mentality' also takes centre stage when trying to make sense of women's abilities to network with one another, as the next chapter demonstrates.

Chapter 6

Being in the sisterhood (with no sisters)

This final chapter addresses the extent to which senior policewomen themselves are actively working to make gender and equality issues visible and central to police organisational agendas. It is here that Bartlett's (1990) final element for challenging the gendered order comes into effect. To recap briefly, her proposition rests on the notion that for meaningful change to take place, individuals need to be engaged in three broad areas: first, they must be involved in 'asking the woman question'; second, they should use a degree of 'feminist practical reasoning'; and, lastly, they must be involved in 'consciousness-raising'. Some of the ways in which senior policewomen use 'feminist practical reasoning' in their leadership styles was outlined in Chapter 5. The extent to which they are involved in 'asking the woman question' and 'consciousness-raising' will form the basis of this chapter.

In conjunction with Bartlett's ideas, I have also found it useful to draw on the framework utilised by Ledwith and Colgan (1996) in attempting to assess women's involvement in effecting change. Investigating women's activism in organisations more closely, they argue that the degree and nature of women's activism can be influenced, first, by their consciousness and awareness of gender politics within the organisation; second, by their reading of organisational dynamics; and, third, by their willingness to actively challenge organisational inequalities. The starting point for my search for sisterhood in policing began with an attempt to trace senior policewomen's 'gender consciousness' through an examination of their involvement in equality initiatives, together with an investigation into the extent to which senior policewomen identify with each other as a group. Challenging and bringing about change to the gendered order of policing demands a specific kind of woman: one with a strong consciousness and awareness of the gender politics that govern the police organisation; one who is willing to take action to address organisational inequalities; and one who attempts to transform the individual experience of discrimination into a collective experience through consciousness-raising.

Searching for sisterhood

In searching for this woman, and this idea of sisterhood, I am returning to the early writings of the Women's Liberation Movement. The voices of the 1960s proclaimed a political unity among women, grounded in a common experience of oppression with a commitment to equality of power, status, and participation within the movement for change. If I had encountered the presence of such women I would have expected to find individuals whose work was informed by feminist debates, women whose values, knowledge, and gender awareness was being used to work towards putting women's rights at the centre of their work, becoming what Sawer (1995) calls 'femocrats' – that is, advocates of feminism. The objectives of feminists are likely to be about 'both removing obstructions to women's attempts to participate and prog-ress remodel the world of work, and the transforming of patriarchal structures and cultures' (Ledwith and Colgan 1996: 28). Participants here operate as a pressure group, campaigning around women's issues with a sense of reciprocity and sisterhood. There is a willingness to be identified both as feminists and as part of the women's movement in pursuit of a more radical long-term approach to equality.

Unlike Kanter (1977), who has suggested that women need to make up at least 25 per cent of the workforce before they can begin to effect change, I have argued that a focus on numbers, albeit critical, is also somewhat misleading. I have pushed for a reading in which a small number of women critically placed within organisations possessing a degree of gender consciousness can potentially influence how that organisation works. Gender consciousness, here, is defined as the recognition that 'one's political world is shaped in important ways by the physical fact of one's sex' (Chow 1987, cited in Rinehart 1992). In addition, gender consciousness is defined as an awareness of one's self as having certain gender characterisations and the identification with others who occupy a similar position. The possession of a gender consciousness brings with it the potential to politicise women, generating insights into how power relations and processes are created and maintained (Rinehart 1992). In order for women to take advantage of the opportunities in the police organisation, they must not only occupy more as well as key positions in the organisation but they must also possess a degree of gender consciousness.

Doing consciousness and activism in policing

In Chapter 3 I noted the substantially altered agenda for British policing brought about as a result of the changes in 'equality' and 'quality'. In addition to equal opportunities initiatives, the value of networking and collaboration in organisations also brings potential benefits for minority groups. Both the opportunities provided by and the difficulties of establishing coalitions and alliances in pursuit of equality initiatives have been fruitfully raised by feminist and other equity-seeking activists (Anthias and Yuval-Davis 1993, Ben-Tovim *et al.* 1992, Tatchell 1992). The very presence of networks, be they formal, informal, social or political in their objective, play an important role in the stimulation of debate and activism. They offer a forum within which individuals can realise their shared experiences and they may also act as a vehicle for driving forward change initiatives.

Before outlining the networks available to women in policing, it is worth reminding ourselves that there are various minority groups in British policing working to make their experiences heard and their presence more visible. In 1990, the Metropolitan Police Assistant Commissioner in charge of Personnel and Training summoned over 350 black and Asian Metropolitan Police officers to a series of seminars at Bristol University. His concern was the high rate of wastage among the service's ethnic minority police officers. One of the outcomes of these seminars was that they provided an opportunity for black and Asian police officers to meet one another and share experiences. In 1993, a number of these police officers and members of the Metropolitan Police's civil staff came together to form the Black Police Association, now known as the National Black Police Association (NBPA).

Holdaway (1996: 152) claims that such an alliance poses a significant challenge to the majority in policing, proving to be 'one of the, if not the most effective reforms within the police'. In the same way that possessing a consciousness of one's sex does not automatically translate into a feminist consciousness, being part of the NBPA will not necessarily heighten members' willingness to take action. It does, however, offer significant benefits for the future of black police officers, strengthening the racialised identity of its members, providing them with 'a stronger power base to argue from' (*ibid.*: 194). Interestingly, Holdaway picks out the importance of gender, observing that black and Asian women working within the police service have a rather different experience of employment than their male peers. While that experience has yet to be described or analysed, the establishment of the Black Police Association Women's Forum (BPAWF) in 2000 will hopefully act as a platform from which such a dialogue can begin. A more integrated approach to understanding the racialised and gendered elements of identity will further enhance our appreciation of the multiplicity of experience and identity within policing.

Other minority groups in policing also provide clues to the processes of networking in policing. As with ethnic minority officers, lesbian and gay officers have the opportunity to share experiences through the Lesbian and Gay Police Association (LAGPA). LAGPA offers support and advice for lesbian and gay officers and works towards better relations between the police and the gay community (Burke 1993).

The development of such networks demonstrates a positive step forward in the acknowledgement and appreciation of difference in policing, but a few words of caution deserve re-emphasis here. In Chapter 3 I noted the complexity of the processes of change and argued that at times the effects of change may be contradictory, unexpected, and even unintended. This might be particularly true for the development of such networks. It might be the case that in working to make themselves more visible and heard in policing, minority groups could be contributing to the development of a hierarchy of oppressions. The reality of such a situation, however, resides in the future organisation and conduct of such groups. My intention here is simply to highlight it as an issue with potentially latent consequences.

Some of the most wide-ranging and oldest collaborations in policing can be found in a range of networks and resources that promote women's status in policing. At an international level, women can access the International Association of Women Police (IAWP).[1] The IAWP currently acts as a world-wide forum for research and seminars, providing a strong network of support and training for women and men. Primarily established to benefit women, it was decided in 1976 that in order to ensure cohesiveness, professionalism, and good communication between all officers, male officers should also be eligible to join (IAWP 2002). The work of the IAWP is further bolstered by the work of the National Centre for Women and Policing (NCWP). The NCWP is the first nation-wide resource for women police headed by a retired chief, Penny Harrington, the first woman chief of police of a major US city. Since its inception in 1995, the NCWP has been a leading force behind the drive to increase the number of women in policing, raising awareness of the positive impact of women in policing, including the reduction of police brutality, the increased efficacy in the police's response to domestic violence, and the increased emphasis on conflict resolution over the use of force (NCWP 1999). Given the feminist underpinnings of NCWP – it is sponsored by the Feminist Majority Foundation (FMF) – one might expect to find evidence of an increasing presence of gender, even a potentially feminist consciousness, and possibly the development of a shared consciousness. Heidensohn (1992) has argued that, despite the international scope of IAWP, the reality is such that members from the US dominate. Any attempt to build a global sisterhood is more likely to result in the development of sisterhood among American policewomen.

Further afield, the Australasian Council of Women and Policing (ACWAP) was initiated in 1997 with the aim of creating an Australasian link in the global network of women in policing. Its commitment to providing a forum for discussion on policing and gender issues is evident in its facilitation of international conferences and through the development of an excellent Internet-based discussion group. Relatively new to the scene of networking, the future of ACWAP looks promising, providing an effective forum through which to pursue important debates about women in policing. Moreover, in working closely with women throughout the world the likelihood of achieving a sense of international gender consciousness looks increasingly possible.

At a European level, we can see the development of the European Network of Policewomen (ENP) founded at the International Conference for policewomen held in the Netherlands in 1989. Through the development of conferences and seminars for policewomen and men, officers are able to exchange knowledge, information, and experiences on the position of women in various European countries. Working within a framework of mutual support between European policewomen, ENP has encouraged the formation of national networks for policewomen. It has also successfully built a database of information on policewomen throughout Europe (ENP 1998).

Inspired by the work of the ENP, Action E (the Association for Communication, Trends, Information Opinion, and Networking on Equality) was founded in Britain in 1993. All aspects of diversity are undertaken by Action E and initiatives to ensure that gender, race and ethnicity, sexuality, and (to a lesser extent) disability are encouraged. Since 1997, the Association of Chief Police Officers (ACPO) Personnel and Training Committee have used Action E as a means of research for the Equalities Subcommittee. More recently, the development of the Gender Agenda in 2001 is a significant addition to policewomen's networks, offering perhaps the most likely initiative capable of shifting the paradigm of policing. Brown (2003: 185) notes that:

> By asking 'the woman question', the Gender Agenda raises consciousness about the long hours culture, including breakfast and twilight meetings. It challenges stereotypical thinking and offers alternative practices. Its vision is that of a 'moral' and 'ethical' approach which ensures that all staff, regardless of their membership of any identifiable category, are neither advantaged nor disadvantaged in pursuing their duty or their career.

It might be somewhat premature to assess the impact of the Gender Agenda, but early indications from the British Association of Women Police (BAWP)'s (2003) *Gender Agenda Force Survey* suggest that a more coherent and forceful approach to developing the role of women in policing is taking place.

The existence of such national and international networks serves to confirm the idea that police organisations throughout the world have signed up for a better future for women in policing, *doing* activism through a number of global networks. Above all, the presence of international networks reminds us that the project for women police, begun nearly a century ago, is still ongoing. In reflecting on her research conducted into policewomen's contemporary global networks, Heidensohn (2000: 122) notes the process of recording and observing women as they 'developed the distinctive international "sisterhood" of policing by women, a phenomenon already a century old yet still in formation'.

'Sisters' in a past life

I have emphasised the significance of drawing parallels between contemporary pioneer policewomen and their early pioneering counterparts. The idea of women forging alliances and networks that go beyond friendships with each other is not a new phenomenon in policing. There is much to suggest from historical accounts that early pioneer policewomen in Britain lobbied hard and fought vigorously together for their cause. The impetus for the women's policing movement came from women themselves, 'from a very large, diverse, sometimes antagonistic range of organizations who formed (and also broke) improbable alliances across class, age, politics, and views on feminism to press their cause' (Heidensohn 1992: 52). More specifically, the campaign for women police came from women who were in some shape or form connected to the suffrage movement in Britain (Carrier 1988). Heidensohn (1992: 236) notes that these early pioneers were often 'committed feminists' and thus almost certainly possessed a gender consciousness, potentially even a 'feminist consciousness'.

In many ways, early pioneer policewomen fulfilled the requirements of working within a framework of 'sisterhood'. Not only did they fight vigorously for recognition as a group but their campaign was also to a large extent 'remarkably international in character', with policewomen engaged in the setting up of international forms of networks and collaborations to promote their cause and existence (Brown and Heidensohn 2000, Heidensohn 2000). Early pioneer policewomen sought to construct a 'concept of the international woman police officer' (Heidensohn 2000: 2). From early accounts, there is evidence to suggest that women involved in the work of policing were interested in each other on a global level. Brown and Heidensohn (2000) and Heidensohn (2000) point to the work of Cornelia Beaujon, who in 1911 was commissioned to undertake a survey and produce a report on the work of women in policing by the National Women's Council of the Netherlands. Despite being restricted to sixteen 'Germanic' cities in Austria, Germany, and Switzerland, her grouping of policewomen resulted in an appreciation of a 'transEuropean phenomena'. The significance of Beaujon's work is that it was one of the first international comparative studies of policing (*ibid*.: 49).

Much of the impetus for an increased profile for women in policing then came from policewomen themselves, who lobbied hard in advocating their cause. Heidensohn (1992) details the manner in which women worked tirelessly pursuing their cause, 'proselytising' their case, urging others to follow their example. Alice Stebbins Wells, America's first officially designated policewoman, for example, took full advantage of her reputation as the first policewoman in the country by launching a nation-wide speaking tour funded by local women's organisations (Segrave 1995). In Britain, Margaret Damer Dawson also addressed meetings of local committees as well as a range of other societies including the National Union of Women Workers (NUWW) for Great Britain and Ireland (later renamed the National Council of Women), the Women's Institute, the Penal Reform League and the

British Women's Temperance League. In a meeting with the Home Secretary, she also demonstrated an awareness and consciousness of other women's strategies beyond Britain. In emphasising the importance of women being sworn in, she cited the fact that policewomen were already employed in the US, Holland, and Denmark (Carrier 1988: 18). Her successor, Mary Allen, also invested much time in advocating the cause of women police, perhaps most notably stopping the traffic in New York wearing her distinctive monocle, breeches, and knee-high boots (Lock 1979: 150).

Throughout the 1920s and 30s *The Policewoman's Review* published by Allen and her supporters further promoted the case by reporting on international visits and links, producing accounts of the work of policewomen in Germany, Sweden, Sydney, and the US. Indeed, many of the skills that Allen and her colleagues sustained and developed were 'remarkable and resemble those of contemporary spin doctors' (Heidensohn 2000: 57). In their battle for recognition, early policewomen displayed acute gender awareness. They also displayed a willingness to take action to address organisational inequalities by transforming the individual experience of discrimination into a collective one through international alliances.

This is not to suggest that early policewomen did not suffer from internal differences and conflicts; they did. Heidensohn (2003: 10) reminds us that the pioneer days in Britain were marked by 'sharp rivalries' between various volunteer groups – characteristic of 'turf' wars between competing groups. At this time, women involved in policing in Britain came from two separate and distinct voluntary organisations. The first group came from the NUWW. Members set up a committee composed of representatives from various groups interested in moral welfare to agitate the introduction of women police. The NUWW recruited women in various parts of the country, organised and trained them for what was to become the Voluntary Women Patrols (VWP). Patrol work in London began in October 1914, and by 1916 the number of women patrols had reached about 2,000 (Segrave 1995). Their role was one of maintaining order in the streets, parks, and other public areas, particularly in the areas near military camps. Members of the women patrols did not hold police powers and no uniforms were worn; their only visible official denotation was an armband bearing the letters NUWW. From the beginning this work was seen only as a wartime measure, a manpower emergency, and hence temporary.

The second group of female police started at around the same time with two formidable women, Margaret Damer Dawson and Nina Boyle at the helm. Together they assembled a group of some forty like-minded women to organise a body of policewomen into what became known as the Women's Police Volunteers (WPV). Headed by Damer Dawson and Boyle, this group was by far the more radical of the two. Both women were of good education and came from middle-class backgrounds. Damer Dawson, a member of the Criminal Law Amendment Committee, and Boyle, a militant suffragette, had been engaged in the campaign for votes for women as supporters of the Women's Freedom League (Lock 1979: 14–15). From the outset, however, it was clear that the WPV did not see their role as temporary; rather, 'members did not assume their organisation would end with the war ... they were against voluntary service, the WPV wanted their workers to be paid a salary' (Segrave 1995: 38). In drawing out the differences in their purpose, Allen (1925: 12) cites a letter addressed to *The Times* in October 1917 by Mrs M. G. Carden, the Honorary Secretary of the Patrols Committee. It read as follows:

> The Voluntary patrols are neither police nor rescue workers, but true friends of the girls, in the deepest and holiest sense of the word ... the Women Police Volunteers, on the other hand, were from the outset conceived of as a trained body of professional women, who were to give their whole time to the job, to be ready to answer a call day or night, or to go to any part of the United Kingdom ... The whole programme of their labours was thus designed to prove their contentions – now more and more taken for granted that women are an indispensable adjunct to any well-ordered policy force.

In acknowledging the differences between these two groups, Carrier (1988: 2) points out that these two groups were to 'conflict with one another in an eccentric scramble for acceptance as the official and legitimate force of women police'. Perhaps predictably, it was the less radical group, the VWP, whose members were eventually accepted as the official women police in the Metropolitan Police area. Considered more radical than other groups of women in policing, members of the WPV associated themselves strongly with the ideologies of first-wave feminism. Of these pioneers, Heidensohn (1992: 231) notes that they 'were often allied to feminism even though they faced conflicts of principal about dual standards of morality'. The conflict that was to emerge within the WPV itself over the policing of Grantham in 1914 provides a powerful illustration of women's internal conflicts and tells us much about the nature of women's early activism.

In November 1914, three volunteers were entrusted with the task of policing in Grantham. The General Officer Commanding (GOC) the area had imposed a curfew on the women of the area. In agreeing to police Grantham, the volunteers' main role was to search houses under the order of the GOC and to seek out and prevent the entertaining by women of the troops. It was this acceptance to police the women of Grantham by enforcing the curfew that was to lead to a showdown between Damer Dawson and Boyle. Boyle considered that Damer Dawson had sold out of the feminist movement and had 'become involved in controlling women for the sake of men (rather than their own) and for public order' (Heidensohn 1992: 48). While the remit of policewomen was to control and protect women and children, Bland (1985: 23) argues that policewomen became involved in the control over women when, as feminists, they had wished to protect them from men. In many respects, women in Britain and America had become involved in a form of 'gendered control'. Heidensohn (1992) notes that in seeking to protect their own sex, women in this period were at times involved in protecting 'wayward' women, or policing them. It was this difference in standpoint that was to lead to a split between Damer Dawson and Boyle. The outcome of Grantham was to break up the WPV, with Damer Dawson immediately forming the Women Police Service (WPS), taking with her the vast majority of members, leaving Boyle free to use the title of WPV (Radford and Stanko 1989, Lock 1979, Carrier 1988).

Early women's conflict and rivalries were predominantly grounded within disagreements over their perceived roles within policing. Carrier (1988) notes the inherent contradiction in the campaign for women police. On the one hand, it was seen as an encroachment on a distinctly male preserve. Hardline feminists, such as Damer Dawson, Boyle and Allen, believed that this was the purpose of their campaign. On the other hand, there were those who saw women police as vital in the battle against the increasing levels of vice and immorality brought about by the war. Carrier (1988) notes that the success of the women police campaign was largely due to the propagation of the latter view of women's specialist role rather than the feminist aim of encroachment. In this way, it is possible to see the appointment of women police as an anti-feminist step designed to protect traditional family life and to reinforce the view that women needed specialist treatment and supervision.

It is undeniable that women involved in policing were awarded the label 'feminist' irrespective of whether or not they allied themselves with the feminist movement. In 1918, Sir Nevil Macready, Commissioner of the Metropolitan London Police, noted his intention to appoint 100 policewomen as an experiment in his force. On November 21 1918, a division of Women Police Patrols came into effect. Under this structure, the commissioner did not call on the expertise of the WPS. Instead, he took direct control over recruitment, training, and all other aspects of employment himself (*ibid.*). Outlining his reasons to the *Baird Committee*, Sir Nevil Macready's suspicion of Damer Dawson's involvement with the suffragette movement, with its attendant feminist attitude and method of work, is clear when he writes:

> The main point was to eliminate any women of extreme view – the vinegary spinster or blighted middle-aged fanatic – and to get broad-minded, kindly, sensible women who would bring to bear common-sense in their dealings with their sisters who had taken a wrong turning, more often from desire to lighten a dull existence than from inherent vice. (Cited in *ibid.*: 85)

Indeed, such beliefs about feminism and feminists continue to be sustained in contemporary policing.

Gender consciousness in contemporary policing

All of the senior policewomen interviewed in this study were conscious of their gender playing a significant part in their careers. This was particularly apparent from their accounts of being 'pioneers' in some shape or form. Indeed, the very fact of occupying such pioneering space might have provided a basis upon which women could begin the process of identifying with each other as women, developing some sense of shared and collective experience and consciousness. The experience of being a pioneer, with its heightened sense of visibility, was to have the opposite effect, encouraging a greater sense of individualism among women. An appreciation of women's pioneering status is useful when trying to make sense of women's engagement with activism.

If we are to understand policewomen's lack of activism it is perhaps best understood through the concept of being the 'first and only'. The 'extra visibility' to which women are subjected, by virtue of their small number, creates a state in which women experience a heightened perception of surveillance over their work by both male and female colleagues. This heightened sense of regulation serves to increase their consciousness of their own successes and failures. The following women's narratives demonstrate a clear concern with the impact that their pioneering status could have for women who might be following them through the ranks. Standing as beacons for all women's achievements, and their failures, was not a position with which most felt comfortable:

> You are very noticeable, being a lone women, you are much more on show, people will notice your mistakes far more than they would if you were male. This brings its pressures, I find myself, working longer hours, putting more time in to reach a higher standard to make sure that I never make those mistakes. I am sure that once I do someone will pick up on it and put it down to the fact that I am a woman.

> You are conscious that if you cock it up, people will possibly attribute it to your gender. It's not just because you are bad at your job, it's because you are a woman.

> The last thing you need is an ACC [Assistant Chief Constable] who is female and useless.

> When you're a failure they define it as a result of you being a woman, when you're a success, then all of a sudden me being a woman isn't such an issue.

Articulating their gender consciousness, women described their consciousness more in terms of a 'forced' awareness. Women were made aware of their presence as women in a male-dominated organisation and occupation. Women recognise the barriers they experience, as women, within the police organisation and are aware that they are working in a male-dominated environment that requires its participants to display a masculine ethic. Though gender consciousness may carry a sense of individual women's identification with other women as a group, this sense of gender consciousness does not necessarily lead to an automatic sense of feminist consciousness. For it is gender consciousness that is logically prior, and necessary and sufficient for, feminism, and not the reverse (Rinehart 1992). Hence, all feminists possess gender consciousness, yet not all gender conscious women would call themselves feminists. Although senior policewomen demonstrated a strong sense of individual gender consciousness, there was little evidence to suggest that this had translated into a collective gender consciousness. Despite the knowledge of the barriers that they face as women in policing by virtue of their gender, senior policewomen broadly accepted the procedural and structural forms that govern the police organisation. In doing so, they share much in common with the 'traditional women' described by Ledwith and Colgan (1996). Such women are the least likely to be involved in any form of change and indeed might even be resistant to it. There is a high level of tolerance and conformity with the dominant male organisational culture.

Few of the senior policewomen associated themselves with feminism; indeed, many of them were hostile to the concept and actively disassociated themselves from it, avidly demonstrating a distaste for feminist aims, strategies, and actions in challenging gender inequalities. This was found to be the case particularly among some of the younger women, who in principle share the values of the women's movement. Among senior policewomen there appeared to be a blanket rejection of feminism's negative social image. A strong consensus of the meaning of feminism emerged from their narratives. Using their own definitions, feminism is something that is equated with radicalism. The following views reflect the majority of women's views of feminism:

I dislike the feminist movement generally.

Feminism is a dirty word I think in policing.

For me, the real feminists are the ones who want to take over the world.

I suppose my idea of feminism is women charging around saying we are in charge, get men out of the way, we can do this, that and the other. I am not that sort of banner waver but rather [a] quietly determined sort of person; if I decide I want to do something I will do it. I never sit back and think this is feminist.

I absolutely hate the word feminism. If someone called me a feminist I would be hurt, I would be insulted . . . I would not want to call myself a feminist, the connotations that the word has is that you champion the rights of women at all costs to the exclusion of everything else and I think that is lovely in theory but it's not reality.

The rejection of feminism is mirrored in a number of studies on women in management. Such views are, for example, reminiscent of Ledwith and Colgan's (ibid.) 'women in transition' who appear to possess an awakening gender consciousness yet are unsure about their identity and role. As a result, they are often anxious to distance themselves from being labelled as feminists and try not to be singled out as 'women'. Nicholson's (1996) study found that senior women in management and the professions are often isolated and tend to reject feminist ideology, theory, and practice. Sheppard (1992) also notes women's reluctance and ambivalence about engaging in organisational gender politics. Women in her study were less inclined to be politically aware and frequently avoided playing political games.

Despite the less than positive images of feminism held by senior policewomen, many of them are in some way engaged with the project of pushing forward equal opportunities. In part, women defined their role in terms of 'asking the woman question' (Bartlett 1990), consisting of identifying and challenging those elements of existing doctrine that leave out or disadvantage women. I have already argued that in principle this is a powerful task; it can involve the unmasking of the so-called gender-neutral organisation and its accompanying gender-neutral norms, practices, rules, and values (Acker 1992). It also challenges claims that male normative values and practices are necessary and correct (Hearn and Parkin 1987). Senior policewomen are more involved in 'inserting' the woman question than in 'asking' it. The majority of women were involved in setting some form of agenda for women's progression. Such agendas were, however, short-term and organisationally driven by the demands to monitor equal opportunities issues as a result of policy demands.

Working within the existing parameters, the nature of the norms, practices, rules, and structures that govern the police organisation have not been questioned. Conceptualisations of the pathways to leadership and the meaning of 'success' remain static and unchallenged. There has been no real attempt to critically identify the structural arrangements of the organisation that enable the male model of policing to dominate and flourish. Rather, 'inserting' women was envisioned in terms of encouraging women to enter policing, supporting existing women with networks, information and personal contacts, and using organisations to gain access to resources and professional support. Such strategies focus on helping women to cope with discriminatory structures rather than disassembling or critiquing those structures. There is little exposure of the way in which gendered processes at work operate to disadvantage women.

Those women who are engaged in pro-women initiatives possess a good understanding of how feminism is perceived organisationally. Many articulated that there was no space for feminism in the police organisation; much of feminism was perceived to be outdated and of little value, given current debates about diversity. What we can see emerging is a skilful attempt by some senior women to repackage women's issues into a more negotiable package of 'diversity for all'.

> I don't know if there is any room for feminism in policing, they're all men. I am not trying to be pessimistic, but if you mentioned the word feminism or that you hold feminist ideas, though, even ideologies, you would be seen as subject material for ridicule. However, if you have the ability to repackage that into a fairness and justice language this will get you further, people are not so scared of this, when it is phrased in this way.

> I am not a rampant feminist, but I want to be taken seriously. There is always the danger that you may encounter more resistance as you will be labelled a 'feminist'. That word just conjures up a lot of negative images for people, let alone police officers, you'll be seen as outrageous.

> I don't go around promoting a woman's agenda, a women's flag, but while I think that women have needs it is also important not to go over the top, the other way. It is very important to recognise that everyone as an individual should have access to equal opportunities and I just see that it is important that we ensure that all of us have the opportunities for positions and that women have those opportunities equally that men have.

In Chapter 1 I noted that as a researcher conducting an enquiry into women police, I was automatically awarded the label of 'feminist'. Ironically, while the majority of the women did not see or classify themselves in terms of feminism, many argued that they were probably perceived to be so by their colleagues. Earning or acquiring the label of 'feminist' is an easy task in policing and can be achieved simply by challenging the use of the male pronoun 'he' in language. This was often perceived to be the language of radicalism. There is evidence of an emerging consciousness among women of the rules that govern the promotions game, albeit too late for some. Being in possession of a long, full-time, and continuous career profile grounded in operational work is imperative for police officers seeking to achieve the badges of credibility and commitment. There are also signs to suggest that some women are consciously and actively 'playing the game by the rules', joining in the race to accumulate competence, skill, and merit in order to progress through the ranks (returning to full-time working before a promotion, seeking out short-term operational posts to fill profiles).

Like their pioneering counterparts, modern policewomen also demonstrate a gender consciousness; this time, however, they appear less likely to show a willingness to take action. In addressing issues of equality, senior policewomen are adopting a cost and benefit approach to their activism, consciously calculating the costs of speaking out. The ability to demonstrate loyalty to one's rank is one more essential ingredient in the recipe for becoming a police leader. Demonstrating loyalty to rank, identifying with managerial peers and not with other managerial women, is essential for achieving credibility and commitment in the climb to the top. Noting the rigorous selection procedures and lengthy socialisation period that police officers undergo before appointment to senior ranks, Wall (1998) argues that the most effective form of accountability that senior officers experience is to their peers. Without peer recognition, he states,

> it is unlikely that they would rise to a position to be appointed as chief constable ... the lengthy and unsupervised, professional socialisation ... ensures that all senior police managers possess a similar *weltanschauung*, speak a common professional language and share broad assumptions about policing. (*Ibid*.: 85, 315)

The common professional language to which Wall refers does not involve speaking the 'gender speak'.

Senior policewomen have adapted to the gendered patterns of job segregation and the masculine culture within which they work by developing individualist strategies. Women's willingness to be involved in pushing forward an equality agenda is in many cases directly related to their understanding of the requirements necessary to become a police leader. Given the ease of acquiring the label of being a feminist in policing, we should not be surprised at women's lack of willingness to engage with collective consciousness-raising. All of the following women's narratives demonstrate a 'knowingness' of what happens to these kinds of women:

> Radicalism you need, but those who become very feminist, I don't think survive in the long term. Certainly those who stick their heads above the parapet and take on the organisation, they may survive for a short period of time but not for very long, we all know this.

> You cannot be too outspoken about women's issues all of the time, you'll just never get anywhere. I do realise that if I aspire to the

next rank then, yes, I would have to accept certain things and not criticise.

I am not a great believer of rocking the boat; if you rock it too much, it will capsize and you will drown, it's as simple as that. I am far happier to keep my head down and to duck and dive than to actually want to put my head over the parapet . . . I think to be successful you would have to be very, very careful.

If there is an issue which is in my mind in principle and morally absolutely wrong, I will stand up for it. I feel the same about male issues, but I will not go out on a limb for feminist issues. I will not be a feminist and I will not shout and scream in every direction I go because if I sit in meetings and do that I will not be accepted.

You don't really think I got here by speaking the gender speak do you? You have to know what's going to get you on and up and that isn't it . . . Have I sold out? Yes probably.

Identifying too closely with women's issues or speaking the 'gender speak' is not a useful contribution to the career profile of a police leader. I am not suggesting that senior policewomen felt that women's situations in policing were acceptable and that change was not required; simply that women have made rational and conscious calculations about the degree to which they are prepared to engage in collective action. The decision to engage in such action is mapped out against a determination to move up the career ladder.

There were some women in the study who had been entrusted with the specific task of representing and networking with other women working towards change. Yet these women appear reluctant and ambivalent about being regarded as agents of change for other women who are also aspiring to senior leadership positions. They appear uncomfortable at the prospect or reality of being seen as role models for anyone and do not see it as part of their mission to be responsible for the overt development of other women. While accepting the inevitability of being perceived as role models for other women, they simultaneously resisted any overt strategy towards women's development, preferring a more informal approach. Women's activism is best described as engaging in 'activism by default'. These women felt increasingly uncomfortable with their roles, and spoke of being 'catapulted into it', of 'going down this track without really wanting to', and being 'bullied' into these roles:

I have now committed myself, and I don't feel very comfortable about this, going to women's organisations, talking to women's groups, going to conferences.

I actually went on to the direction of women's groups . . . I have got myself into that and I wish I hadn't . . . So I have found myself going down this track without really wanting to. I find myself at the forefront of it yet I know very little about the issues or the legislation.

Because I am female they have made me equal opportunities representative on the management team . . . I suppose I may be a bit typecast into roles.

I am directly involved with an equal opportunities agenda, but that's more to do with being catapulted into it. Someone has got to do it, and no one wanted to do it, so I took up the responsibility.

The previous rep. retired and I suppose I was bullied into it.

These policewomen's involvement in the promotion of equality appears largely driven by external pressures and individualist considerations. As a result, they are unlikely to bring about any significant changes in organisational gender relations. For significant change to take place there must be recognition of the value of sharing the personal experience of all women as a starting point from which to envisage and fight for change. Women's activism may depend on the possession of a gender consciousness but there also needs to be a willingness to transform this into a shared consciousness. The presence of groups such as the IAWP, ENP and the BAWP by their very nature indicate evidence of a shared consciousness among women in policing. In contrast to the optimistic findings of Brown and Heidensohn's (2000) study into networking among policewomen in a global context, my findings present a rather gloomier picture. Many of the senior policewomen I interviewed were unaware of the existence of broad networks such as the ENP and IAWP and had little intention of joining such networks on a national or international level. However welcome and encouraging Brown and Heidensohn's sense of optimism may be, they too are cautious of their own findings, adding an important caveat to their work. They note that their sample was drawn from women attending a conference aimed at improving the position of policewomen. They also point to the difference in motives between conference participants, stating that:

Most of the North American officers had paid their own way to the conference, often taking annual leave in order to be there. This is their normal practice. Delegates from Europe and the rest of the world were much more likely to have been officially selected and sponsored by their agencies. (*Ibid.*: 142)

In highlighting the partial nature of their sample, they note the significance of missing populations at the conference, observing the low number of women officers from Germany for example. In spite of women's differential motives for attendance, arguably these women were already in possession of a gender consciousness, potentially a feminist one.

There was some evidence of alliance and network building among senior policewomen. Such alliances tended to be informal in nature and are better conceptualised as relationships based on friendship than formal networking groups. Some of the more senior women in this study were also part of specifically designated senior policewomen's groups. All of these groups were advisory in nature, with no terms of reference or accountability mechanisms, and none acted as a pressure group. The following policewoman notes the lack of clear direction, knowledge, and purpose of such groups:

I do have a problem with what we do, what we are trying to do. We seem to be stumbling around in the dark a bit. I don't know whether people know who we are or what we are here for. I don't even know sometimes what we are trying to do.

Unsure of their roles, members suffered from a lack of confidence in their ability to facilitate change and some found it difficult to justify their existence. It was felt that senior women's initiatives had failed to introduce the voice of women into the male discourse at decision-making levels in the organisation, with the reality being that:

Male officers don't really want to entertain us [the senior women's group], they don't see us or hear us.

Women also expressed a sense of powerlessness and frustration as networks lost momentum as senior women left their jobs, reducing the number of network participants back into single figures.

You are made an automatic member when you are a chief inspector. I knew nothing about the group when I got promoted.

155

I got a letter saying well done and welcome to the group, really exclusive membership as you can see, it just happens automatically. So you see they were desperate, there were only six of them, and a wave of us got promoted and all of a sudden, the group doubled our numbers.

One of the key obstacles for these groups was the issue of 'time'; all of them operated in their own time and within their own budgets. It is not surprising that activism, then, is something that takes place in addition to their normal duties; it is perceived in terms of being a 'selfish luxury'. Attendance had become increasingly difficult as performance targets and workloads for individuals increased. Unlike most organisations, the concept of networking around a single issue such as gender becomes even more pronounced in the police organisation, which is governed and bound by codes of hierarchy and loyalty. In addition to realising the potential benefits of networking, King (1993: 56) offers some cautionary advice when she notes that:

> women gravitating towards other women for support is fine, and as long as it controlled . . . women managers may be great friends and allies but need to be careful that they are not labelled as a formidable team bound by gender rather than profession.

Where separate women-only structures and networking between senior policewomen did take place, both male and female colleagues often perceived this with suspicion.

> Any form of network by women I think is seen by many as a great challenge, they [men] are very suspicious of networking.

> They perceive more than two of us together with suspicion and fear. There is a lack of understanding, perhaps a wilful misunderstanding, that it's all girls together again and that we are all ganging up on them.

> I don't think that anyone knows the senior women's group exists, this is not a bad thing, not that it is a secret society or anything.

> I have had the odd comment, I don't brandish it, it has been publicised, it's no secret. I don't put a note on my door but it's not a group that immediately comes to the lips of either men or women.

> I still think that although [senior] women are much more accepted now than they were in the past, it is not seen now as an issue so

much. But when three of us had lunch together last week, people were commenting about it, you know 'what's going on'. I think it must have been a bit of a formidable sight, if there had been four men having lunch no one would have commented on them, it's because we were women. The boss of one of the women walked in and said 'I have obviously interrupted something'. You know he was obviously nervous because there were two women in the room alone, I suppose I should be grateful really. It was like a little triumvirate. I think he felt very uncomfortable, yet as individuals he would have been fine, but his behaviour towards us as a group was really noticeably different.

Holding the position of femocrat (Sawer 1995) or being associated with a network of women brings the potential to be identified as a 'feminist', a role perceived to be incompatible with the duty of an unbiased police officer. As such, women's loyalty and discretion is likely to be questioned. Loyalty here is composed of both loyalty to the organisation and loyalty to rank. In demonstrating loyalty to the organisation, women were conscious of the effects of their association with specific causes such as those based on sex and/or race. Given the upsurge in public scandals involving sexism and racism, women spoke at length of the need for the police organisation to 'stick together' and present a 'united front in the face of mounting criticism and external attack'. The need to demonstrate a unified front is echoed in the broader police literature that emphasises the marked internal solidarity of the police. In appreciating more fully the dynamic nature of loyalty, Waddington (1999a: 10) notes the complex pattern of 'vertical and horizontal division within the police organisation that qualifies the loyalty that the officer is expected to show'.

Rank gets in the way

The purpose of networking by its very nature is an attempt to encourage commonality between participants – to engender a forum within which experiences can be shared. The realities of women's experiences of networks, however, demonstrate the problematic nature of trying to achieve commonality across the differences brought about by rank. As a result of their small number, women's networks (even those dedicatedly termed 'senior women's groups') are often made up of women from a range of managerial ranks. Despite the commonality of womanhood, the lives of lower and middle management in policing differ greatly from their senior counterparts. Raising and debating issues in the presence of direct/indirect line management or subordinates often proved problematic for members. One policewoman notes the divisiveness of such groups and her reluctance to engage fully:

> There is still the rank structure between us; despite the fact we were trying to be together there appears to be this inability to move away from the hierarchical structure. If I want to kick my shoes off, I felt I couldn't because of the lower ranks. I don't want to do it, the rank gets in the way, I would like to see it working more as a team than as a hierarchical structure.

Organising across difference poses a number of significant challenges that often inhibit coalition building even when participants appear to share common standpoints. Waddington (*ibid.*: 100) also notes that police officers as a group are notoriously unwilling to 'share information about anything with anyone'. Punch (1985: 183) draws heavily on the features of solidarity and secrecy that characterise the culture of policing in explaining police corruption, arguing that 'there is a deep dichotomy between the values, styles and vulnerability of lower ranks and senior officers which is characterised by social distance, mutual distrust, and varying levels of manipulation, control and acquiescence'. Such features of solidarity might also go some way in explaining the difficulties that women might encounter in trying to join forces across ranks in the name of womanhood. There was little evidence of any attempt to eliminate 'rank mentality' by policewomen.

Officers quickly learn the cultural attributes that govern their membership of the culture of management. Adlam's (2002: 29) data points to the patterns of interaction that underline how individual officers are inducted into cultural forms that are 'hierarchical and status laden'. Rituals and routines serve to ensure that officers 'know their place', with clear 'markers of subordination' in operation. While further strengthening the association that police officers have with rank and hierarchy, the markers of 'knowing one's place' simultaneously serve to weaken officers' ability to organise across such divisions.

Further acknowledgement of the racial differences among women also holds significant clues about the ability to organise collectively as women. Research from Martin (1992, 1994) and Pogrebin *et al.* (1999) detailing the American experience provides valuable material for understanding the complexity of women organising across difference. Martin (1994) argues that the lack of unity among black and white women in policing could be attributed to racial differences. She claims that white women police, like black male police officers, are perceived to trade on their racial and gender solidarity with higher status white policemen. With the arrival of black women in policing, black men trade on their masculinity to distance themselves from both black and white women police officers and align themselves with the dominant majority of white men. Distancing themselves from women provides the means for acceptance of black male officers by white male officers. In turn, white women officers racially distance themselves from minority women police, thereby providing themselves with the opportunity to utilise their racial similarity to align themselves with white male officers.

In much the same way that senior policewomen in my study do not ally themselves with feminism, black policewomen in Pogrebin *et al.*'s (1999) study also sought to distance themselves from anything political in nature. Instead, they maintained a 'neutral' stance and attempted to 'blend' in. Their work suggests that black policewomen occupy an anomalous position, finding that they are unable to ally themselves with their black sisters, their white sisters-in-law, their black brothers, or their white brothers-in-law. Achievement of upward mobility for minorities within police organisations requires competition with the dominant white males. As a result, Pogrebin *et al.* note that 'Divisiveness between all groups, both dominant and minority, as well as male and female, is maintained throughout the entire organisation as a result of the competition for rank and sustained control of the department' (*ibid.*: 34). It is apparent from their respondents' views that the relationship with white female officers can best be described as one based on 'self interest first and unification as women with common employee problems as a distant second' (*ibid.*: 36). The reason for this lack of unification is summed up by one of their respondents when she states: 'It's not the in thing to do, to be supportive to one another because we are in a sense *dividing the pie*' (*ibid.*: 37, emphasis added).

My findings add further weight to such works. There was little evidence of senior policewomen acting as a group; even where there were common views and experiences, there was no sense of a shared consciousness, of an overall solidarity. As one of my respondents observed:

It's like being in the sisterhood with no sisters.

In an interesting study, Gherardi (1995) examines the construction of gender in the workplace, drawing upon Greek mythology with its female and male divinities and showing how these goddesses and gods

159

correspond to specific embodiments of femaleness and maleness in modern organisational cultures. Drawing on Gherardi's analysis, it is Athena (the goddess of wisdom and of the arts) as a cultural model who best represents senior policewomen in this study. As a cultural model, Athena is both a trusted accomplice of leaders and a spokeswoman for the established order. The cultural model of the woman as 'right hand man' does not necessarily require her to conceal herself or to become invisible. Despite the diversity between senior policewomen in this study, one of the key issues that bind them together is their acceptance of policing in its present form, working within existing frameworks of male power. The Athenian model of femaleness normally rules out sisterhood, and the professional success of an Athena rarely prompts other women to follow in her footsteps. By representing the patriarchal order, the Athena model of femaleness defends the status quo. It demonstrates acceptance of established norms of 'professional behaviour' – that is, self-control, objectivity, impersonality, logical thought, and the development of specific skills (*ibid.*).

It would be unfair, however, to characterise senior policewomen as strangers, for they are not. Their relationship is perhaps better characterised as resembling a state of 'sibling rivalry'. When placed within broader debates about the emergence of the risk society, the idea that individuals adopt highly individualistic approaches to getting to the top should come as no surprise. Beck *et al.* (1994) reminds us that collective and group-specific sources of meaning in the culture of industrial society are suffering from break-up, and that, as a result, 'individuals are being expected to live with a broad variety of different mutually contradictory, global and personal risks' (*ibid.*: 7). Individuals experience less certainty, security, and stability and are faced with a different set of relationships in society; indeed, 'the whole notion of "society" in modernity is abstract, characterised not by the concrete and particular relationships of the *Gemeinschaft* but by abstract relationships such as impersonality, achievement and universalism' (Lash 1994: 115).

In an ongoing climate of police reform in Britain, it is clear that the police service of the future will be characterised by fewer officers, together with less opportunity to achieve rank. In an attempt to climb the organisational ladder to secure scarce senior positions, women are joining the competitive race to accumulate the necessary profile for leadership. Policewomen's lack of activism needs to be understood against this backdrop of organisational restructuring. At more senior levels, women find themselves in a situation of increased competition with men (and women), a state of 'sibling rivalry', over a diminishing number of jobs. As a result, in many ways 'staying there' does equate with 'staying quiet'. Panzarella (2003: 130) reminds us that although non-conforming may be a highly desirable trait in some organisations, police organisations tend not to be inclined to 'pass the reins to people who break the rules ... They are looking for a kind of leader who follows the rules and will prompt subordinates to do the same.' In this case, it is predicted that women will continue to adopt a cost and benefit approach to activism, with the cost of being an active gendering agent proving too high a price to pay and the job of policing worth playing the game for without changing the rules.

While the findings of this study point to a lack of shared consciousness among senior policewomen, the findings of Heidensohn (2000) and Brown and Heidensohn (2000) are worth reiterating as they suggest grounds for future optimism. In detailing the value of sisterhood at an international level, their work demonstrates that linking internationally is one way to achieve a 'critical mass of colleagues with whom one can network, gain support and build resistance to abuse' (Heidensohn 2000: 60). The challenge of such networks and groups, however, will be to reach out and harness the support of those women who are disinterested or in some way have become disaffected by what sisterhood, and by implication feminism, has to offer.

An appreciation of early policewomen also serves to demonstrate that the fight to find a permanent place in policing came from women themselves. Despite internal conflicts between early policewomen, the vigour with which they fought serves as a reminder of the power of agency in working towards change. Their attempts to work towards establishing a sense of sisterhood also provide valuable lessons for some of their modern-day counterparts who are involved in the search for sisterhood. In the development of a long-term equal opportunities agenda, early policewomen undertook a dual strategy of organising separately as women while at the same time continuing to work within mainstream structures and systems. Women inside and outside the police lobbied hard for the instatement of women into policing. Historically, it was the existence of 'well-placed insiders' in the political machinery that was to have a substantial impact on the position of women in policing. In 1920s Britain, the support and influence of two women MPs, Lady Astor and Mrs Wintringham, together with support from a group of sympathetic male MPs and members of the House of Lords was to ensure that a nucleus of women patrols were allowed to remain. Early in 1923, twenty women constables were sworn in with Lilian Wyles appointed in 1922 to Scotland Yard (Carrier 1988). In Australia, Irene Longman, the first women MP elected in 1929 in Queensland, was to provide increased support and impetus for the case of women in policing (Prenzler 1998: 4). For policewomen in America a key source of support was to come from 'women's clubs'. Drawn from college-educated, middle-class women, these clubs were to play a significant role in articulating the increased need for women's presence in policing. A further global stamp of support for policewomen came in 1923 at Geneva, Switzerland, in which the League of Nations assembly adopted a resolution in favour of the employment of females in police work throughout the world (Segrave 1995).

There was also significant male support in the shape of male MPs, as well as help from some chief constables who chose to employ women on an experimental basis. Allen (1925) details a key point in which all members of the WPV were requested to vote whether policewomen should join with men or go it alone; with two exceptions the whole body of women voted solidly for cooperation with men. She goes on to note that Damer Dawson represented the point of view that:

> women must of necessity, work in closest co-operation with, and in staunchest loyalty to, their male colleagues; that the public service is one and indivisible, that it demands the united efforts of both men and women, and that these efforts should dovetail but never conflict. (Cited in *ibid*.: 15)

In working towards improving women's position in policing, there is much to suggest that women must continue to work with the majority group – that is, men – in pursuing their cause. At the same time, women in policing need to continue to strive for an increased sense of sisterhood with each other, working together in developing a shared consciousness. Continuing with a plan of 'interim separatism' (Colgan and Ledwith 1996), working and organising with other women is a necessary strategy for building a collective feminist awareness and consciousness. It might also serve to 'empower women in their struggle to alter existing, mainstream political and organisational structures' (*ibid*.: 164). With 50 per cent of women from the public sector union UNISON identifying themselves as feminists, Colgan *et al.* (1996) extol the value of working in such a state. In developing an increased sense of shared consciousness, women should also work towards developing stronger links with other minority groups in policing. In doing so, it is hoped that the trend towards a hierarchy of oppressions may be lessened.

A further source of optimism for modern networks and collabor-ations comes from Heidensohn (2000) who notes that the significance of collaboration lies not only in their international nature but also in the nature of their relationship to mainstream policing. That modern networks are inside the police is a source of confidence for the future position of women in policing. Observing the early international policewomen's movement, Heidensohn (*ibid.*) stresses that although the cause of women police was strongly supported by well-placed insiders, '. . . leadership consisted of only a few people, often indepen-dent minded and sometimes too highly individual to work well with others or within organisations'. In addition:

> the international movement was *external* to police organizations and could not exercise effective influence upon them . . . [As a result] while initially it was a strength to have bases and support outside the police, the failure to move on from this position was ultimately a weakness. (*Ibid.*: 58, original emphasis)

The potential of women's activism in policing may also benefit from an acknowledgement of the broader context within which change takes place. Chan (1997) emphasises the significance of this wider appreci-ation. In her analysis she demonstrates that, despite having undergone major organisational and cultural reforms for some years, police and race relations in New South Wales remained poor, with condemnations against police racism being widely cited by the media, politicians, and community groups. By drawing on the work of Bourdieu, Chan contends that the key to understanding why substantial reforms introduced within the police organisation have had such a limited impact is related to the fact that reform efforts were principally directed at changing the 'habitus' rather than the 'field'.[2] She argues that during the time of police reform, many of the elements of the 'field' remained substantially the same. As a result, she contends, organisational changes intended to affect the 'habitus' without altering the 'field' will inevitably fail. Her analysis strongly urges researchers to appreciate the power of the field – that is, the social, economic, legal, and political sites in which policing takes place.

Much of this book has been concerned with documenting the power of individual agency, encouraging a reading in which individual officers are held accountable as active gendering agents. Mindful of Chan's (*ibid.*) advice, the final part of this chapter situates the possibilities of change for women in policing within a broader context. I have already made reference to some of the resources that exist in police organisations which promote women's status and enable police-women to *do* activism at an institutional level. What I want to do in this last section is to investigate the extent to which the wider 'field' – in this instance, the state – is involved in pushing an agenda of equality for women forward. By drawing attention to the nature and level of gendered activism at a state level we can begin to comprehend the importance of structure in its abilities to both aid and constrain individual action.

Doing activism on a state level

Stetson and Mazur (1995) provide an interesting starting point with their review of institutionalised feminism – that is, 'state feminism'. Here the concept of state feminism refers to the 'activities of government structures that are formally charged with furthering women's status and rights' (*ibid.*: 2). Their analysis is grounded in the earlier work of Scandinavian and Australian theorists. It was the Scandinavian literature that first referred to state feminists as 'both feminists employed as administrators and bureaucrats in positions of power and to women politicians advocating gender equality policies' (Siim 1991: 189, cited in Stetson and Mazur 1995). It was, however, Australian writers who coined the term 'femocrat' in the 1970s (Sawer 1995) to describe the individuals referred to by Siim. The term referred to feminists who took up women's policy positions that were being created in government; it was also used for feminists who moved into mainstream positions in bureaucracies. Sawer notes that while the term 'femocrat' was originally used as a term of abuse or ironic self-deprecation, it is now an icon of the Australian experiment with feminist interventions in the workings of the state.

Through a comparative analysis, Stetson and Mazur (1995) offer a comprehensive overview of the role that state structures play in promoting feminist political agendas in the contexts of the different political, social, and cultural traditions of various countries. An appreciation of their framework provides an interesting backdrop for an analysis of the changing fortunes of an equal opportunities agenda in Britain. Their classification of women's policy machinery is governed by two criteria: the degree of policy influence and the degree of policy access.

Policy influence refers to the participation of each women's policy office in the formation of feminist policies that promote the status of women and/or undermine patterns of gender hierarchy. It is measured by determining the impact of women's policy offices on equal employment policy (EEP). Women's policy machineries are classified as having high policy influence if 'they have had a clear role in determining the content of EEP at any stage in the policy formation, including, pre-formulation, formulation, implementation and evaluation' (ibid.: 275).

Policy access refers to the degree to which women's policy machineries develop opportunities for society-based actors, feminist and women's advocacy organisations, to exert influence on feminist policies. The policy access dimension of state feminism focuses on the way women's policy offices might advance the feminist political agenda, through helping women's advocacy organisations find access to policy-making arenas inside the state. They note that offices can do this directly by recruiting organisation leaders into policy networks or by forging alliances with relatively powerful and well-organised society-wide actors.

The argument is that through the joint action of 'well placed insiders and outsiders, women's equality policies will rise onto the political agenda, to be formalised and implemented' (ibid.: 276). Policy machineries that score high on the policy access dimension are those that have provided access directly or indirectly to feminist groups, interests, and activists in such a way that they become more powerful actors in the policy process. Those machineries that fail to reach out to feminist interests, or that tend to make interest subservient to the goals and fortunes of official versions of feminism, are classified as low on the dimensions of policy access.

They go on to develop a classification of countries according to the dichotomous measures of high/low policy influence and policy access: Type 1 – high influence/high access (the most feminist); Type 2 – high influence/low access; Type 3 – low influence/high access; and Type 4 – low influence/low access (the least feminist). Britain is classified as Type 2: high influence/low access – that is, women's policy machineries have had a clear role in determining the content of employment policy but have failed to empower feminist and women's advocacy organisations to exert an influence by formulating feminist policies.

In light of the recent political changes brought about by the election of the New Labour government in May 1997, it may be that this classification needs revisiting. Since taking office, the New Labour government has done much to fuel a sense of increased optimism for women. As part of an attempt to modernise government, we can see a host of welcome initiatives that address the position of women. A new infrastructure for pursuing women's issues in government has emerged. There is new machinery to address women's needs, including Ministers for Women in the Cabinet, a new Women's Unit in the Cabinet Office, and a Cabinet subcommittee responsible for ensuring that the whole of government takes into account women's needs and aspirations. The Women's Unit has commissioned a series of research projects exploring the experiences of women. Current government discourse on issues of equality has both encompassed and gone beyond the principles of social justice being strongly couched in the 'business' case for efficiency. Government has acknowledged a changing form of economy, characterising the new economy as knowledge based, entrepreneurial, productive, and inclusive. As such, it has also asserted that it is an economy in which women are increasingly active and that the skills that women excel in, for example project management, interpersonal skills, and high standards of customer service, are all skills that are highly valued in this changing economy (CEDAW 1999).

In attempting to secure the advancement of women, government has also set up institutional mechanisms to create and strengthen national and other governmental bodies; to integrate gender perspectives in legislation, public polices, programmes, and projects; and to generate and disseminate gender-disaggregated data and information for planning and evaluation. It has recognised that the production of such data is a precondition for researching and monitoring the development of gender issues which cover all aspects of society and the policy-making process. The UK's Governmental Statistical Service (GSS) has taken an active lead in pursuing this goal, working with others across government and beyond in developing gender-related statistics and making them more easily accessible.

In tackling women's representation in public life, the government is committed to the principle of a 50:50 ratio of women and men in public appointments, and to appoint on merit using fair selection procedures, including those that recognise skills acquired through non-traditional career patterns as suitable qualifications for appointments. All departments are now required to produce individual action plans with specific goals and objectives for increasing the representation of women. In meeting legal and international obligations, the aim is to ensure that Britain carries forward the government's agenda in international forums, broadening and strengthening links with women across the country and beyond. In terms of power and decision making, it has also taken measures to ensure women's equal access to and full participation in power structures, increasing women's capacity to participate in decision making and leadership.

Perhaps the most visible manifestations of such efforts are best reflected in the increase of women candidates returned in the 1997 General Election, with the highest number of women MPs ever recorded at 122.[3] Such an increase was due, in part, to the Labour Party adopting a policy of women-only shortlists – roughly half had been selected in this way. All-women shortlists were to fall foul of employment laws in 1998. This legal challenge stopped their use in the 2001 election, reducing the number of women returned to 117. Following more recent amendments to the Sex Discrimination Act (SDA) (1975), to enable political parties to take action to reduce inequality in the number of women and men, it seems that shortlists are back (House of Commons 2003).

By introducing a structural element here, I am trying to clarify and give a greater context to the limits of what is possible for women in policing. Research has repeatedly pointed to the striking differences in the levels of state consciousness and activism between nation states. In comparison with Britain, the state in Canada, the US, Australia, and some parts of Europe, in its role as employer, has taken much bolder legislative and structural measures to assist the progression towards equity for women and other disadvantaged groups.

In his study of the recruitment of black Americans into the police, Leinen (1984) argues that the United States' legal framework of positive discrimination was crucial for the significant advances made by black officers. Civil disturbance acted as a catalyst to a public consciousness of civil rights and a protest movement among black Americans. Legal change followed, first within a framework of equal opportunities. Affirmative action then developed as a prelude to the acceptance of positive discrimination and the setting of formal employment quotas. Fielding's (1999) research on American policing notes the existence of separate but parallel promotion structures for officers of white and minority groups. He notes that while the idea of separate structures might have 'uncomfortable resonances', they 'appear to work', citing cases where the post of chief of police is held by a member of an ethnic minority, signalling important changes in the make-up of police organisations.

The effect of a robust legal framework in the US has ensured that political and policy approaches to equality issues have been far more radical and far-reaching than in Britain (Heidensohn 1992). Despite this, the outcome for policewomen in the US is not as good as in Britain. Mindful of the fragmentary nature of US police organisations,[4] statistics for 2001 show a downward trend in the overall percentage of women in law enforcement, falling from a peak of 14.3 per cent in 1999 to 13 per cent in 2000, and to 12.7 per cent in 2001. Such a trend leads Lonsway *et al.* (2002: 6) to note that 'At best, this pattern can be seen as a stall in the glacial pace of progress for women in policing. At worst, it demonstrates that women are actually losing ground in their representation within sworn law enforcement.' In explaining the decline in women's representation, they point firmly to the decrease in the number of consent decrees mandating the hiring and/or promotion of women and/or minorities.[5] They go on to argue that without consent decrees imposed to remedy the discriminatory hiring and employment practices by law enforcement agencies, even the most marginal gains for women in policing would not have been possible.

Scandinavian systems have also been praised for the significant gains made by women. Sweden, for example, has a high level of female representation within its national parliament, with women accounting for 42.7 per cent of positions (EOC 2002). While grounded in the principles of democratic justice, resource utilisation, and interest representation[6] (Nordeval 1985), actual gains for women in Scandinavian parliaments have stemmed largely as a result of structural factors such as electoral systems, methods of selection, and initiatives such as quota-based reforms.[7]

The potential impact that structural arrangements such as employment quotas could have on the position and number of women in organisations, then, is considerable. Indeed, the substantial increase of women elected to parliament in 1997 and their subsequent decline in 2001 outlined earlier is evidence enough to recognise the power of all-women shortlists. The arguments against quotas are well rehearsed but are worth repeating briefly. In short, it has been argued that quotas often have unintended consequences, reinforcing rather than eroding the damaging stereotypes that already characterise minority groups – in this case, women. Through the existence of quotas, members of the 'majority' population – men – may express feelings of unfairness and disadvantage, fuelling an increased sense of antipathy towards those being served by quotas. It might also be the case that 'quota' people are perceived to be less able than their 'non-quota' counterparts, achieving success solely by virtue of their sex. All too aware of the mantra that chants 'she only got the job because she's a woman', I am not advocating a return to the development of quotas[8] for women in policing. Such a position remains fundamentally flawed for the future development of women in policing. It remains a strategy that is ultimately locked into a myth which suggests that increasing the number of women inevitably results in change. Any increase in the number of women in policing is welcome. Nevertheless, bringing about change to the gendered order of policing requires a much more complex solution than that offered by the development of quotas.

Activism among senior policewomen in this study is weak and there is no so-called 'feminist' presence in policing to speak of. This perhaps should come as no surprise given that there seems little doubt from the literature that the visible national feminist movement is in decline. Lovenduski and Randall (1993) note that the second half of the 1980s heard numerous assertions that feminism had once again declined, that it was a spent force, that many of its aims had been met, and that those still outstanding were ridiculous. Perhaps it is worth questioning here whether the idea of sisterhood is still a valid basis for working with women. The notion of organising based simply on ideas of 'sisterhood' might seem simplistic and quite problematic given the development of more sophisticated feminist analyses. In recent years, fierce debates about race, sexuality, and class have posed serious questions within the women's movement in relation to the idea of sisterhood. On the one hand it could be argued that if the feminist movement cannot exhibit a form of unity, the search for sisterhood could be a fruitless one. On the other hand, and perhaps more convincingly, the reality might be that the so-called fragmentation of the women's national movement is better understood as a progressive and positive move. The plurality of feminism and diversity might be more suggestive of vitality and dynamism in which many complex debates are still to be had. Ironically, sisterhood does not mean obscuring the issue of difference, but should accommodate recognition of difference. In summing up, it would appear that at a structural level there is much to be optimistic about at the beginning of the twenty-first century in Britain. In terms of *doing* activism at a state level, a shifting political terrain has led to a greater degree of access, with an increased ability to influence the development of a stronger agenda for women. There appear to be a number of 'well placed insiders' in the 'field' who can push the project of equality forward with greater vigour.

Notes

1   Founded in 1915 in the US, the International Association of Women Police (IAWP) was formerly the International Policewomen's Association (IPA).
2   Here the 'field' consists of a set of objective, historical relations between positions anchored in certain forms of power (or capital), while 'habitus' consists of a set of historical relations 'deposited' within individual bodies

169

in the form of mental and corporeal schemata of perception, appreciation, and action (Chan 1997).

3   A total of 120 women were returned after the main election but a further two women MPs were elected at by-elections during the 1997 parliament.

4   Made up of numerous large and smaller police agencies, the number of sworn female officers across them varies enormously. For example, although Terrebonne Parish Sheriff, Los Angeles, rates the highest number of women officers at 41.71 per cent (78 women officers out of a total of 187 officers), Lorain Police, Ohio, has only 0.95 per cent of women officers (1 woman officer out of a total of 105). For a comprehensive list detailing percentages for all states, see Lonsway et al. (2002).

5   Among the 247 agencies surveyed, Lonsway et al. (2002) demonstrate that forty indicated that they had once been under such a consent decree. Only twenty-two currently remain in effect. Moreover, there is evidence that consent decrees are expiring and not being implemented at the same rate as they were in the 1970s and 1980s. Eight consent decrees expired in the period of time from 1999 to 2002, yet only two consent decrees were implemented since 1995, and only six were implemented in the entire decade.

6   Nordeval (1985) argues that in Scandinavian countries arguments for increased female representation have relied on three main principles. The first is democratic justice – that justice is an important principle, and that it is unjust for women to be under-represented on decision-making bodies. The second is resource utilisation – that valuable human resources are wasted when half the population is not involved in politics. The third is interest representation – that because of the different experiences of women and men (in relation to economic and social structures) they have different political interests, implying that in politics women will employ a different set of values and pursue different interests from men.

7   Countries that have made the most significant advances are those where the electoral system is based on Proportional Representation (PR) and not on majoritarian systems (first past the post). Research shows that women are twice as likely to be elected under PR as under majoritarian systems (EOC 2002). Party reform, based on quotas, has been widely adopted in Norway, where the Socialist Left, Labour, and Liberal parties each require at least 40 per cent representation of each sex at all levels of party activity.

8   The study conducted by the Policy Studies Institute (PSI) in 1983 reported that the Metropolitan Police were operating a quota system in the recruitment of female officers (Smith and Gray 1983).

Chapter 7

Conclusion

This final section contributes to some of the ongoing debates about change in the police organisation. I will be revisiting the site of equal opportunities to assess the extent to which the police can lay claim to organisational change. I will also review the role that women in police leadership are playing in the change process, and offer some observations on the potential of current and future change initiatives.

I began this book by suggesting that there is much to be happy about in the twenty-first century in relation to equal opportunities. As an investigative site, it has allowed us to observe in real terms the police organisation's attempt to push forward an agenda of change. At the same time, it has enabled us to witness some of the ways in which an organisation and its inhabitants are able to resist such a movement. Reflecting on the transformations of police organisations, Jones and Newburn (2002) argue that Bayley and Shearing's (1996) proposition of radical change across police organisations is an overstated one. In support of their position, the current discourses on the development of equal opportunities within policing disguises some important continuities. There have been a number of welcome changes in equal opportunities policy and substantial inroads made to advance the integration of women within policing. At a policy level, at least, attempts to bring about change through the twin doctrines of 'equality' and 'quality' can be identified.

Structurally, the systems necessary to bring about change to the gendered order of policing have been set in place. Yet, despite the optimism brought about through changes in policy, the need to remain vigilant about their effects remains constant – policy does not always easily translate into practice. We need to continue to be wary of the powerful mantra which informs us that 'things are equal now'. Gender remains a crucial division in society, albeit in a more inconsistent way – men still dominate. In realising the sources of change for policing, the languages of 'equality' and 'quality' have, for the most part, been driven more by a concern with image, than by a philosophy of social justice. Policewomen in Britain and throughout the world continue to encounter resistance and the discriminatory effects of working in a male-dominated occupation. Unlike those policewomen who have gone before them, modern policewomen's discrimination is less blatant, less visible, and as a result, more insidious.

The base of equal opportunities policies and programmes remains fundamentally flawed with discrimination framed as an individual problem of rogue officers and not as a systemic condition. Culture continues to be framed as 'out there', a distinct entity to be tackled – that is, something that an organisation *has* rather than *is* (Bate 1996). The essence of equal opportunities continues to concentrate on the distribution of opportunities for certain jobs, promotion, rewards, training, and development. Its message remains one that allows women to compete effectively for existing jobs and one in which men are encouraged to accept that competition. By encouraging the notion that women *can* and *are* as capable as men, the police service appears to be moving towards an organisational logic characterised by gender neutrality in line with the notion of the abstract and disembodied worker (Acker 1992). This concentration is at the expense of a critical examination of the job itself.

Just as the police role remains intact and unchallenged, the culture, climate, and values of police leadership remain untouched with a steadfast and unchanging perception of women as unsuitable leaders in policing. The theory and practice of gender neutrality continues to cover up and obscure the underlying gendered substructure, allowing practices that perpetuate it to continue (*ibid.*). The police service is not a gender-neutral organisation, but is deeply gendered at structural, cultural, and individual levels. In this sense, the police organisation through its enactment of equal opportunities both *embodies* and *disembodies* its officers. Much of the project of change regarding equality has been about organisational development rather than organisational change. What we see so far in the development of equal opportunities in policing is a change 'in' strategy, rather than a change 'of' strategy (Bate 1996).

The ability to bring about meaningful and sustainable change in the police organisation continues to cause problems for those involved in its implementation. I have called for greater caution in the reading and interpretation of the effects of change. Guided by some of the recent ideas about the potential of organisational restructuring, I began this book with an optimistic projection of the effects that restructuring in organisations could bring for women in management. The breakdown of the traditional career structure has provided an important opportunity to revisit the concept of career in terms of gender. It was anticipated that organisational restructuring towards less hierarchy, more team functioning, and greater flexibility might be working towards reducing some of the disadvantages that senior women in policing face. The reality, however, suggests a very different picture.

The police organisation continues to pay reverence to the concepts of 'time' and 'place' and, rather than representing an opportunity for change, restructuring has worked to maintain gendered identities in the police organisation. The removal of layers of management, combined with the intensification of managerial work, holds serious implications for women in policing. Women have been afforded opportunities to compete on equal terms with men for promotion to senior management positions and while gender alone is no longer a barrier to even the most senior police management position, the characteristics required of leaders in this new order are leaving their mark. Changes brought about as a result of the movement towards greater quality of service have served to create a 'smart macho' culture of police management.

In order to develop a more accurate reading of the gendered nature of policing, I have also urged a greater appreciation of the multiplicity of cultures and identities that exist in the police organisation. More research on diverse populations within policing should serve to expose these multiple cultures, which will, in turn, give rise to the multiplicity of police identities. Such a prospect has led Waddington (1999a: 105) to write that, 'Faced with all this diversity, it seems that culture – as a set of shared artefacts – almost disappears entirely and the monolith crumbles into a pile of rubble. Subculture disappears into a near infinity of multiple subcultures.' In emphasising the multiplicity of participants in policing, my aim is to encourage a cautionary approach to reading existing accounts and to offer a more constructive approach to exploring new ones.

The importance of acknowledging a multiplicity of cultures in policing lies in its ability to unlock a multiplicity of masculinities, as well as femininities. In doing so, it is anticipated that a more complex appreciation of what it seems has become a 'convenient label' (Chan 1996) for a range of behaviours that characterise police officers and police work will be developed. It is anticipated that this will lead to more sophisticated analyses of the intersections of gender, race, class, and sexuality in experiencing policing. Such analyses will further deconstruct the differential experiences of officers within policing.

There is a pressing need to conduct more research on both women and men in senior management. Not only will this serve to enhance the study of missing populations in policing, but such analyses will also provide rich data on the construction and meaning of gendered identities. The failure to acknowledge the existence of multiple cultures, and, in turn, multiple gendered identities, in the police organisation could contribute further to the failure of police reform packages.

The current structure of the police organisation, together with the continued importance it attaches to rank, impacts in a particularly damning way for women. The 'smart macho' culture of police leadership has impacted on policewomen's decisions to move up the ranks. The reduction of management posts appears to have strengthened the predominant male culture of long working hours and aggressive and competitive behaviour. The ability to work long hours, to 'give time', has become one of the most desired management attributes and in an increasingly competitive environment Rutherford (2001) reminds us that time can be seen as a resource to be drawn on in order to progress in an organisation. The inclusion of long working hours into the profile required of police leaders continues to be justified on the grounds of operational necessity; in turn, this contributes to the ongoing processes of gender demarcation and exclusion.

The long-hours culture remains an important barrier to women's progress in organisations. Working long hours is bound up with a specific form of masculinity; in this case, 'time' is a key constituent of the 'smart macho' culture of police leaders. The use of more flexible working practices should be encouraged by the police organisation. It provides an important strategy for ensuring the retention of trained staff, and at the same time offers workers the opportunity to balance the demands of work and home life. The development of policy alone, however, will not achieve the open and flexible working environment that officers need if they are to take up such working options. Part-time work continues to be characterised by a mentality that constructs those who assume flexible forms of working as 'part-able and part-committed' (Julie Spence, President of the British Association of Women Police, cited in Jenkins 2000: 23).

If part-time work is not considered to be 'real' policing then flexible working policies will have limited real effect for those who wish to take advantage of them (both men and women). Particular attention needs to be paid by senior management in their role as communicators of the messages about job worth. Those in senior management need to actively demonstrate a commitment to flexible forms of working by taking action to ensure that information awareness and the potential to undertake different ways of working are more fully supported, both by the officers they manage and among their managerial peers. There also needs to be the development of a more creative dialogue on the possibilities of working more flexibly at all ranks; only then can women in senior management sustain their roles more ably. Above all, engaging in flexible ways of working should be recast as evidence of officers' ability and not inability to perform the job of policing.

In thinking more broadly about the concept of *doing* 'time', the impact of the strict linear career in policing holds serious implications for policewomen. In negotiating the climb to the top, women experience the true force of structural constraint. By strictly adhering to such a model, the police organisation continues to successfully achieve social closure for women. The interrupted nature of policewomen's career profiles, together with their lack of time spent on operational duty, results in a situation where they are unable to display the right amount or type of commitment and credibility. Policing scholars spend much time making reference to commitment and credibility, yet there is no real sense of the way in which either of these are informally defined, constructed or accomplished. The need to understand this more fully is supported by Metcalfe and Dick (2000: 400) when they state that 'policy developments should consider what shapes commitment and ensure that these factors are addressed in human resources management systems and procedures'. Only by understanding more fully the way in which both credibility and commitment are developed informally can we begin to reconcile more accurately the complex processes involved in the shaping of police identities.

There is clear evidence to suggest that women have a tacit understanding of what is required to make it to the top and in some cases are clearly enacting their own agency to achieve this. Some women who are in the race to accumulate skill and merit are employing strategic planning in the management of time during their careers, especially in their movement in and out of part-time work during maternity leave. These tactics, however, tend to be short-term with planning confined to transitional events or phases. The visions offered by Bayley (1994) in Chapter 4 hold considerable significance for women in policing. Challenging the single entry scheme, together with reconstructing policing along function rather than rank lines, may serve to weaken the control men hold in policing. Since authority is directly determined by one's position in the police hierarchy, any change to the power structure in policing requires a major paradigm shift and restructuring of existing rank structures. Through redesigning police decision-making and accountability processes across the ranks, lower-level officers may become responsible for a broader range of police decisions and activities (Metcalfe and Dick 2000).

Research should continue to challenge the single entry scheme in the police organisation. It is anticipated that more flexible forms of entry will serve to enhance women's progression through the ranks. Conducting more work on women and policing on a 'world stage' (Bayley 1999) will enable us to challenge the way things are in our own current system and has the potential to lead to significant changes in policy. Investigating Sweden, for example, which is one of the few countries in which women hold a good percentage of senior positions, may enable us to assess more accurately how police organisations are improving the position of policewomen.

Such analyses have already been set in motion by Brown and Heidensohn's (2000) international comparative work on women in policing; the challenge now is to progress and advance this. In the meantime, for those women who aspire to achieve high rank, working within existing systems, a greater awareness of the timeframe that governs the police career in its present form should be fostered. In order to progress and get to the top in policing, women need to be alert to the power of structural constraints involved in 'getting there'. Such awareness should serve to encourage women to engage in more strategic planning for carving out a long-term future in policing. In addition, the police organisation should step up its campaign to attract more women into the work of policing. Given the length of time it takes to achieve promotion and a management post in the police career, Baxter and Wright (2000) show mathematically that to effect even a small increase in the proportional representation of women in senior management levels there must be a substantial increase in the representation of women in lower levels.

The significance of rank is a strong and recurring theme throughout this book. It has been central both to defining rank-oriented cultures ('smart macho' police culture) and rank-oriented identities (managerial masculinity). Despite an organisational discourse that suggests the movement away from a militaristic model, the police service remains underpinned by a philosophy of militarism. At a structural level, the police organisation remains governed and demarcated by hierarchy and rank. At a more cultural level, officers still undergo a series of rituals that continue to symbolise an association and yearning for a lost militarism. The 'passing out' parade that new recruits experience; band playing and marching; the use of the salute; the ritual reference to senior officers as 'Sir' and 'Ma'am'; the attention to uniform and the various insignia of different ranks are all ways in which the police organisation bolsters and emphasises a military model in the way that it works.

In much the same way that officers in the military collect medals for their achievements, police officers collect badges of their accomplishments. On a more conceptual level, in the route to becoming a police leader, women are also involved in the process of collecting badges – badges that symbolise achievement and serve to distinguish them from their peers. The narratives of policewomen in many ways are testimonies of that collecting process. In the movement upwards, policewomen are involved in the collection and wearing of various badges. Being 'the first' is worn as a badge, symbolising pioneering and groundbreaking achievements. Those who posses a long and uninterrupted career in policing are able to use the concept of 'doing time' as a badge to demonstrate commitment to the organisation. Those women who have strong operational and public order skills can demonstrate credibility through wearing a badge of 'doing place'. However, it is the ability to demonstrate 'loyalty to rank' that is probably the most powerful badge, symbolising a combination of commitment and credibility to a career in policing.

Maintaining loyalty to rank remains an important impediment to women's ability to push forward change to the gendered order of policing through networking with other women. Women organising together as women in policing will continue to face the inherent problem that accompanies a group structured through hierarchical power – that is, the reality that 'rank gets in the way'. If the aim of developing women's networks is to encourage open and free communication between participants, then there is a need to overcome the 'rank mentality' that so clearly exists between officers. For ' "rank mentality" does little to foster openness and honesty, nor does it allow a team based approach to problem solving . . . Rank culture reinforces a management style that is distant and unsupportive' (Metcalfe and Dick 2000: 413, 414). The movement away from hierarchy through rank to a more function-based model might also serve to lessen the stronghold that demands 'loyalty' from its officers.

At first glance, the findings of this study might appear to offer pessimistic conclusions for examining women's careers in policing; this is not my intention. On the contrary, the narratives of senior policewomen can and should in many ways be interpreted as diaries of their 'secrets of success'. Ambitious to rise through the ranks, women are faced with a number of dilemmas. Since the choices made by senior policewomen in this study have ensured that they have reached the top, their narratives should be read as testaments of their success. The majority of women in this study who articulated success grounded their achievements in their own individual drive, commitment, determination, and hard work. In the face of structural constraints, senior policewomen have used innovative routes and have carefully crafted their way to the top. They have skilfully made judgements about the direction of their careers and the behaviour they exhibit in order to achieve success. The secret of their success has involved weaving in and out of positions, often minimising their high visibility as women. In many ways, senior policewomen have negotiated a path of contradictions, conflicts, and dilemmas; in essence, these individuals are 'wise' women (Ledwith and Colgan 1996).

Despite the lack of formal mentoring, some women did stress the encouragement they received from colleagues – sometimes from other women but predominantly from male officers. Their routes, however, do not necessarily follow the path outlined by feminism. Their choices have been realistic ones made in the face of strong structural constraints. This sense of realism has for them made way for a more effective route than that offered by following a more feminist path. The findings of this study send out an important message to those women who want to progress in policing: speaking the 'gender speak' is not the language of those who want to move on and climb the career ladder. It might be the case, then, that 'sisterhood' is the support group for those women who are unable to get on and move up.

In *doing* leadership, senior policewomen *are* active gendering agents involved in doing both 'masculinity' and 'femininity' in order to achieve their goals. The majority of senior policewomen are involved in promoting a different kind of police leadership. Women are using and developing consultative, participatory, and holistic styles – styles not traditionally associated with the police organisation. In many ways, they are drawing on leadership styles that are akin to some of the virtues of feminist practice and transformational leadership. In supporting the idea that women might be engaged in doing leadership differently to men, I am conscious of my part in colluding in the project that perpetuates the distorted binary world of 'feminine' and 'masculine'. Though problematic, the idea of a feminine leadership can act as a critical concept challenging traditional notions of organisation, hierarchy, management, and leadership. Developing the notion of a 'feminine' leadership is both misleading and risky in terms of working towards gender equality, but as Billing and Alvesson (2000: 151,155) contend:

It also has the virtue of putting gender on the leadership agenda in a, for many, appealing and pedagogical manner, thus problematizing male domination. It may contribute to the de-masculinization of management . . . not necessarily meaning a feminization of it, but loosening up management being culturally connected to men and given a masculine meaning.

In spite of the contemporary demands for inspirational and transformative styles of management and leadership, Maddock (2002: 12) argues that the disparity between the 'fantasy of the strategic and visionary manager' and the reality of how managers actually behave could not be greater. With reference to police leadership more specifically, Adlam and Villiers (2003: xi) note that, despite talking the talk of reform, police leaders fail to 'think strategically and act positively'. The police organisation remains 'bland in its statements and fundamentally averse to achieving radical change in its actions' (*ibid.*).

The use of different leadership styles evidenced by senior policewomen in this study should be strongly encouraged by the police organisation. Such styles emphasise that transformational leadership is a possibility for the police service. The value of transformational over transactional approaches to leadership are now well established within organisational and management circles (Bass and Avolio 1990). Continued reliance and emphasis on the transactional approach to leadership is deficient for long-term development or change. Transformational leadership approaches offer much more effective strategies in the development of long-term change and a greater emphasis on transformational leadership behaviours will place senior police officers in a position where they can more effectively cope with, and even facilitate, change.

The leadership styles exhibited by senior policewomen have the potential to effect change on the internal relationships between police officers, as well as improving external relations with those whom they police. Inherent within transformational approaches is the potential to inject a higher degree of emotion into *doing* leadership. Thus, police officers may become more emotionally aware of themselves and others; in turn, this can become the basis for a 'new emotional orientation that seeks creative solutions to issues confronting police' (Drodge and Murphy 2002: 432). As a result, it is envisaged that such styles will result in a more sensitive and humane form of policing.

Sharing power and encouraging more team-based decision making suggests that rank would lose some of its power status, since police tasks and solutions would be planned and carried out in a collaborative way. In addition, team-based arrangements also encourage supportive and cooperative behaviours between ranks (Metcalfe and Dick 2000). Given the increased competition for the scarce number of senior positions, together with the understanding that using more participatory and consultative approaches do not count towards earning the profile needed to be a police leader, we should not be surprised if senior policewomen choose to use more transactional approaches, to *do* 'masculinity' in their role as police leaders in the twenty-first century.

A continued emphasis on rank predisposes the police organisation to perceive of itself as different and distinct from other organisations. Carving out such a detached identity serves to bolster police officers', and in this case police leaders', sense of uniqueness. It is this sense of 'detachment' and 'uniqueness' that continues to undermine attempts at police reform. The view that policing is not so unique is summed up by Blair (2003: 170) who argues that 'police leadership is not essentially different from leadership in almost all other spheres of activity'. He suggests that in the same way that leaders in other organisations undergo leadership training, 'police officers can be and indeed need to be taught leadership skills ... good leadership needs to be one that learns'. Police leaders must be encouraged to abandon their long-held association with military models of leadership. In an interesting analysis of the military model in law enforcement, Cowper (2000) dispels the notion that police officers and their departments are patterned after the real military. He proposes that a careful and open-minded examination of military theory and practice will reveal an approach to organisation and leadership that is radically different from what both advocates of the military model and its critics within law enforcement currently believe. He writes:

> The modern military is not the top-down, centrally controlled monolith that many traditional police managers cherish and forward thinking police progressives decry ... For many decades, the modern military has actively and purposely worked to develop leaders who can think independently, take action without detailed supervision and create solutions to complex and rapidly changing problems. (*Ibid.*: 231, 236)

In spite of the superficial similarities that lend themselves to the military comparison, Cowper argues that the adoption by policing of this 'grossly inaccurate model of leadership and organization, mistakenly attributed to the military, has distorted police perceptions and leadership methodologies' (*ibid.*: 237). With limited leadership training and skills to draw on, police leaders automatically resort to using more militaristic styles of leadership as a means to achieve order and control. One of the key objectives of those involved in the training of police leaders should be to end the long-held association between police leadership and more militaristic models and styles of working.

Given the precarious position in which police organisations continue to find themselves, there may be serious consequences for those police organisations that do not embrace styles that are more transformational. The value of more transformational leadership styles should be encouraged for *all* police leaders at *all* levels of the organisation. We should be heartened by the fact that through the development of the National Police Leadership Faculty and the Police Leadership Development Board, the pursuit of organisational change has been grounded within the domain of training and education. Unlike other approaches, Bate (1996) argues that using education offers the most explicit and organised framework for creating cultural change, for it is not simply concerned with effecting change at a 'performance' level – that is, 'first order' change. Rather, adopting an educative approach is concerned with actually changing the form – the meta-directions, the guiding principles, the philosophical frameworks of organisational life, more simply the 'frame within which reality is defined' – that is, 'second order' change.

The educative approach works at the level of meta-directions, devoting itself to changing the underlying frame of meanings and values, and leaving performance to follow on naturally and developmentally. The argument thus follows: change the meta-directions that are the frames in which reality is defined and so the whole definition of reality changes (*ibid.*: 198). There is, of course, always doubt as to whether a change in the meta-directions always works through into the day-to-day performance. The purpose, nonetheless, is to transform and change culture, seeking discontinuity not continuity, dealing with second order change, leading to a fundamental change of cultural identity rather than simply an improvement or development of it.

In thinking about the sorts of knowledge that police leaders could undergo to alter their frame of meanings and values and increase their professional practice, Adlam (2003a), Vickers (2000), and Blair (2003) all call for a review of the police leadership curriculum, encouraging police leaders to develop 'reflective' and 'critical' thinking. Sceptical of the police organisation's ability to achieve this, Adlam (2002) observes that no genuinely comprehensive and critical doctrine of police leadership is evident in the current police leadership curriculum. A consequence of not exploring questions of social and political philosophy and questions in the philosophy of law and ethics is that 'the doctrinal (as opposed to the doctrinaire) aspects of policing remain impoverished' (*ibid.*: 34).

In order to ensure the accomplishment of critical leaders, such proponents are resolute in demanding that a strong theoretical base underpins management education. The police leadership curriculum should be developed upon strong foundations – foundations that can be provided through an engagement with applied philosophy. Such a philosophical underpinning, they argue, would encourage

> a more holistic theoretically based approach to education [which] possesses the structure and focus on the whole in relation to its parts, rather than taking an atomistic approach which is inclined to distort the structure, focusing on the parts as segments of the whole. (Ramsden 1992: 43, cited in Vickers 2000: 52)

Without the development of critical police leaders, Vickers argues that police organisations will miss out on a number of opportunities, including the ability to: identify and challenge unexamined assumptions; imagine and explore useful and previously acknowledged alternatives; and challenge and understand the importance of context in any situation. While improving the calibre of police leaders, encouragement of more higher educational training among police officers may also serve to strengthen the role of women in policing. Research by Heidensohn (1992, 2000), Wimshurst (1995) and McGuigan *et al.* (2002) has reported that, in academic terms, women tend to be better equipped than their male counterparts. Given such findings, the movement towards greater professionalism through a growing investment in education in policing provides grounds for an optimistic future for women in policing. In much the same way that early pioneer policewomen exploited the opportunities brought about by the conditions created by the First World War to expand their numbers, their modern pioneering counterparts should also seize the opportunities offered in the current climate of growing credentialism. In this sense, women are in a good position to be able to contribute to the professionalising project of the police.

In trying to produce a more realistic account of change, I have also urged a greater appreciation of the wider context within which change occurs. Although not necessarily predictive of the future success or failure of equality programmes, greater attention to the nature and level of state feminism will allow for more accurate readings of what achievements might be possible. In reflecting on the major transformations in policing that took place in the very early part of this century and again during the late 1960s and 1970s, Heidensohn (1992) reminds us that these were best characterised as periods of 'active and vocal' feminism. Currently, the Netherlands, Australia, and Sweden all have 'femocrats', state sponsored networks and a strong culture of equal opportunities. In Britain, the New Labour government has done much to encourage a greater confidence in the future of equality initiatives. While there are good grounds for embracing this optimism, adopting a more cautious approach will enable us to remain alert to the unpredictable nature of change. According to a recent internal brief from the government's Women and Equality Unit, attempts to recruit more women to take up posts on public bodies are failing, with the plan to achieve a 50:50 ratio of women and men now being extended until 2020 (*Guardian* 13/2/03). Indeed, the government itself looks set to fall short of its own target of 35 per cent women MPs by the next election. The ability to engage long-lasting and meaningful support for equality initiatives inside government looks somewhat less certain.

The shifting and changeable nature of the 'field' suggests that the fight for a place in policing must continue to come from women themselves. Brown (2003) points to the potential of the Gender Agenda in reforming working practices within the police. Despite this potential, she remains cynical about its abilities to do so, suggesting that based on past experience, the police occupational culture will absorb and neutralise such an attempt at reform. In order to ensure that real change occurs, she urges a more radical shift towards better styles of leadership and greater numbers of women at senior rank. In the same way that Adlam (2003b) has argued that police management education requires a strong theoretical base from which to operate, so too do the initiatives of change. If initiatives such as the Gender Agenda are to have any chance of real and long lasting success, their work needs to be underpinned by a stronger philosophical position informed by a feminist theory of structural oppression.

The mantra of calling for more women, more minority groups, to engage in the policing task will no doubt provide useful currency for those dealing with the aftermath of organisational crises that continue to plague the police. The most recent critique of 'macho' policing is reported by Heidensohn (2003) who cites Lord Laming's report into the murder of eight-year-old Victoria Climbié. In his report, Lord Laming identifies a number of management failures across a range of organisations responsible for child protection. With particular reference to the police organisation, he notes the low status awarded to child protection work within policing. As one senior officer told the Inquiry:

> there was a significant amount of 'macho nonsense' in the force concerning the work of Child Protection Teams, which were sometimes referred to in a derogatory way such as 'cardigan squads'. One of the consequences of this low status was that the best detectives would be put off from applying to join these teams. (Laming 2003: 334, cited in Heidensohn 2003: 25)

Recruitment of more female officers and of more female senior managers will not in and of itself impact upon the deep-rooted gendered assumptions on which policing, more generally, and management practice, more specifically, are based. To achieve meaningful change within policing, we need to think beyond the numerical. The call for more women, however, continues to be made in the absence of more sophisticated analyses of the reasons why such outcomes are desirable to us as a community. Heidensohn (2003) points to the strength of works carried out by the National Centre for Women and Policing (NCWP) in the US. Recent works have highlighted the higher economic costs of employing men over women in the task of policing. Studies have suggested that 'the average male officer on a big city police agency cost taxpayers somewhere between two and a half and five and half times more than the average woman officer in excessive force liability lawsuit payouts' (NCWP 2002, cited in Heidensohn 2003: 29). A cost benefit analysis of employing more women in policing is particularly welcome. It could provide the necessary evidence and rationale for encouraging more women into policing and for shifting the conceptualisation of police work as men's work. It will also no doubt appeal to those involved in promoting quality of service and value for money in policing.

The perception that women managers enter organisations with the intention of representing other women and their interests is naïve. This will depend on their consciousness, their reading of the situation, and their willingness to take action to address organisational inequalities. The fact that the majority of senior policewomen rejected feminist identification, and that most of those who did accept it were liberal feminists pushing for progress within existing systems, means that most respondents lack the conceptual vocabulary to analyse the overall situation for women in policing. Without access to such a feminist theory, strategies based around representation and retention issues will do little to change women's experience of policing. Together with this, an approach that emphasises success through achieving merit and competence continues to foster the myth that if women work hard(er) they will succeed. The rejection of the idea that social structures mediate women's professional achievement in policing meshes with the effective social stigmatisation of the feminist to ensure that radical gendered change will be rejected before it even begins. Without a more radical and systematic critique of women's position in policing, and openness to feminist ideas about these issues, long-term change and improvement for women is unlikely to take place.

While it may be true that the glass ceiling in policing has been cracked, as Yearnshire (2002: 5) reminds us 'the cracks by the small number of women who do achieve, soon repair themselves'. In order to develop a stronger gender consciousness within the police organisation, the benefits of sharing experiences through both single and mixed-sex networking need to be exploited more boldly. Networking as broadly as possible with both men and other groups in policing will allow women the broadest platform from which to engage support. At the same time, women who have broken through the glass ceiling need to be willing to act as mentors and role models for those officers who follow in their footsteps. Senior policewomen need to take an active and lead role in emphasising the importance of challenging the gendered order that continues to govern policing. More specifically, they need to find a way to reach those officers, both women and men, who seem disinterested in gender issues. The challenge will also be to harness the support of those officers who might be the current beneficiaries of improved equal opportunities policies and institutional arrangements. For these officers, the battle for equality might seem to have already been won, and as a result they are less willing to engage with such issues. Senior policewomen's task then is a formidable one – to make known the inconspicuous yet strongly embedded forms of gendered discrimination that officers might encounter as they rise through the ranks.

References and further reading

Acker, J. (1989) *Doing Comparable Worth: Gender, Class and Pay Equity*, Philadelphia: Temple University Press.

Acker, J. (1990) 'Hierarchies, jobs, bodies: a theory of gendered organisations', *Gender and Society*, vol. 4, no. 2, pp. 139–58.

Acker, J. (1992) 'Gendering organizational theory' in Mills, A. and Tancred, P. (eds.) *Gendering Organizational Analysis*, London: Sage.

Acker, J. (1998) 'The future of "gender and organization": connections and boundaries', *Gender, Work and Organisation*, vol. 5, no. 4, pp. 195–206.

Acker, J. and Van Houten, D. R. (1992) 'Differential recruitment and control: the sex structuring of organisations' in Mills, A. and Tancred, P. (eds.) *Gendering Organizational Analysis*, London: Sage.

Acker, J., Barry, J. and Esseveld, K. (1983) 'Issues in feminist research', *Women's Studies International Forum*, vol. 6, no. 4, pp. 423–35.

ACPO (1990) *Strategic Policy Document: Setting the Standards for Policing: Meeting Community Expectations*, London: New Scotland Yard.

ACPO (1993) *Quality of Service Committee Getting Things Right*, London: New Scotland Yard.

ACWAP (2002) http://www.auspol-women.asn.au/council.html

Adams, K. (2001) *Women in Senior Police Management*, Payneham, South Australia: Australasian Centre for Police Research.

Adlam, R. (2002) 'Governmental rationalites in police leadership: an essay exploring some of the "deep structure" in police leadership praxis', *Policing and Society*, vol. 12, no. 1, pp. 15–36.

Adlam, R. (2003a) 'Nice people, big questions, heritage concepts' in Adlam, R. and Villiers, P. (eds.) *Police Leadership in the Twenty-first Century: Philosophy, Doctrine, and Developments*, Winchester: Waterside Press.

Adlam, R. (2003b) 'This complex thing, leadership' in Adlam, R. and Villiers, P. (eds.) *Police Leadership in the Twenty-first Century: Philosophy, Doctrine and Developments*, Winchester: Waterside Press.

Adlam, R. and Villiers, P. (eds.) (2003) *Police Leadership in the Twenty-first Century: Philosophy, Doctrine and Developments*, Winchester: Waterside Press.

Alderson, J. (2003) 'Police leadership' in Adlam, R. and Villiers, P. (eds.) *Police Leadership in the Twenty-first Century: Philosophy, Doctrine and Developments*, Winchester: Waterside Press.

Allen, M. (1925) *The Pioneer Policewoman*, London: Chatto and Windus.

Alimo-Metcalfe, B. (1995) 'An investigation of female and male constructs of leadership and empowerment', *Women in Management Review*, vol. 10, no. 2, pp. 3–8.

Anderson, R., Brown, J. and Campbell, E. (1993) *Aspects of Sex Discrimination within the Police Service in England and Wales*, London: Home Office Police Research Group.

Anthias, F. and Yuval-Davis, N. (1993) *Racialized Boundaries*, London: Routledge.

Appier, J. (1998) *The Sexual Politics of Law Enforcement and the LAPD*, Philadelphia: Temple University Press.

Audit Commission (1990) *Effective Policing: Performance Review in Police Forces. Police Paper 8*, London: Audit Commission.

Avolio, B. (1999) *Full Leadership Development*, London: Sage.

Baker Miller, J. (1988) *Toward a New Psychology of Women*, Boston, MA: Beacon Press.

Balkin, J. (1988) 'Why policemen don't like policewomen', *Journal of Police Science and Administration*, vol. 16, no. 1, pp. 29–36.

Baril, G., Elbert, N., Mahar-Porter, M. and Reavy, G. (1989) 'Are androgynous managers really more effective?', *Group and Organizational Studies*, vol. 14, no. 2, pp. 234–49.

Barker, H. (1986) 'Recapturing sisterhood: a critical look at "process" in feminist organising and community work', *Critical Social Policy*, vol. 16, pp. 80–90.

Baron, J. N. and Davis-Blake, A. (1986) 'The structure of opportunity: how far promotion ladders vary within and among organisations', *Administrative Science Quarterly*, vol. 31, pp. 248–73.

Barry, C. (1998) 'Choosing qualitative data analysis software', *Sociological Research Online*, vol. 3, no. 3: http://www.socresonline.org.uk/3/3/4/html

Bartlett, K. T. (1990) 'Feminist legal methods', *Harvard Law Review*, vol. 103, pp. 829–88.

Bass, B. M. and Avolio, B. (1990) *Transformational Leadership Developments*, Palo Alto, CA: Consulting Psychologists Press.

Bate, P. (1996) *Strategies for Cultural Change*, Oxford: Butterworth Heinemann.

BAWP (2002) *The Gender Agenda*, London: British Association of Women Police.

BAWP (2003) *Gender Agenda Force Survey Report*, London: British Association of Women Police.

Baxter, J. and Wright, E. O. (2000) 'The glass ceiling hypothesis: a comparative study of the United States, Sweden and Australia', *Gender and Society*, vol. 14, no. 2, pp. 275–94.

Bayley, D. H. (1985) *Patterns of Policing: A Comparative Analysis*, New Brunswick: Rutgers University Press.

Bayley, D. H. (1991) *Forces of Order: Police Behaviour in Japan and the United States*. Berkeley, CA: University of California Press.

Bayley, D. H. (1994) *Police for the Future*, New York: Oxford University Press.

Bayley, D. H. (1999) 'Policing the world stage' in Mawby, R. (ed.) *Policing Across the World: Issues for the Twenty-first Century*, London: UCL Press.

Bayley, D. H. and Shearing, C. (1996) 'The future of policing', *Law and Society Review*, vol. 30, no. 3, pp. 285–606.

Beck, U., Giddens, A. and Lash, S. (1994) *Reflexive Modernization*, Cambridge: Polity Press.

Belknap, J. and Shelley, J. K. (1992) 'The new lone ranger: policewomen on patrol', *American Journal of Police*, vol. 12, pp. 47–75.

Bell, C. and Roberts, H. (1984) (eds.) *Social Researching: Politics, Problems, Practice*, London: Routledge.

Bell, D. J. (1982) 'Policewomen: myths and reality', *Journal of Police Science and Administration*, vol. 10, no. 1, pp. 112–20.

Ben-Tovim, G., Gabriel, J., Law, I. and Streder, K. (1992) 'A political analysis of local struggles for racial equality' in Braham, P. H., Rattansi, A. and Skellington, R. (eds.) *Racism and Antiracism*, Buckingham: Open University Press.

Bernard, H. R. (1994) *Research Methods in Anthropology*, Newbury Park, CA: Sage.

Bielby, W. T. and Baron, J. N. (1987) 'Men and women at work: sex segregation and statistical discrimination', *American Journal of Sociology*, vol. 91, pp. 759–99.

Billing, Y. and Alvesson, M. (2000) 'Questioning the notion of a feminine leadership: a critical perspective on the gender labelling of leadership', *Gender, Work and Organization*, vol. 7, no. 3, pp. 144–57.

Blair, I. (2003) 'Leadership that learns' in Adlam, R. and Villiers, P. (eds.) *Police Leadership in the Twenty-first Century: Philosophy, Doctrine and Developments*, Winchester: Waterside Press.

Blakemore, J. L., Barlow, D. and Padgett, D. (1995) 'From the classroom to the community: introducing process in police diversity training', *Police Studies*, vol. 18, no. 1, pp. 71–83.

Bland, L. (1985) 'In the name of protection: the policing of women in the First World War' in Brophy, L. and Smart, C. (eds.) *Women in Law*, London: Routledge.

Bland, N., Mundy, G., Russell, J. and Tuffin, R. (1999) *Career Progression of Ethnic Minority Police Officers*, Police Research Series Paper 107, London: Home Office.

Bloch, P. and Anderson, D. (1973) *Policewomen on Patrol: Major Findings: First Report*, Washington, DC: Police Foundation.

Bourlet, A. (1990) *Police Intervention in Marital Violence*, Buckingham: Open University Press.

Bowling, B. and Phillips, C. (2002) *Racism, Crime and Justice*, London: Longman.

Boyd, M., Mulvihill, M. and Myles, J. (1991) 'Gender, power and post-industrialism', *Canadian Review of Sociology and Anthropology*, vol. 28, pp. 407–36.

Brandser, G. C. (1996) 'Women – the new heroes of the business world?', *Women in Management Review*, vol. 11, no. 2, pp. 3–17.

Brazil, W. (1978) 'The attorney as victim: toward more candour about the psychological price tag of litigation practice', *Journal of the Legal Profession*, vol. 3, pp. 107–17.

Brewer, J. (1990) 'Sensitivity as a problem in field research', *American Behavioural Scientist*, vol. 33, no. 5, pp. 578–93.

Brewer, J. (1991) 'Hercules, Hippolyte and the Amazons – or policewomen in the RUC', *British Journal of Sociology*, vol. 42, no. 2, pp. 231–47.

Bridges, W. (1995) *Jobshift: How to Prosper in a Workplace Without Jobs*, London: Nicholas Brealey.

Brittan, A. (1989) *Masculinity and Power*, Oxford: Blackwell.

Britton, D. (1997) 'Gendered organizational logic: policy and practice in men's and women's prison', *Gender and Society*, vol. 11, no. 6, pp. 796–818.

Brown, J. (1992) 'Changing the police culture', *Policing*, vol. 8, pp. 307–23.

Brown, J. (1994) 'Equality environment in the Central Scotland Police', Paper presented at an equal opportunities seminar, Stirling: Central Scotland Police, 12–13 May.

Brown, J. (1995) 'Networking in Europe', *Newsletter of the European Network*, vol. 1, pp. 2–4.

Brown, J. (1996) 'Police research: some critical reflections' in Leisham, F., Loveday, B. and Savage, S. (eds.) *Core Issues in Policing*, London: Longman.

Brown, J. (1997a) 'Equal opportunities and the police in England and Wales, past, present and future possibilities' in Francis, P., Davies, P. and Jupp, V. (eds.) *Policing Futures*, Macmillan: London.

Brown, J. (1997b) 'European policewomen: a comparative research perspective', *International Journal of the Sociology of Law*, vol. 25, no. 1, pp. 1–19.

Brown, J. (1998) 'Aspects of discriminatory treatment of women police officers serving in forces in England and Wales', *British Journal of Criminology*, vol. 38, no. 2, pp. 265–83.

Brown, J. (2002) 'You can't have it both ways: being an officer and a lady (woman) in a male dominated occupation', Paper presented at *Women and Policing Globally Conference*, Canberra, Australia, 20–23 October 2002.

Brown, J. (2003) 'Women leaders: A catalyst for change' in Adlam, R. and Villiers, P. (eds.) *Police Leadership in the Twenty-first Century: Philosophy, Doctrine and Developments*, Winchester: Waterside Press.

Brown, J. and Campell, E. (1991) 'Less than equal', *Policing*, vol. 7, pp. 324–34.

Brown, J. and Funelle, R. (1993) *Rank and Role Disposition of Ethnic Minority Officers in England and Wales*, Winchester: Hampshire Constabulary.

Brown, J., Maidment, A. and Bull, R. (1993) 'Appropriate skill-task matching or gender bias in deployment of male and female police officers?', *Policing and Society*, vol. 3, no. 1, pp. 121–36.

Brown, J., Hazenberg, A. and Ormiston, C. (1999) 'Policewomen: an international comparison' in Mawby, R. (eds.) *Policing Across the World: Issues for the Twenty-first Century*, London: UCL Press.

Brown, J. and Heidensohn, F. (2000) *Gender and Policing*, London: Macmillan.

Bruijn, J. and Cyba, E. (eds.) (1994) *Gender and Organisations – Changing Perspectives*, Amsterdam: VU University Press.

Brumlop, E. (1994) 'Women at the top – more than just a passing fad' in Bruijn, J. and Cyba, E. (eds.) *Gender and Organisations – Changing Perspectives*, Amsterdam: VU University Press.

Brunskill, H. (1998) 'Feminist methodology' in Seale, C. (ed.) *Researching Society and Culture*, London: Sage.

Bryant, L., Dunkerely, D. and Kelland, G. (1995) 'One of the boys?', *Policing*, vol. 1, no. 4, pp. 236–44.

Bryett, K. (1999) 'The policing dynamic', *Policing: An International Journal of Police Strategies and Management*, vol. 22, no. 1, pp. 30–44.

Bryman, A. (1992) *Charisma and Leadership in Organizations*, London: Sage.

Bull, R. and Horncastle, P. (1989) 'An evaluation of human awareness training' in Morgan, R. and Smith, D. J. (eds.) *Coming to Terms with Policing*, London: Routledge.

Bunyard, R. (2003) 'Justice, integrity and corruption' in Adlam, R. and Villiers, P. (eds.) *Police Leadership in the Twenty-first Century: Philosophy, Doctrine and Developments*, Winchester: Waterside Press.

Burke, M. E. (1992) 'Cop culture and homosexuality', *The Police Journal*, January, pp. 30–9.

Burke, M. E. (1993) *Coming out of the Blue*, London: Cassell.

Burris, B. (1996) 'Technocracy, patriarchy and management' in Collinson, D. and Hearn, J. (eds.) *Men as Managers, Managers as Men*, London: Sage.

Burton, C. (1992) 'Merit and gender: organizations and the mobilization of masculine bias' in Mills, A. and Tancred, P. (eds.) *Gendering Organizational Analysis*, London: Sage.

Butler, A. J. P. (1996) 'Managing the future: a Chief Constable's view' in Leisham, F., Loveday, B. and Savage, S. (eds.) *Core Issues in Policing*, Essex: Longman.

Cain, M. (1973) *Society and the Policeman's Role*, London: Routledge.

Cancian, F. (1987) *Love in America: Gender and Self-Development*, Cambridge: Cambridge University Press.

Carrier, J. (1988) *The Campaign for the Employment of Women as Police Officers*, Aldershot: Avebury Gower.

CEDAW (1999) *United Nations Convention on the Elimination of all forms of Discrimination against Women (CEDAW)*, London: HMSO.

Chan, J. B. L. (1996) 'Changing police culture', *British Journal of Criminology*, vol. 36, no. 1, pp. 109–34.

Chan, J. B. L. (1997) *Changing Police Culture: Policing in a Multicultural Society*, Cambridge: Cambridge University Press.

Chapman, J. (1993) *Politics, Feminism and the Reformation of Gender*, London: Routledge.

Charman, S., Savage, S. and Cope, S. (1999) 'Getting to the top: selection and training for senior managers in the police service', *Social Policy and Administration*, vol. 33, no. 3, pp. 281–301.

Chase, S. (1995) 'Taking narrative seriously: consequences for method and theory in interview studies' in Josselson, R. and Lieblich, A. (eds.) *Inter-preting Experience: The Narrative Study of Lives*, Newbury Park, CA: Sage.

Cheng, C. (ed.) (1996) *Masculinities in Organizations*, London: Sage.

Christopher, W. (1991) *Report of the Independent Commission on the Los Angeles Police Department*, Los Angeles.

Clarke, J., Cochrane, A. and McLaughlin, E. (eds.) (1994) *Managing Social Policy*, London: Sage.

Clarke, J. and Newman, J. (1993) 'Managing to survive: dilemmas of changing organisational forms in the public sector' in Deakin, N. and Page, R. (eds.) *The Costs of Welfare*, Aldershot: Avebury.

Cockburn, C. (1983) *Brothers: Male Dominance and Technological Change*, London: Pluto.

Cockburn, C. (1985) *Machinery of Dominance: Women, Men and Technical Know-How*, London: Pluto.

Cockburn, C. (1988) 'The gendering of jobs: workplace relations and the reproduction of sex segregation' in Walby, W. (ed.) *Gender Segregation at Work*, Buckingham: Open University Press.

Cockburn, C. (1991) *In the Way of Women: Men's Resistance to Sex Equality in Organizations*, London: Macmillan.

Coe, T. (1992) *The Key to the Men's Club*, Corby: Institute of Management.

Coffey, S., Brown, J. and Savage, S. (1992) 'Policewomen's career aspirations: some reflections on the roles of and capabilities of women in policing in Great Britain', *Police Studies*, vol. 15, no. 1, pp. 13–19.

Coffey, A., Holbrook, B. and Atkinson, P. (1996) 'Qualitative data analysis: technologies and representations', *Sociological Research Online*, vol. 1, no. 1: http://www.socresonline.org.uk.uk/1/1/4.html

Cohn, S. (1985) *The Feminization of Clerical Labor in Great Britain*, Philadelphia: Temple University Press.

Colgan, F. and Ledwith, S. (1996) 'Women as organisational change agents' in Ledwith, S. and Colgan, F. (eds.) *Women in Organisations: Challenging Gender Politics*, London: Macmillan.

Colgan, F., Johnstone, S. and Shaw, S. (1996) 'On the move – women in Toronto public transport sector' in Ledwith, S. and Colgan, F. (eds.) *Women in Organisations: Challenging Gender Politics*, London: Macmillan.

Collins, H. (1992) *Equality Matters: Equal Opportunities in the 1990s: Background and Current Issues*, London: Library Association.

Collins, P. H., Maldonado, L. A., Takagi, D. Y., Thorne, B., Weber, L. and Winant, H. (1995) 'Symposium on West and Fenstermaker's "Doing Difference"', *Gender and Society*, vol. 9, no. 4, pp. 491–513.

Collins, P. (1998) 'Negotiating selves: reflections on 'unstructured' interviewing' *Sociological Research Online*, vol. 3, no. 3: http://www.socresonline.org.uk/socresonline/3/3/2.html

Collinson, D. and Collinson, M. (1989) 'Sexuality in the workplace: the domination of men's sexuality' in Hearn, J., Sheppard, D. L., Tancred-Sheriff, P. and Burrell, G. (eds.) *The Sexuality of Organizations*, London: Sage.

Collinson, D. and Hearn, J. (1994) 'Naming men as men: implications for work, organization and management', *Gender, Work and Organization*, vol. 1, no. 1, pp. 2–21.

Conger, J. and Kanungo, R. (1998) *Charismatic Leadership in Organisations*, London: Sage.

Connell, R. (1987) *Gender and Power: Society, the Person and Sexual Politics*, Stanford, CA: Stanford University Press.

Cowper, T. (2000) 'The myth of the "military model" of leadership in law enforcement', *Police Quarterly*, vol. 3, no. 3, pp. 228–46.

Coyle, A. (1988) 'The limits of change: local government and equal opportunities for women', *Public Administration*, vol. 67, pp. 39–50.

Coyle, A. (1995) *Women and Organisational Change*, Manchester: Equal Opportunities Commission.

Crank, J. P. (1998) *Understanding Police Culture*, Cincinnati, OH: Anderson.

Crawford, A., Jones, T., Woodhouse, T. and Young, J. (1990) *The Second Islington Crime Survey*, London: Middlesex Centre for Criminology.

Critchley, T. (1978) *A History of Police in England and Wales*, London: Constable.

Cromack, V. (1995) 'The policing of domestic violence: an empirical study', *Policing and Society*, vol. 5, no. 3, pp. 185–99.

Crompton, R., Gallie, D. and Purcell, K. (eds.) (1996) *Changing Forms of Employment: Organisations, Skills and Gender*, London: Routledge.

Crowther, C. (2000) 'Thinking about the "underclass"', *Theoretical Criminology*, vol. 4, no. 2, pp. 149–67.

Cunningham, R., Lord, A. and Delaney, L. (1999) 'Next steps for equality? The impact of organizational change on opportunities for women in the civil service', *Gender, Work and Organization*, vol. 6, no. 2, pp. 67–78.

Dahlerup, D. (1992) 'From a small to a large minority: women in Scandinavian politics', *Scandinavian Political Studies*, vol. 11, no. 4, pp. 21–39.

Davies, A. (1998) *The Restructuring of Police Forces: Implications for Command Resilience*, Pangbourne: Police Superintendents' Association of England and Wales.

Davies, C. (1982) 'Sexual taboos and social boundaries', *American Journal of Sociology*, vol. 87, pp. 1032–63.

De La Garde, G. and Arney, E. (1998) 'The evaluation of police training', *The Police Journal*, vol. LXXI, no. 4, pp. 284–96.

DeMatteo, L. A. and Stern, L. N. (1994) 'From hierarchy to unity between men and women managers: towards an androgynous style of management', *Women in Management Review*, vol. 9, no. 7, pp. 21–8.

Densten, I. (1999) 'Senior Australian Law enforcement leadership under examination' *Policing: An International Journal of Police Strategies and Management*, vol. 22, no. 1, pp. 45–57.

Dixon, B. and Stanko, E. (1995) 'Sector policing and public accountability', *Policing and Society*, vol. 5, no. 3, pp. 171–83.

Dobbins, G. and Platz, S. J. (1986) 'Sex differences in leadership: how real are they?', *Academy of Management Review*, vol. 1, no. 11, pp. 118–27.

Donnell, S. M. and Hall, J. (1980) 'Men and women as managers: a significant case of no difference', *Organisational Dynamics*, vol. 1, no. 6, pp. 67–71.

Drodge, E. N. and Murphy, S. A. (2002) 'Interrogating emotions in police leadership', *Human Resource Development Review*, vol. 1, no. 4, pp. 420–38.

Dunphy, D. C. and Stace, D. A. (1988) 'Transformational and coercive strategies for planned organisational change: beyond the OD model', *Organisation Studies*, vol. 9, no. 3, pp. 317–34.

Edwards, S. (1989) *Policing Domestic Violence*, London: Sage.

Edwards, S. (1994) 'Domestic violence and sexual assault' in Stephens, M. and Becker, S. (eds.) *Police Force, Police Service: Care and Control in Britain*, London: Macmillan.

Eisenstein, H. (1985) 'The gender of bureaucracy: reflections of feminism and the state' in Goodnow, J. and Pateman, C. (eds.) *Women, Social Science and Public Policy*, Sydney: Allen and Unwin.

Ely, R. J. (1996) 'The role of the dominant identity' in Jackson, S. and Ruderman, M. (eds.) *Diversity in Work Teams*, Washington, DC: American Psychology Association.

Emsley, C. (1996) *The English Police: A Political and Social History* (2nd edn), London: Longman.

England, P. (1989) 'A feminist critique of rational-choice theories: implications for sociology', *The American Sociologist*, vol. 20, pp. 14–28.

ENP (1998) *European Network of Policewomen*, Netherlands: European Network of Policewomen: http://www.enp.nl

EOC (2002) *Women in Parliament: A Comparative Analysis*, Manchester: Equal Opportunities Commission.

Equal Opportunities Unit (1992) *Guide to Part-time Working for Police Officers – Experimental Scheme*, London: Metropolitan Police Service.

Equal Opportunities Unit (1993) *Equal Opportunities: A Collection of Documents*, London: Metropolitan Police Service.

Ericson, R. (1994) 'The division of expert knowledge in policing and security', *British Journal of Sociology*, vol. 45, no. 2, pp. 149–75.

Ericson, R. and Haggerty, D. (1997) *Policing the Risk Society*, Oxford: Oxford University Press.

Evetts, J. (1998) 'Gender and career in engineering', Working paper 122, Nottingham: University of Nottingham.

Feinman, C. (1986) 'Women in law enforcement' in Feinman, C. (ed.) *Women in the Criminal Justice System* (2nd edn), New York: Praeger.

Felknes, G. and Schroedel, F. (1993) 'A case study of minority women in policing', *Women and Criminal Justice*, vol. 4, no. 1, pp. 65–89.

Feminist Majority Foundation (1995) 'FMF launches National Centre for Women and Policing', *Feminist Majority Newsletter*, vol. 7, no. 1: http://www.feminist.org/news/newsletters.html

Feminist Majority Foundation (1997) 'Women redesign policing', *Feminist Majority Newsletter*, vol. 8, no. 2: http://www.feminist.org/news/newsletters.html

Ferguson, K. (1984) *The Feminist Case Against Bureaucracy*, Philadelphia: Temple University Press.

Ferrario, M. (1994) 'Women as managerial leaders' in Davidson, M. J. and Burke, R. (eds.) *Women in Management: Current Research Issues*, London: Paul Chapman Publishing.

Fielding, N. (1988) *Joining Forces: Police Training, Socialisation and Occupational Competence*, London: Routledge.

Fielding, N. (1994a) 'Cop canteen culture' in Newburn, T. and Stanko, E. (eds.) *Just Boys Doing the Business: Men, Masculinity and Crime*, London: Routledge.

Fielding, N. (1994b) 'The organizational and occupational troubles of community police', *Policing and Society*, vol. 4, no. 4, pp. 305–22.

Fielding, N. (1995) *Community Policing – Clarendon Studies in Criminology*, Oxford: Clarendon Press.

Fielding, N. (1999) 'Policing's dark secret: the career paths of ethnic minority officers', *Sociological Research Online*, vol. 4, no. 1: http://www.socresonline.org.uk/socresonline/4/lawrence/fielding.html

Fielding, N. and Fielding, J. (1992) 'A comparative minority: female recruits to a British constabulary force', *Policing and Society*, vol. 2, no. 3, pp. 205–18.

Fitzgerald, A. (1989) *Report of a Commission of Inquiry Pursuant to Orders in Council: Commission of Inquiry into Possible Illegal Activities and Associated Police Misconduct*, Brisbane: Queensland Government Printer.

Fleming, J. and Lafferty, G. (2002) 'Equality confounded? New managerialism, organisational restructuring and women in Australian police services', Paper presented at *Women and Policing Globally Conference*, Canberra, Australia, 20–23 October.

Flynn, E. E. (1982) 'Women as criminal justice professionals: a challenge to change tradition' in Rafter, N. H. and Stanko, E. (eds.) *Judge, Lawyer, Victim, Thief: Women, Gender Roles and Criminal Justice*, Boston, MA: Northeastern University Press.

Foster, J. (1989) 'Two stations: an ethnographic analysis of policing in the inner city' in Downes, D. (ed.) *Crime and the City*, London: Macmillan.

Foster, J. (1999) 'Talking the talk: walking the walk', Paper presented at *British Society of Criminology Southern Branch Seminars*, London, 22 March.

Francis, P., Davies, P. and Jupp, V. (eds.) (1997) *Policing Futures: The Police, Law Enforcement and the Twenty-First Century*, London: Macmillan.

French, K. (1992) 'Men and locations of power, why move over?' in Itzen, C. and Newman, J. (eds.) (1995) *Gender, Culture and Organizational Change*, London: Routledge.

Gaston, K. C. and Alexander, J. A. (1997) 'Women in the police: factors influencing managerial advancement', *Women in Management Review*, vol. 12, no. 2, pp. 47–55.

Gelsthorpe, L. (1990) 'Feminist methodology in criminology: a new approach or old wine in new bottles?' in Gelsthorpe, L. and Morris, A. (eds.) *Feminist Perspectives in Criminology*, Buckingham: Open University Press.

Gherardi, S. (1995) *Gender, Symbolism and Organizational Cultures*, London: Sage.

Giddens, A. (1984) *The Constitution of Society: Outline of the Theory of Structuration*, Berkeley, CA: University of California Press.

Giddens, A. (1990) *The Consequences of Modernity*, Oxford: Polity Press.

Glucksmann, M. A. (1995) 'Why work? Gender and the total social organization of labour', *Gender, Work and Organization*, vol. 2, no. 2, pp. 63–75.

Gold, M. E. (2000) 'The progress of women in policing', *Law and Order*, vol. 48, no. 6, pp. 159–61.

Gooch, L. and Ledwith, S. (1996) 'Women in personnel management – re-visioning of a handmaiden's role?' in Ledwith, S. and Colgan, F. (eds.) *Women in Organisations: Challenging Gender Politics*, London: Macmillan.

Goode, J. and Bagihole, B. (1998) 'The social construction of gendered equal opportunities in UK universities: a case study of women technicians', *Critical Social Policy*, vol. 18, no. 2, pp. 175–92.

Grace, S. (1995) *Policing Domestic Violence in the 1990s*, Home Office Research Study no. 139, London: HMSO.

Grant, J. (1988) 'Women as managers: what they can offer to organisations', *Organisational Dynamics*, vol. 16, no. 3, pp. 56–63.

Grant, J. (1993) *Fundamental Feminism*, New York: Routledge.

Gregory, J. and Lees, S. (1999) *Policing Sexual Assault*, London: Routledge.

Grennan, S. A. (1987) 'Findings on the role of officer gender in violent encounters with citizens', *Journal of Police Science and Administration*, vol. 15, pp. 78–85.

Halford, A. (1987) 'Until the 12th of Never', *Police Review*, vol. 2109, 9 October.

Halford, A. (1993) *No Way Up the Greasy Pole*, London: Constable.

Halford, S., Savage, M. and Witz, A. (1997) *Gender, Career and Organisations: Current Developments in Banking, Nursing and Local Government*, London: Macmillan.

Hall, E. (1993) 'Smiling, deferring, and flirting: doing gender by giving "good service" ', *Work and Occupations*, vol. 20, no. 4, pp. 452–71.

Handy, C. (1991) *Gods of Management: The Changing Work of Organisations*, London: Arrow Books.

Handy, C. (1994) *The Empty Raincoat*, London: Hutchinson.

Hanmer, J. and Maynard, M. (eds.) (1987) *Women, Violence and Social Control*, London: Macmillan.

Hanmer, J. and Saunders, S. (1990) *Women, Violence and Crime Prevention: A Study of Changes in Police and Practices in West Yorkshire*, Violence, Abuse and Gender Relations Unit Research Paper 1, Bradford: Bradford University.

Hanmer, J. and Saunders, S. (1991) 'Policing violence against women: implementing policy changes', Paper presented to the *British Criminology Conference York*, July.

Hanmer, J., Griffiths, S. and Jerwood, D. (1999) *Arresting Evidence: Domestic Violence and Repeat Victimisation*, Research Paper 104, London: Police and Reducing Crime Unit, Home Office.

Hanmer, J., Radford, J. and Stanko, E. (eds.) (1989) *Women, Policing and Male Violence*, London: Routledge.

Hansard Society Commission (1990) *The Report of the Hansard Society Commission on Women at the Top*, London: Hansard Society for Parliamentary Government.

Hantrais, L. and Walters, P. (1994) 'Making it in and making out: women in professional occupations in Britain and France', *Gender, Work and Organization*, vol. 1, no. 1, pp. 23–32.

Harding, S. (ed.) (1987) *Feminism and Methodology*, Buckingham: Open University Press.

Harlow, E. and Hearn, J. (1995) 'Cultural constructions: contrasting theories of organisational culture and gender construction', *Gender, Work and Organization*, vol. 2, no. 4, pp. 180–91.

Harlow, E., Hearn, J. and Parkin, W. (1995) 'Gendered noise: organizations and the silence and din' in Itzen, C. and Newman, J. (eds.) *Gender, Cultures and Organizational Change*, London: Routledge.

Hartley, S., Stevenson, K. and Rogerson, J. (2002) *Sex Differences in the OSPRE® Part II Assessment Centre*, Harrogate: Centrex.

Harris, J. M. (1995) *Messages Men Hear*, London: Taylor & Francis.

Hearn, J. (1992) *Men in the Public Eye*, London: Routledge.

Hearn, J. and Collinson, D. (eds.) (1996) *Managements and Men*, London: Sage.

Hearn, J. and Parkin, W. (1987) *'Sex' at 'Work': the Power and Paradox of Organization Sexuality*, New York: St Martin's Press.

Hearn, J. and Parkin, W. (1992) 'Gender and organizations: a selective review and a critique of a neglected area' in Mills, A. and Tancred, P. (eds.) *Gendering Organizational Analysis*, London: Sage.

Hearn, J., Sheppard, D. L., Tancred-Sheriff, P. and Burrell, G. (eds.) (1989) *The Sexuality of Organization*, London: Sage.

Hegelson, S. (1990) *The Female Advantage*, New York: Doubleday.

Heidensohn, F. (1989) *Women in Policing in the USA*, London: Police Federation.

Heidensohn, F. (1992) *Women in Control: The Role of Women in Law Enforcement*, Oxford: Oxford University Press.

Heidensohn, F. (1994a) 'From being to knowing: some issues in the study of gender in contemporary society', *Women and Criminal Justice*, vol. 6, pp. 13–37.

Heidensohn, F. (1994b) ' "We can handle it out here": women officers in Britain and the USA and the policing of public order', *Policing and Society*, vol. 4, no. 4, pp. 293–303.

Heidensohn, F. (1996a) 'Comparing charges: comparative studies of policing and gender', Paper presented at the *American Society of Criminology*, 20–23 November.

Heidensohn, F. (1996b) 'Making it even: equal opportunities and public order' in Critcher, C. and Waddington, D. (eds.) *Policing Public Order*, Aldershot: Avebury Press.

Heidensohn, F. (1998) 'Translations and refutations: an analysis of changing perspectives in criminology' in Holdaway, S. and Rock, P. (eds.) *Thinking about Criminology*, London: UCL Press.

Heidensohn, F. (2000) *Sexual Politics and Social Control*, Buckingham: Open University Press.

Heidensohn, F. (2003) 'Gender and policing' in Newburn, T. (ed.) *The Handbook of Policing*, Devon: Willan Publishing.

HMIC (1992) *Equal Opportunities in the Police Service*, London: HMSO.

HMIC (1993) *Thematic Inspection on Equal Opportunities*, London: Home Office.

HMIC (1994) *A Report of HMIC (into the) Cleveland Constabulary*, London: Home Office.

HMIC (1995) *Developing Diversity in the Police Service: Equal Opportunities Thematic Inspection Report*, London: Home Office.

Hochschild, A. (1973) 'Making it: marginality and obstacles to minority consciousness' in *Annals of the New York Academy of Science*, vol. 208, pp. 79–82.

Hochschild, A. (1983) *The Managed Heart: Commercialization of Human Feeling*, Berkeley, CA: University of California Press.

Hochschild, A. (1997) *The Time Bind: When Work becomes Home and Home becomes Work*, New York: Metropolitan Books.

Holdaway, S. (1983) *Inside the British Police*, Oxford: Basil Blackwell.

Holdaway, S. (1991) *Recruiting a Multiracial Police Force*, London: HMSO.

Holdaway, S. (1996) *The Racialisation of British Policing*, London: Macmillan.

Holdaway, S. and Barron, A. (1997) *Resigners: The Experience of Black and Asian Police Officers*, London: Macmillan.

Holdaway, S. and Parker, S. (1998) 'Policing women police: uniform patrol and representation in CID', *British Journal of Criminology*, vol. 38, no. 1, pp. 40–60.

Holdaway, S. and Rock, P. (1998) *Thinking about Criminology*, London: UCL Press.

Hollway, W. (1996) 'Masters and men in the transition from factory hands to sentimental workers' in Collinson, D. and Hearn, J. (eds.) *Men as Managers, Managers as Men*, London: Sage.

Homant, R. J. (1983) 'The impact of policewomen on community attitudes toward police', *Journal of Police Science and Administration*, vol. 11, pp. 16–22.

Homant, R. J. and Kennedy, D. B. (1985) 'Police perceptions of spouse abuse: a comparison of male and female officers', *Journal of Criminal Justice*, vol. 13, pp. 29–47.

Home Office (1983) Circular 114/1983, *Manpower, Effectiveness and Efficiency in the Police Service*, London: Home Office.

Home Office (1986) Circular 69/1986, *Violence Against Women: Treatment of Victims of Rape and Domestic Violence*, London: Home Office.

Home Office (1989) Circular 87/1989, *Equal Opportunities Policies in the Police Service*, London: Home Office.

Home Office (1989) *Higher Police Training and the Police Staff College: Home Affairs Committee*, Third Report, London: HMSO.

Home Office (1990) Circular 60/1990, *Domestic Violence*, London: Home Office.

Home Office (1991) Circular 98/1991, *Appointment to ACPO Ranks*, London: Home Office.

Home Office (1993) *Police Reform: A Police Service for the Twenty-First Century*, Cm 2281, London: HMSO.

Home Office (1995a) *Review of Police Core and Ancillary Tasks*, London: HMSO.

Home Office (1995b) *Chief Appointments in the Police Service: Guidelines on Selection Procedures*, London: HMSO.

Home Office (2000) Circular 19/2000, *Domestic Violence: Revised Circular to the Police*, London: Home Office.

Hopton, J. (1999) 'Militarism, masculism and managerialisation in the British public sector', *Journal of Gender Studies*, vol. 8, no. 1, pp. 71–82.

Hoskyns, C. (1994) 'Gender issues in international relations: the case of the European community', *Review of International Studies*, vol. 20, pp. 225–39.

Hough, M. (1985) 'Organization and resource management in the uniformed police' in Heal, K., Tarling, R. and Burrows, J. (eds.) *Policing Today*, London: HMSO.

House of Commons (2003) *Women in the House of Commons, Factsheet M4*, London: HMSO.

Hunt, J. (1984) 'The development of rapport through the negotiation of gender in field work among police', *Human Organization*, vol. 43, no. 4, pp. 283–96.

Hunt, J. (1990) 'The logic of sexism among police', *Women and Criminal Justice*, vol. 1, no. 2, pp. 3–30.

IAWP (2002) *A Brief History of the International Association of Women Police*: http://www.iawp.org/history.html

Irving, B. (1986) *Independent Evaluation of an Experiment in Neighbourhood Policing in Notting Hill*, London: Police Federation.

Itzen, C. and Newman, J. (eds.) (1995) *Gender, Culture and Organizational Change*, London: Routledge.

Itzen, C. and Phillipson, C. (1995) 'Gendered ageism: a double jeopardy for women in organizations' in Itzen, C. and Newman, J. (eds.) *Gender, Culture and Organizational Change*, London: Routledge.

Jackall, R. (1988) *Moral Mazes: The World of Corporate Managers*, New York: Oxford University Press.

Jefferson, T. (1988) 'Race, crime and policing', *International Journal of the Sociology of Law*, vol. 16, no. 4, pp. 521–39.

Jefferson, T. and Walker, M. (1992) 'Ethnic minorities in the criminal justice system', *Criminal Law Review*, vol. 81, no. 140, pp. 83–96.

Jenkins, C. (2000) 'Gender just', *Police Review*, vol. 108, pp. 22–3.

Johnston, L. (2000) *Policing Britain: Risk, Security and Governance*, Harlow: Longman.

Joint Consultative Committee of the Police Staff Associations (1990) *Operational Policing Review*, London: Police Federation.

Jones, S. (1986) *Policewomen and Inequality*, London: Macmillan.

Jones, T. and Newburn, T. (1997) *Policing After the Act: Police Governance after the Police and Magistrates' Courts Act 1994*, London: Policy Studies Institute.

Jones, T. and Newburn, T. (2002) 'The transformation of policing? Understanding current trends in policing systems', *British Journal of Criminology*, vol. 42, no. 1, pp. 129–46.

Jones, T., Newburn, T. and Smith, D. (1994) *Democracy and Policing*, London: Policy Studies Institute.

Jordan, J. (2002) 'Will any woman do? Police, gender and rape victims', *Policing: An International Journal of Police Strategies and Management*, vol. 25, no. 2, pp. 319–44.

Jurik, N. (1985) 'An officer and a lady: organizational barriers to women working as correctional officers in men's prisons', *Social Problems*, vol. 32, no. 3, pp. 375–88.

Jurik, N. (1988) 'Striking a balance: female correctional officers, gender role stereotypes, and male prisons', *Sociological Inquiry*, vol. 58, pp. 291–305.

Kanter, R. M. (1977) *Men and Women of the Corporation*, New York: Basic Books.

Kennedy, D. B. and Homant, R. J. (1981) 'Non-traditional role assumption and the personality of the policewoman', *Journal of Police Science and Administration*, vol. 9, pp. 346–55.

Kerfoot, D. and Knights, D. (1993) 'Management, masculinity and manipulation: from paternalism to corporate strategy in financial services in Britain', *Journal of Management Studies*, vol. 30, no. 4, pp. 659–77.

Kessler, S., Ashensden, D., Connell, R. and Dowsett, G. (1985) 'Gender relations in secondary schooling', *Sociology of Education*, vol. 58, pp. 46–69.

Kiesler, S., Sproull, L. and Eccles, J. S. (1985) 'Pool halls, chips, and war games: women in the culture of computing', *Psychology of Women Quarterly*, vol. 9, pp. 451–62.

King, C. (ed.) (1993) *Through the Glass Ceiling*, Sevenoaks: Tudor Business Publishing.

Kinsey Lord (1994) *Development of an Equal Opportunities Strategy (for) the Metropolitan Police Service*, London: Kinsey Lord Management Consultants.

Kirkcaldy, B. and Cooper, C. (1992) 'Cross-cultural differences in occupational stress among British and German managers', *Work and Stress*, vol. 6, no. 2, pp. 177–90.

Kirkcaldy, B., Brown, J. and Cooper, C. (1998) 'The demographics of occupational stress among police superintendents', *Journal of Managerial Psychology*, vol. 13, nos 1/2, pp. 90–101.

Laming, Lord H. (2003) *The Victoria Climbié Inquiry: Report of an Inquiry by Lord Laming*, Cm 5730, London: HMSO.

Lanier, M. (1996) 'An evolutionary typology of women police officers', *Women and Criminal Justice*, vol. 8, no. 2, pp. 35–55.

Lash, S. (1994) 'Reflexivity and its doubles: structure, aesthetics, community' in Beck, U., Giddens, A. and Lash, S. *Reflexive Modernization*, Cambridge: Polity Press.

Ledwith, S. and Colgan, F. (eds.) (1996) *Women in Organisations: Challenging Gender Politics*, London: Macmillan.

Leidner, R. (1983) *Fast Food, Fast Talk: Service Work and the Routinization of Everyday Life*, Berkeley, CA: University of California Press.

Leidner, R. (1991) 'Selling hamburgers and selling insurance: gender work and identity in interactive service jobs', *Gender and Society*, vol. 5, no. 2, pp. 154–77.

Leinen, S. (1984) *Black Police: White Society*, New York: New York University Press.

Leisham, F., Cope, S. and Starie, P. (1996) 'Reinventing and restructuring: towards a "new policing order"' in Leisham, F., Loveday, B. and Savage, S. (eds.) *Core Issues in Policing*, Harlow: Longman.

Leisham, F., Loveday, B. and Savage, S. (eds.) (1996) *Core Issues in Policing*, Harlow: Longman.

Liff, S. and Cameron, I. (1997) 'Changing equality cultures to move beyond "women's problems"', *Gender, Work and Organization*, vol. 4, no. 1, pp. 35–46.

Linden, R. (1983) 'Women in policing – a study of lower mainland Royal Canadian Mounted Police detachments', *Canadian Police College Journal*, vol. 7, pp. 212–29.

Loader, I. and Mulcachy, A. (2001) 'The power of legitimate naming: part one – Chief Constables as social commentators in post-war England', *British Journal of Criminology*, vol. 41, no. 1, pp. 41–55.

Lock, J. (1979) *The British Policewoman: Her Story*, London: Hale.

Loden, M. (1985) *Feminine Leadership or How to Succeed in Business without Being One of the Boys*, New York: Times Books.

Lonsway, K., Carrington, S., Aguire, P. and Wood, M. (2002) *Equality Denied: The Status of Women in Policing, 2001*, Los Angeles: National Center for Women and Policing.

Lord, L. K. (1986) 'A comparison of male and female peace officers: stereotypic perceptions of women and women peace officers', *Journal of Police Science and Administration*, vol. 14, no. 2, pp. 83–91.

Lovenduski, J. and Norris, P. (eds.) (1996) *Women in Politics*, Oxford: Oxford University Press.

Lovenduski, J. and Randall, V. (1993) *Contemporary Feminist Politics: Women and Power in Britain*, Oxford: Oxford University Press.

Low, P. C. (1993) 'Reflections on the Halford Inquiry', *Police Journal*, vol. 9, Spring, pp. 5–16.

Lunnenborg, P. W. (1989) *Women Police Officer: Current Career Profiles*, Springfield, IL: Thomas.

Macpherson, Sir W. (1999) *The Stephen Lawrence Inquiry: Report of an inquiry by Sir William Macpherson of Cluny*, London: HMSO.

Maddock, S. (2002) 'Modernization requires transformational skills: the need for a gender-balanced force', *Women in Management Review*, vol. 17, no. 1, pp. 12–17.

Maddock, S. and Parkin, D. (1993) 'Gender cultures', *Women in Management Review*, vol. 8, no. 2, pp. 3–9.

Maguire, M., Morgan, R. and Reiner, R. (eds.) (2002) *The Oxford Handbook of Criminology* (3rd edn), Oxford: Oxford University Press.

Maile, S. (1995) 'The gendered nature of managerial discourse: the case of the local authority', *Gender, Work and Organization*, vol. 2, no. 2, pp. 76–87.

Manning, P. (1977) *Police Work*, Cambridge, MA: MIT Press.

Manning, P. (1989) 'Occupational culture' in Bailey, W. G. (ed.) *The Encyclopaedia of Police Science*, London: Garland.

Margetts, H. (1996) 'Public management change and sex equality within the state' in Lovenduski, J. and Norris, P. (eds.) *Women in Politics*, Oxford: Oxford University Press.

Margolick, D. (1988) 'At the bar: Rambos invade the courtroom', *New York Times*, 5 August.

Marsden, P. V., Kalleberg, A. L. and Cook, C. (1993) 'Gender difference in organisational commitment', *Work and Occupations*, vol. 20, no. 3, pp. 368–90.

Marshall, J. (1984) *Women Managers: Travellers in a Male World*, Chichester: Wiley.

Marshall, J. (1995) *Women Managers Moving On*, London: Routledge.

Martin, C. (1996) 'The impact of equal opportunities policies on the day to day experiences of women police constables', *British Journal of Criminology*, vol. 36, no. 4, pp. 510–28.

Martin, P. Y. (1993) 'Feminist practice in organisations: implications for management' in Fagenson, E. A. (ed.) *Women in Management: Trends, Issues and Challenges in Managerial Diversity*, London: Sage.

Martin, P. Y. (1997) 'Gender accounts and rape processing work', *Social Problems*, vol. 44, no. 4, pp. 464–82.

Martin, S. E. (1980) *Breaking and Entering: Policewomen on Patrol*, Berkeley, CA: University of California Press.

Martin, S. E. (1990) *On the Move: The Status of Women in Policing*, Washington, DC: The Police Foundation.

Martin, S. E. (1992) 'The interactive effects of race and sex on women police officers', *The Justice Professional*, vol. 6, pp. 155–72.

Martin, S. E. (1994) 'Outsider within the station house: the impact of race and gender on black women police', *Social Problems*, vol. 41, pp. 393–400.

Martin, S. E and Jurik, N. (1996) *Doing Justice, Doing Gender*, London: Sage.

Mavin, S. (1996) 'An appraisal related pay scheme for the UK police service', *Policing and Society*, vol. 6, no. 2, pp. 101–11.

Mawby, R. (1990) *Comparative Policing Issues: The British and American System in International Perspective*, London: Unwin Hyman.

Mawby, R. (ed.) (1999) *Policing Across the World: Issues for the Twenty-first Century*, London: UCL Press.

May, T. (1997) *Social Research: Issues, Methods and Process*, Buckingham: Open University Press.

Maynard, M. and Purvis, J. (eds.) (1994) *Researching Women's Lives from a Feminist Perspective*, London: Taylor & Francis.

McConville, M., Sanders, A. and Leng, R. (1991) *The Case for the Prosecution*, London: Routledge.

McConville, M. and Shepherd, D. (1992) *Watching Police, Watching Communities*, London: Routledge.

McElhinny, B. (1994) 'An economy of affect: objectivity, masculinity and the gendering of police work' in Cornwall, A. and Lindisfarne, N. (eds.) *Dislocating Masculinity: Comparative Ethnographies*, London: Routledge.

McGuigan, C., Sampson, F. and Rogerson, J. (2002) *A Soft Touch?* Harrogate: Centrex.

McKenzie, I. K. (1993) 'Equal opportunities in policing: a comparative examination of anti-discrimination policy and practice in British policing', *International Journal of the Sociology of Law*, vol. 21, no. 2, pp. 159–74.

McLaughlin, E. and Murji, K. (1993) 'Controlling the Bill: restructuring the police in the 1990s', *Critical Social Policy*, vol. 37, no. 2, pp. 95–103.

McLaughlin, E. and Murji, K. (1995) 'The end of public policing? Police reform and "the new managerialism" ' in Noaks, L., Levi, M. and Maguire, M. (eds.) *Contemporary Issues in Criminology*, Cardiff: University of Wales.

McLaughlin, E. and Murji, K. (1997) 'The future lasts a long time: public policework and the managerialist paradox' in Francis, P., Davies, P. and Jupp, V. (eds.) *Policing Futures: The Police, Law Enforcement and the Twenty-First Century*, London: Macmillan.

Messerschmidt, J. W. (1993) *Masculinities and Crime: Critique and Reconceptualisation of Theory*, Lanham, MD: Rowan and Littlefield.

Messerschmidt, J. W. (1996) 'Managing to kill: masculinities and the space shuttle *Challenger* explosion' in Cheng, C. (ed.) *Masculinities in Organizations*, London: Sage.

Metcalfe, B. and Dick, G. (2000) 'Exploring organisation commitment in the police: implications for human resources strategy', *Policing: An International Journal of Policing Strategies and Management*, vol. 24, no. 3, pp. 399–419.

Metropolitan Police Service/Equal Opportunities Commission (1990) *Managing to Make Progress Report: A Collaborative Exercise*, London: Metropolitan Police Service.

Metropolitan Police Service (1992) *Focusing on Fair Treatment for All: A Handbook to Support Learning in the Area of Equal Opportunities in Probationer Training*, London: Metropolitan Police Service.

Millen, D. (1997) 'Some methodological and epistemological issues raised by doing feminist research on non-feminist women', *Sociological Research Online*, vol. 2, no. 3: http://www.socresonline.org.uk/2/3/3.html

Miller, S. L. (1999) *Gender and Community Policing: Walking the Talk*, Boston, MA: Northeastern University Press.

Miller, S. and Palmer, M. (2003) 'Authority, leadership and character' in Adlam, R. and Villiers, P. (eds.) *Police Leadership in the Twenty-first Century: Philosophy, Doctrine and Developments*, Winchester: Waterside Press.

Mills, A. (1989) 'Gender, sexuality and organization theory' in Hearn, J., Sheppard, D. L., Tancred-Sheriff, P. and Burrell, G. (eds.) *The Sexuality of Organization*, London: Sage.

Mills, A. and Tancred, P. (eds.) (1992) *Gendering Organizational Analysis*, London: Sage.

Miner, R. (1988) 'Lawyers owe one another', *National Law Journal*, 19 December, pp. 13–14.

Mitchell, T. (2003) 'The real business of policing' in Adlam, R. and Villiers,P. (eds.) *Police Leadership in the Twenty-first Century: Philosophy, Doctrine and Developments*, Winchester: Waterside Press.

Mollen Commission (1994) *Report of the Commission to Investigate Allegations of Police Corruption and the Anti-Corruption Procedures of the Police Department*, New York: New York City.

Mooney, J. (1993) *The Hidden Figure: Domestic Violence in North London*, London: Islington Council.

Morash, M. and Greene, J. R. (1986) 'Evaluating women on patrol: a critique of contemporary wisdom', *Evaluation Review*, vol. 10, no. 2, pp. 230–55.

Morgan, R. (1986) *Images of Organizations*, Beverly Hills, CA: Sage.

Morgan, R. and Newburn, T. (1997) *The Future of Policing*, Oxford: Clarendon Press.

Morley, R. and Mullender, A. (1994) *Preventing Domestic Violence to Women*, London: Home Office Police Research Group.

Morris, C. (1994) *Bearing Witness: Sexual Harassment and Beyond*, New York: Little, Brown and Company.

Murji, K. and Cutler, D. (1990) 'From a force into a service? The police, racial attacks and equal opportunities', *Critical Social Policy*, vol. 29, no. 3, pp. 92–9.

National Police Training (1998) *Strategic Command Course*, Hampshire: Bramshill Police Staff College.

NCWP (1999) *Equality Denied – the Status of Women in Policing*, Los Angeles: National Centre for Women and Policing.

Neiderhoffer, A. (1974) *New Directions in Police Community Relations*, Rinehart Press.

Newburn, T. (1999) *Understanding and Preventing Police Corruption: Lessons from the Literature*, Police Research Series Paper 110, London: Home Office.

Newburn, T. and Stanko, E. (1994) *Just Boys Doing Business?* London: Routledge.

Newman, W. (1982) 'Pay equity emerges as top labor issues in the 1980s', *Monthly Labor Review*, vol. 105, no. 4, pp. 49–51.

Neyroud, P. and Beckley, A. (2001) *Policing, Ethics and Human Rights*, Devon: Willan Publishing.

Nichols, N. A. (1993) 'Whatever happened to Rosie the Riveter?', *Harvard Business Review*, July/August, pp. 54–62.

Nicholson, P. (1996) *Gender, Power and Organisations: A Psychological Perspective*, London: Routledge.

Nicholson, P. and West, M. (1989) *Managerial Job Change*, Cambridge: Cambridge University Press.

Noaks, L., Levi, M. and Maguire, M. (eds.) (1995) *Contemporary Issues in Criminology*, Cardiff: University of Wales.

Nordeval, I. (1985) 'Party and legislative participation among Scandinavian women' in Bashevkin, S. (ed.) *Women and Politics*, London: Macmillan.

Norris, N. (1992) 'Problems in police training', *Policing*, vol. 8, no. 3, pp. 210–21.

Norris, P. (1996) 'Women politicians: transforming Westminster?' in Lovenduski, J. and Norris, P. (eds.) *Women in Politics*, Oxford: Oxford University Press.

Northouse, P. (1999) *Leadership: Theory and Practice* (2nd edn), London: Sage.

Oakley, A. (1981) 'Interviewing women: a contradiction in terms' in Roberts, H. (ed.) *Doing Feminist Research*, London: Routledge.

Oerton, S. (1996) 'Sexualising the organization, lesbianizing the woman: gender, sexuality and the "flat" organization', *Gender, Work and Organization*, vol. 3, no. 1, pp. 26–37.

Ott, E. M. (1989) 'Effects of the male–female ratio at work', *Psychology of Women Quarterly*, vol. 13, pp. 41–57.

Owen, B. (1988) *The Reproduction of Social Control: A Study of Prison Workers*, New York: Praeger.

Owings, C. (1925) *Women Police: A Study of the Development and Status of the Women Police Movement*, Hitchcock, NY: Bureau of Social Hygiene.

Pagon, M. (2003) 'The need for a paradigm shift' in Adlam, R. and Villiers, P. (eds.) *Police Leadership in the Twenty-first Century: Philosophy, Doctrine and Developments*, Winchester: Waterside Press.

Panzarella, R. (2003) 'Leadership myths and realities' in Adlam, R. and Villiers, P. (eds.) *Police Leadership in the Twenty-first Century: Philosophy, Doctrine and Developments*, Winchester: Waterside Press.

Pierce, J. (1996) 'Rambo litigators: emotional labor in a male-dominated occupation' in Cheng, C. (ed.) *Masculinities in Organizations*, London: Sage.

Plotnikoff, J. and Woolfson, P. (1998) *Policing Domestic Violence: Effective Organisational Structures*' Police Research Paper 100, London: Police Research Group.

Pogrebin, M., Poole, E. and Chatman, H. (1999) 'A negotiated identity: African-American policewomen's dual marginalization', Paper presented at the *American Society of Criminology Conference*, Toronto, Canada, 17–20 November.

Police Central Planning and Training Unit (1994) *Community, Fairness and Quality Review Team: Final Report: Minimum Training Levels*, London: Home Office.

Police Promotion Examinations Board (1999) *Rules and Syllabus – Qualifying Examinations for Promotion to the Ranks of Sergeant and Inspector*, London: Improvement and Development Agency.

Pollock, J. M. (1986) *Sex and Supervision: Guarding Male and Female Inmates*, New York: Greenwood.

Powell, G. (1990) 'One more time: do female and male managers differ?', *The Academy of Management Executive*, vol. 4, pp. 68–75.

Prenzler, T. (1994) 'Women in Australian policing: an historical overview', *Journal of Australian Studies*, vol. 42, pp. 78–88.

Prenzler, T. (1997) 'A problem oriented approach to preventing sex discrimination in police recruitment', *Crime Prevention Studies*, vol. 7, pp. 221–37.

Prenzler, T. (1998) 'Concession and containment: the establishment of women in the Queensland Police, 1931–1965', *Australian and New Zealand Journal of Criminology*, vol. 31, no. 2, pp. 1–16.

Prenzler, T. and Wimshurst, T. (1996) 'Reform and Reaction: women and politics in the Queensland Police 1970–87', *Journal of Australian Studies*, vol. 6, pp. 23–56.

Pringle, R. (1989) *Secretaries Talk: Sexuality, Power and Work*, London: Verso.

Pritchard, C. (1996) 'Managing universities: is it men's work?' in Collinson, D. and Hearn, J. (eds.) *Men as Managers, Managers as Men*, London: Sage.

Punch, K. F. (1998) *Introduction to Social Research*, London: Sage.

Punch, M. (1985) *Conduct Unbecoming: The Social Construction of Police Deviance and Control*, London: Tavistock Publications.

Punch, M. and Naylor, T. (1973) 'The police – a social service', *New Society*, 17 May.

Puwar, N. (1997) 'Reflections on interviewing women MPs', *Sociological Research Online*, vol. 2, no. 1: http://www.socresonline.org.uk/2/1/4.html

Quinton, P. and Miller, J. (2003) *Promoting Ethical Policing: Summary Findings of Research on New Misconduct Procedures and Police Corruption*, Home Office Online Report 12/03, London: Home Office: http://www.homeoffice.gov.uk

Quirk, M. (2002) 'Flirting with the Gender Agenda', Paper presented at *Women and Policing Globally Conference*, Canberra, Australia, 20–23 October.

Radford, J. (1987) 'Policing male violence – policing women' in Hanmer, J. and Maynard, M. (eds.) *Women, Violence and Social Control*, London: Macmillan.

Radford, J. and Stanko, E. (1989) 'Policing: men's violence: an introduction' in Hanmer, J., Radford, J. and Stanko, E. (eds.) *Women, Policing and Male Violence*, London: Routledge.

Rao, A. and Stuart, R. (1997) 'Rethinking organisations: a feminist perspective', *Gender and Development*, vol. 5, no. 1, pp. 10–16.

Rawlings, P. (1995) 'The idea of policing: a history', *Policing and Society*, vol. 5, pp. 129–49.

Rawlings, P. (1999) *Crime and Power: A History of Criminal Justice 1688–1998*, London: Longman.

Reiner, R. (1978) *The Blue-Coated Worker*, Cambridge: Cambridge University Press.

Reiner, R. (1989) 'Race and criminal justice', *New Community*, vol. 16, no. 1, pp. 5–22.

Reiner, R. (1991) *Chief Constables*, Oxford: Oxford University Press.

Reiner, R. (1992) *The Politics of the Police* (2nd edn), Brighton: Wheatsheaf.

Reiner, R. (1993) 'Race, crime and justice' in Gelsthorpe, L. and McWilliam, B. (eds.) *Minority Ethnic Groups and the Criminal Justice System*, Cambridge: Cambridge University Press.

Reiner, R. (1994) 'The dialectics of Dixon: the changing image of the TV cop' in Stephens, M. and Becker, S. (eds.) *Police Force, Police Service: Care and Control in Britain*, London: Macmillan.

Reiner, R. (1997) 'Policing and the public' in Maguire, M., Morgan, R. and Reiner, R. (eds.) *The Oxford Handbook of Criminology* (2nd edn), Oxford; Oxford University Press.

Reiner, R. (1998) 'Copping a plea' in Holdaway, S. and Rock, P. (eds.) *Thinking about Criminology*, London: UCL Press.

Reskin, B. F. and Hartmann, H. (1986) *Women's Work, Men's Work: Sex Segregation on the Job*, Washington, DC: National Academy Press.

Reskin, B. F. and Roos, P. (1987) 'Status hierarchies and sex segregation' in Bose, C. (ed.) *Ingredients for Women's Employment and Policy*, Albany, NY: State University of New York Press.

Reskin, B. F. and Roos, P. (1990) *Gender Queues, Job Queues: Explaining Women's Inroads into Male Occupations*, Philadelphia: Temple University Press.

Reskin, B. F. and Ross, C. (1992) 'Jobs, authority and earnings among managers: the continuing significance of sex', *Work and Occupations*, vol. 19, no. 4, pp. 342–65.

Reuss-Ianni, E. and Ianni, F. A. J. (1983) 'Street cops and management cops: the two cultures of policing' in Punch, M. (ed.) *Control in the Police Organization*, Cambridge, MA: MIT Press.

Richards, N. (2003) 'Strategic depth' in Adlam, R. and Villiers, P. (eds.) *Police Leadership in the Twenty-first Century: Philosophy, Doctrine and Developments*, Winchester: Waterside Press.

Rinehart, S. T. (1992) *Gender Consciousness and Politics*, London: Routledge.

Roberts, H. (1981) (ed.) *Doing Feminist Research*, London: Routledge.

Roos, P. and Jones, K. (1993) 'Shifting gender boundaries: women's inroads into academic sociology', *Work and Occupations*, vol. 20, no. 4, pp. 395–428.

Roper, M. (1994) *Masculinity and the British Organization Man since 1945*, Oxford: Oxford University Press.

Roper, M. (1996) 'Seduction and succession: men's networks in management' in Hearn, J. and Collinson, D. (eds.) (1996) *Managements and Men*, London: Sage.

Rose, P. (2002) 'New Zealand Police – flexible employment and best practice', Paper presented at *Women and Policing Globally Conference*, Canberra, Australia, 20–23 October.

Rosenbaum, D. (1988) 'Community crime prevention: a review and synthesis of the literature', *Justice Quarterly*, vol. 5, pp. 323–95.

Rosenbaum, J. E. (1980) 'Hierarchical and individual effects on earnings', *Industrial Relations*, vol. 19, no. 1, pp. 1–14.

Rosenbaum, J. E. (1985) 'Jobs, job status and women's gains from affirmative action' in Hartmann, H. (ed.) *Comparable Worth: New Directions for Research*, Washington, DC: National Academy Press.

Rosenberg, J., Perlstad, H. and Phillips, W. R. F (1993) 'Now that we are here: discrimination, disparagement and harassment at work and the experience of women lawyers', *Gender and Society*, vol. 7, no. 3, pp. 415–33.

Rosener, J. (1990) 'Ways women lead', *Harvard Business Review*, November/December, 119–25.

Rutherford, S. (2001) 'Are you going home already?: The long hours culture, women mangers and patriarchal closure', *Time and Society*, vol. 10, nos 2/3, pp. 259–76.

Ryan, B. (1989) 'Ideological purity and feminism: The US women's movement from 1966–1975', *Gender and Society*, vol. 3, no. 3, pp. 239–57.

Sackamann, S. (1991) *Cultural Knowledge in Organizations*. Newbury Park, CA: Sage.

Saunders, D. and Size, P. (1986) 'An evaluation of policewomen on patrol in a suburban police department', *Journal of Police Science and Administration*, vol. 3, pp. 434–8.

Savage, M. and Witz, A. (eds.) (1992) *Gender and Bureaucracy*, Oxford: Blackwell.

Savage, S. P. and Charman, S. (1996) 'Managing change' in Leisham, F., Loveday, B. and Savage, S. (eds.) *Core Issues in Policing*, Harlow: Longman.

Sawer, M. (1995) 'Femocrats in glass towers?: The office of the status of women in Australia' in Stetson, D. M. and Mazur, A. G. (eds.) *Comparative State Feminism*, London: Sage.

Sayer, R. (1988) 'Rambo litigation: why hardball tactics don't work', *American Bar Association Journal*, vol. 79.

Scarman, Lord (1981) *The Brixton Disorders Report of an Inquiry by the Honourable the Lord Scarman*, London: HMSO.

Schein, E. (1985) *Organizational Culture and Leadership*, San Francisco, CA: Jossey-Bass.

Schulz, D. (1995) *From Social Worker to Crime Fighter: Women in United States Municipal Policing*, Westport, CT: Praegar.

Segrave, K. (1995) *Policewomen: A History*, Jefferson, NC: McFarland.

Sheehy, Sir P. (1993) *Inquiry into Police Responsibilities and Rewards*, Cm 2280, London: HMSO.

Sheppard, D. (1992) 'Women managers: perceptions of gender and organisational life' in Mills, A. and Tancred, P. (eds.) *Gendering Organizational Analysis*, London: Sage.

Sherman, L. (1975) 'Evaluation of policewomen on patrol in a suburban police department', *Journal of Police Science and Administration*, vol. 3, pp. 434–8.

Simpson, R. (2002) 'Gender mix and organisational fit: how gender imbalance at different levels of the organisation impacts on women managers', *Women in Management Review*, vol. 15, no. 1, pp. 15–38.

Simpson, R. and Altman, Y. (2000) 'The time bounded glass ceiling and young women managers: career progress and career success – evidence for the UK', *Journal of European Industrial Training*, vol. 24, no. 2, pp. 190–8.

Skolnick, J. and Bayley, D. (1986) *The New Blue Line*, New York: Free Press.

Smircich, L. (1983) 'Concepts of culture and organisational analysis', *Administrative Science Quarterly*, vol. 28, no. 3, pp. 339–58.

Smith, C., Rundle, S. and Hosking, R. (2002) *Police Service Strength, 10/02*, London: Home Office.

Smith, D. J. and Gray, J. (1983) 'The police in action' in *Police and People in London*, London: Policy Studies Institute.

Smith, D. (1988) *The Everyday as Problematic: A Feminist Sociology*, Buckingham: Open University Press.

Social Trends (2000) *Social Trends 30*, London: Office for National Statistics.

Spillar, K. (1999) A testimony of Katherine Spillar: Police Use of Excessive Force: Taking Gender into Account', National Centre for Women and Policing: http://www.feminist.org/police/kstestim.html

Stanford, J., Oates, B. R. and Flores, D. (1995) 'Women's leadership styles: a heuristic analysis', *Women in Management Review*, vol. 10, no. 2, pp. 9–16.

Stanko, E. (1985) *Intimate Intrusions: Women's Experiences of Male Violence*, London: Routledge.

Stanko, E. (1989) 'Missing the mark: policing battering' in Hanmer, J., Radford, J. and Stanko, E. (eds.) *Women, Policing and Male Violence*, London: Routledge.

Stanko, E. (1995) 'Policing domestic violence: dilemmas and contradictions', *Australian and New Zealand Journal of Criminology*, special supplement, pp. 31–44.

Stanko, E. (1998) 'Making the invisible visible in criminology: a personal journey' in Holdaway, S. and Rock, P. (eds.) *Thinking about Criminology*, London: UCL Press.

Stanko, E., Crisp, D., Hale, C. and Lucraft, H. (1997) *Counting the Costs: Estimating the Impact of Domestic Violence in the London Borough of Hackney*, London: Crime Concern.

Stanley, L. and Wise, S. (1990) 'Method, methodology and epistemology in feminist research processes' in Stanley, L. (ed.) *Feminist Praxis*, London: Routledge.

Stanley, L. and Wise, S. (1993) *Breaking Out Again: Feminist Ontology and Epistemology*, London: Routledge.

Stephens, M. and Becker, S. (eds.) (1994) *Police Force, Police Service: Care and Control in Britain*, London: Macmillan.

Stetson, D. M. and Mazur, A. G. (eds.) (1995) *Comparative State Feminism*, London: Sage.

Stevens, Sir John (2003) Stevens Enquiry 3: Overview and Recommendations, London: Metropolitan Police Service.

Stevens, P. and Willis, P. (1989) *Race, Crime and Arrests*, London: HMSO.

Stollenberg, J. (1990) *Refusing to be a Man*, New York: Meridien.

Stone, R., Kemp, T. and Weldon, G. (1994) *Part-Time Working and Job Sharing in the Police Service*, Police Research Series Paper 7, London: Home Office.

Strati, A. (1992) 'Organizational culture' in Szell, G. (ed.) *Concise Encyclopaedia of Participation and Co-Management*, Berlin: de Gruyter.

Swanberg, E. and O'Connor, P. (1995) 'Paradoxes of participation: textual analysis and organisational change', *Organisation Studies*, vol. 16, no. 5, pp. 769–803.

Symposium on Higher Police Training (1990) *Howard Journal of Criminal Justice*, vol. 29, no. 3, pp. 199–219.

Tancred, P. (1995) 'Women's work: a challenge to the sociology of work', *Gender, Work and Organization*, vol. 2, no. 1, pp. 11–20.

Tang, T. L. and Hammontree, M. L. (1992) 'The effects of hardiness, police stress and life stress on police officers' illness and absenteeism', *Public Personnel Management*, vol. 21, no. 4, pp. 493–510.

Tatchell, P. (1992) 'Equal rights for all: strategies for lesbian and gay equality in Britain' in Plummer, K. (ed.) *Modern Homosexualities*, London: Routledge.

Taylor, C. and McKenzie, I. (1994) 'The glass ceiling at the top of the greasy pole', *Policing*, vol. 10, no. 4, pp. 269–77.

Thacker, S. (1995) 'The next generation', *Policing*, vol. 11, no. 2, pp. 81–9.

Tienari, J. (1999) 'The first wave washed up on shore: reform, feminization and gender resegregation', *Gender, Work and Organization*, vol. 6, no. 1, pp. 1–19.

Tomkins, P. and Brunstrom, R. (1995) 'An unprofessional lottery?', *Policing Today*, April.

Tuffin, R. and Baladi, Y. (2001) *Flexible Working Practices in the Police Service*, Home Office Police Research Paper no. 147, London: Home Office.

Turkle, S. (1984) *The Second Self: Computers and the Human Spirit*, New York: Simon and Schuster.

Turkle, S. (1988) 'Computational reticence: why women fear the intimate machine' in Kramarae, C. (ed.) *Technology and Women's Voices: Keeping in Touch*, New York: Routledge.

Ussher, J. M. (1990) 'Sexism in psychology', *The Psychologist*, vol. 13, no. 9, pp. 31–3.

Vickers, M. H. (2000) 'Australian police management education and research: a comment from "outside the cave"', *Policing: An International Journal of Policing Strategies and Management*, vol. 23, no. 4, pp. 506–24.

Villiers, P. (2003a) 'Philosophy, doctrine and leadership' in Adlam, R. and Villiers, P. (eds.) *Police Leadership in the Twenty-first Century: Philosophy, Doctrine and Developments*, Winchester: Waterside Press.

Villiers, P (2003b) 'Leadership by consent' in Adlam, R. and Villiers, P. (eds.) *Police Leadership in the Twenty-first Century: Philosophy, Doctrine and Developments*, Winchester: Waterside Press.

Waddington, P. A. J. (1999a) *Policing Citizens*, London: UCL Press.

Waddington, P. A. J. (1999b) 'Police (canteen) sub-culture – an appreciation', *British Journal of Criminology*, vol. 39, no. 2, pp. 287–309.

Wajcman, J. (1996) 'Women and men managers' in Crompton, R., Gallie, D. and Purcell, K. (eds.) *Changing Forms of Employment: Organisations, Skills and Gender*, London: Routledge.

Walker, D. and Richards, M. (1996) 'A service under change: current issues in policing in England and Wales', *Police Studies*, vol. 19, no. 1, pp. 53–73.

Walker, N. (1994) 'Care and control in the police organisation' in Stephens, M. and Becker, S. (eds.) *Police Force, Police Service: Care and Control in Britain*, London: Macmillan.

Walker, S. (1985) 'Racial minority and female employment in policing: the implications of "glacial changes" ', *Crime and Delinquency*, vol. 31, no. 4, pp. 555–72.

Walklate, S. (1993a) 'Sexing Sheehy: towards a gendered agenda for policing' in Kimber J. and Stanko, E. (eds.) *Masculinity and Crime: Issues in Theory and Practice*, London: Brunel University.

Walklate, S. (1993b) 'Policing by women, with women, for women', *Policing*, vol. 9 Summer, pp. 101–15.

Walklate, S. (1995) *Gender and Crime*, Hertfordshire: Prentice Hall/ Harvester Wheatsheaf.

Walklate, S. (1996) 'Equal opportunities and the future of policing' in Leisham, F., Loveday, B. and Savage, S. (eds.) *Core Issues in Policing*, Harlow: Longman.

Walklate, S. (2001) *Gender, Crime and Criminal Justice*, Devon: Willan Publishing.

Wall, D. S. (1998) *The Chief Constables of England and Wales: The Socio-legal History of a Criminal Justice Elite*, Aldershot: Dartmouth and Ashgate.

Waters, I. (1996) 'Quality of service: politics or paradigm shift?' in Leisham, F., Loveday, B. and Savage, S. (eds.) *Core Issues in Policing*, Harlow: Longman.

West, C. and Fenstermaker, S. (1995) 'Doing difference', *Gender and Society*, vol. 9, no. 1, pp. 8–37.

West, C. and Zimmerman, D. H. (1987) 'Doing difference', *Gender and Society*, vol. 1, pp. 125–51.

Westmarland, L. (2001) *Gender and Policing*, Devon: Willan Publishing.

White, J. (1995) 'Leading in their own ways: women chief executives in local government' in Itzen, C. and Newman, J. (eds.) *Gender, Culture and Organizational Change*, London: Routledge.

Widerberg, K. (1991) 'Reforms for women on male terms – the example of the Swedish legislation on parental leave', *International Journal of the Sociology of Law*, vol. 19, no. 1, pp. 27–44.

Williams, C. (1989) *Gender Differences at Work*, Berkeley, CA: University of California Press.

Williams, C. (1992) 'The glass escalator: hidden advantages for men in the female professions', *Social Problems*, vol. 39, no. 3, pp. 253–68.

Williams, C. (1995) *Still a Man's World: Men who do 'Women's' Work*, Berkeley, CA: University of California Press.

Willis, C. (1983) *The Use of Effectiveness and Impact of Police Stop and Search Powers*, Home Office Research and Planning Unit Paper no. 15, London: Home Office.

Wimshurst, K. (1995) 'Anticipating the future: the early experiences and career expectations of women police recruits in post-Fitzgerald Queensland', *Australian and New Zealand Criminology*, vol. 2813, pp. 278–97.

Witz, A. (1990) 'Patriarchy and professions: the gendered politics of occupational closure', *Sociology*, vol. 24, no. 4, pp. 675–90.

Witz, A. (1992) *Professions and Patriarchy*, London: Routledge.

Women's Advisory Council to the Los Angeles Police Commission (1993) *A Blueprint for Implementing Gender Equality in the Los Angeles Police Department*, Los Angeles: Los Angeles Police Department.

Wood, J. R. T. (1997) *Final Report of the Royal Commission into the New South Wales Police Service*.

Woodeson, A. (1993) 'The first women police: a force for equality or infringement?, *Women's History Review*, vol. 2, pp. 217–32.

Wright, R. (1996) 'The occupational masculinity of computing' in Cheng, C. (ed.) *Masculinities in Organizations*, London: Sage.

Wyles, L. (1951) *A Woman at Scotland Yard*. London: Faber & Faber.

Yearnshire, S. (2002) 'Improving the position of women in policing: women in management', Paper presented at *Women and Policing Globally Conference*, Canberra, Australia, 20–23 October.

Young, M. (1991) *An Inside Job*, Oxford: Clarendon Press.

Zimmer, L. (1986) *Women Guarding Men*, Chicago, IL: University of Chicago Press.

Zimmer, L. (1987) 'How women reshape the prison guard role', *Gender and Society*, vol. 1, no. 4, pp. 415–31.

Zimring, F. and Hawkins, G. (1997) *Crime is Not the Problem: Lethal Violence in America*, Oxford: Oxford University Press.

Index